In the Hide

In the Hide

How the Natural World Saved My Life

Gordon Buchanan
with Will Millard

Witness Books

UK | USA | Canada | Ireland | Australia
India | New Zealand | South Africa

Witness Books is part of the Penguin Random House group of companies
whose addresses can be found at global.penguinrandomhouse.com

Penguin Random House UK
One Embassy Gardens, 8 Viaduct Gardens, London SW11 7BW

penguin.co.uk
global.penguinrandomhouse.com

First published by Witness Books in 2025
This paperback edition published in 2026
1

Typeset by seagulls.net

Printed and bound in Great Britain by Clays Ltd, Elcograf S.p.A.

The authorised representative in the EEA is Penguin Random House Ireland,
Morrison Chambers, 32 Nassau Street, Dublin D02 YH68

A CIP catalogue record for this book is available from the British Library

ISBN 9781529144277

Contents

You Dancer

The air thickens as the city's street dogs let out a series of explosive barks. They are panicking, and quite rightly so. A night-walking predator is creeping unseen and feline through this Mumbai night. On the fringes of the Indian megacity, the urban leopard finds its ambush cover not through expansive grasslands and forest, but around tight alley corners, sneaking through informal settlements, skulking among the city's most tangled and litter-strewn edges. A large, lethal ghost cat, hunting somewhere in the shadows of skyscrapers as I wait in my hide, poised behind my camera.

These leopards have been captured on the occasional very well-placed camera trap, and a glimpse of its nocturnal form may even be spotted by a pedestrian, but you're far more likely to be completely unaware of its presence – just its calling card: one fewer stray dog, fat rat, pig, goat or chicken, snatched from one of the city's many smallholdings.

Away from Mumbai, the urban leopard felt more anecdote than animal. For the most part, the rumours were all we knew, but here, on the ground, the Mumbai leopard was very much alive. It was writ large in the terror of those yelping dogs and the fears of the people who live around here, some two hundred of whom had been attacked in the last 25 years.

It was 2016 and *Planet Earth II*, narrated by the incomparable Sir David Attenborough, would go on to break audience records, with more than 13 million viewers tuning in from the comfort of their homes. But there were 20 million people living in this Indian city alone, and just 40 leopards for our team to track down. When we began our attempt to capture, for the first time ever on film, a Mumbai leopard successfully making a kill, it felt a bit like looking for a moving needle in the most enormous haystack. With camera traps we narrowed their hunting grounds down to a handful of probable locations, before I climbed into my hide with a thermal camera and began my vigil.

It would become my longest run in a hide ever.

•　•　•

For four weeks, I carried my thermal camera over to my spot on the stroke of each and every sunset. Long nights of watching, punctuated by the noises of the local community: their goats, pigs and chickens, the occasional night-time drumming party, fireworks and all the other ordinary urban strollers and shouters. Then dawn would break, I'd emerge from my den to get some kip and it would start all over again.

At first, it didn't feel like this was an environment that was conducive to a deathly silent stealth predator, but I did befriend a tiny mouse. Admittedly, we didn't get off to the best of starts. In India, whenever you hear a movement in the undergrowth, your immediate thought is *poisonous snake*. It wasn't until this sweet little mousey face peeked out from my biscuit packet that I was able to relax. Every night after that we'd share a biscuit while I continued to wait.

From the outside looking in, you might think you'd have to be a bit of a masochist to enjoy a month spent in a hide. Swatting away the mosquitoes while eating, drinking and performing all bodily functions in conditions so cramped you could easily touch all four canvas walls from your chair. Throw on top the specifics of that particular shoot, with its sleep deprivation, urban noise and the sweltering humidity of the Indian nights, and it really does sound quite mad. But I have always found comfort in the simplicity of this work: the self-containment and the very basic routine. When you know you are in exactly the right place, it's just a case of waiting for the right time to come, so there can never be a question of being bored.

The buzz from all that anticipation helps keep you sharp. It makes you focus on your narrow view from the hide and the wider environment you can sense sweeping around you in the blackness. You become hyper-aware of every movement and sound, tuned in to each rustle, creaking branch and background movement. In readiness for that one moment when all the waiting, work and research comes together and delivers an exceptional meeting with nature. Then it's just up to you to distil the skills you've honed over years of effort into what might only amount to a few seconds of performance.

For me, there's much more to the hide than my collection of experiences within that very singular space. My life triangulated me towards the hide too. It is as much a metaphor for who I am as it is my sometime place of work.

When I was young, if you had granted me one wish, I probably would have chosen to be invisible. If I was invisible, I rationalised, then I could get as close as possible to the earth's most elusive creatures. Moreover, I could comfortably evade all the things that troubled me most in the human world too. Three decades on, the scientists and engineers have partly granted me that wish. I have been closer than I could ever have dreamt to many of the iconic wildlife species I watched on television as a child, and many more that I had zero prior knowledge of. But the evasion of the most difficult aspects of my life? That was one invisibility cloak I could never possess.

Trips to the hide are often escapist though. They allow me to focus purely on the work at hand. In here, at least for a spell, there are no complex people problems to navigate and solve. I can indulge the minutiae. The fleeting temporal moments that gather alongside my wait for the 'moment'. The way the light fades from the land at sunset and creeps back at dawn. The gentle breeze brushing across the leaves, the sound and smell of a rainstorm, a simple swirl in the dust. All of those beautiful tiny things that you could never appreciate if you weren't made to sit still and really watch.

Spend enough time waiting and you might discover you have another sense too. It is a throwback, a primal feeling that is long since buried in most of us. A sort of sixth sense which is attuned to the natural timing of other animals. It can be sharpened through intense observation, experience and plain gut instinct. Get it right, and it can forewarn you of an animal event in the moments before it plays out; I could interpret the clues that the leopard was coming before I could catch it on my thermal camera: those barking dogs, a hush among the humans, the right type of darkness and the intangible atmospherics that signal a switch has been flicked. The scene out front is no longer ours, it's the leopard's.

That's when working the hide can be at its very best: when you just know something is coming and you frame up your camera, focus and gently place your thumb on the record button.

Out from the gloom the slinking form of my first urban leopard appears. It ghosts in from behind a shroud of bushes before appearing in the centre of my thermal camera lens. A spirit-like white against the dark trees and the artificial glow of a quietening cityscape.

'*You dancer!*' I whisper. 'Look at that!'

My eyes widen and my pulse quickens. The hunt is on.

Memory Lane

'There's a worm at the bottom of the garden'

I extend my finger out to a mixed audience of parents, teachers and playschool peers.

'And his name is Wiggly Woo'

I wiggle my finger.

That's it. My earliest childhood memory. My first performance for *any* audience and it was *even* related to wildlife. I mean, we could just wrap this entire childhood section right here, couldn't we?

I was a pale and pasty wee lad with a mop of curly brown hair capping my head and an oddly bulging belly and bulbous forehead – both of which I haven't yet entirely grown into. I can't have been much more than two, but that moment is seared into the core of my memory – no doubt, in part, because I was absolutely terrified to be stood on that stage.

I was a shy young boy who lacked confidence in himself, but I should say, too, that this was not a solo performance. I'm sure

I would've been part of a wider ensemble of snotty-nosed and scabby-kneed Dumbarton kids – all gathered to sing inarguably the greatest garden-based nursery rhyme ever penned, in front of their parents and probably some quite stressed-out teachers.

I don't know precisely why *that* is my first memory. I think it's probably a mix of the fear and me having total investment in the lyrics (and in the quality of my finger-wiggling performance). I'm fairly certain that I would've hugely enjoyed the feeling of having my mum's full attention too.

Finally. No nonsense interruptions or noise from either of my older brothers.

This was all *my* moment. Admittedly a moment of fear and terror, but also my earliest introduction to feeling dread and doing something anyway.

· · ·

Most of my very earliest memories revolve around our time living on Bellsmyre council estate, over on the north-eastern edge of Dumbarton town. It's nestled at the foot of the wide-open Kilpatrick Hills, so a bit of the Scottish high country always felt within reach to the north, but the south took you down through town to the point where the river Leven spills into the tidal waters of the river Clyde, 13 miles downstream of Glasgow. Both confluence and town stand in the shadow of an enormous geological feature visible from miles around. A 73-metre basalt volcanic plug was formed over 300 million years ago and is modestly called the 'Dumbarton Rock'. Scottish people are masters of understatement and boys born in the area are known as 'sons of the rock'.

I was born in 1972, at a time when things were getting tough on Clydeside. The once mighty shipbuilding and steel industries had been on a firm downslide since the end of the Second World War. Industry and community rubbed up almost brick-to-brick alongside the river Clyde's banks. Glasgow ran seamlessly into the shipyards and houses of Clydebank town, with a short two-mile hop flowing on to the shipyards and houses of Dumbarton. During the war, the Naval shipyards and munitions factories had made the area a major target for German bombers through the Blitz – and the Luftwaffe raids on 13 and 14 March 1941, in particular, did some serious damage.

Even with decoy lights placed up on the Kilpatrick Hills, the German bombs rained down on the docklands and shipyards, destroying many people's homes in the process. In Clydebank alone, out of some 12,000 houses, only eight were left without damage – and more than 4,000 were reduced to rubble. In those raids, 1,200 Clydesiders died, and almost half of those victims had lived in Clydebank: a tiny town, less than three miles wide.

By the time the 1960s rolled round, the world-famous Fairfield shipyard had collapsed completely and some of the largest unemployment figures in Scottish history were blighting the wider Glasgow area. After the war, new industrial markets opened up in Asia, forcing Scottish shipyards into an almost unsustainable competition over construction prices. The British government attempted to halt the decline in the early 1970s with a cash injection and the nationalisation of the handful of ship-yards that were still in operation, but the writing was on the wall. Generations of workers lost their jobs in an industry that had, within the span of a single lifetime, gone from being responsible for the construction of one-fifth of all ships launched worldwide, to making almost nothing.

The knock-on effect of all that loss of work was devastating. Not just to those directly involved in building ships or knocking out the steel plate in the wider Lanarkshire region, but to all those businesses that relied on people spending their hard-earned wages too. The pubs, the shops, the cafes, the clubs; widespread closures and unemployment remained rife well into the 1970s. It wasn't that people didn't want to work, there just wasn't anything like enough jobs or money to go around.

Living in Bellsmyre, you could be forgiven for feeling like Glasgow had washed a lot of its inner-city problems downstream. On our estate, the original houses were built as part of the British Iron and Steel Federation scheme, but, come the 1950s, Bellsmyre, and many of the estates just like ours, were rapidly expanded by the Scottish Special Housing Association. These estates would grow as part of an 'overspill' programme that moved families away from Glasgow's over-crowded inner-city districts, places like Gorbals and Hutchesontown, and out into these spots that were being thrown up, almost like entirely new towns in themselves, on the edges of many of Clydeside's established towns.

There were a few council house estate schemes around Dumbarton, and they all, more or less, looked exactly the same as the one I grew up in. Grey concrete slabs meeting the occasional pebble dash, muted yellow or brown block flourish, with uniform windows and communal hallways for packs of kids to scream and thump along in their tribes and clans.

These things are always relative. If you haven't lived on a council estate like Bellsmyre, you could be forgiven for looking at it and thinking that it was pretty grim and a bit dodgy. No place for kids to grow up. Before we moved there, I do have these very faint memories of once being in a nice new-build middle-class bungalow over on the leafier side of the river Leven, and, despite the obvious change of circumstances, I quite honestly can't distinguish between that place being that 'good' and Bellsmyre being that 'bad'. It never felt rough to me back then and it still doesn't now. I was still with my mum, my brothers and my sister. That was good enough for me.

A few years ago, I heard that the part of Bellsmyre I knew was getting bulldozed (or 'redeveloped' if you want to toe the town planner parlance) so I took my daughter Lola to show her where I used to live, before it was all gone for good.

She was pretty young then, and I'd said to her, 'Lola, we are going on a trip down memory lane,' to which she, rather sweetly, replied: 'Oh! I've always wanted to go to memory lane!' In the half an hour drive from our home in Glasgow to the newly condemned section of Bellsmyre, I managed to explain to Lola that 'memory lane' was not, in fact, an actual place – and then there we both were: pulled up, right outside our old council flat.

I don't know what I was expecting. There were a couple of burnt-out cars and a little bit of vandalism, some smashed windows and twisted fences, but it certainly wasn't a warzone. The grass was overgrown in places and some small saplings shot up from the ground immediately in front of the building's plain yellow walls – but it still looked fundamentally okay. The windows and doors were all boarded up, the upstairs with wood, the downstairs with a strong steel sheeting, yet as I stared up at it, I could sense a lot of my old memories and feelings pouring out from that place.

• • •

My parents had us young. My mum was 20 and my dad was 21 when they'd got married and had my eldest brother, the grandly named Walter Alexander Buchanan, who everyone actually just calls the much more down-to-earth sounding 'Sandy'. That was the end of 1969, and then along came big brother Stewart in 1971. I was born a short year after Stewart, and our poor mum, now 23, was caring for three kids under four.

I don't remember my dad being around too much after I'd arrived, and given Sandy was still a toddler and Stewart was really still a baby too, my mum always jokes that for the first year of my life I probably thought the sofa cushion was my mother – as she'd always had to keep propping me up to deal with the demands of the other pair.

After two boys, I think my mum may have secretly, and quite understandably, hoped that I would be a girl. I say 'secretly' – but some early photos show me wearing quite *fluid* baby attire: bonnets, sandals and what can best be described as the occasional frock. It was the seventies so maybe I was a 'glam rock' inspired baby, but more likely they were hand-me-downs from my older female cousins. Then, in 1975, Maggie came along and my mum really did have the girl she'd wanted – my bonnets, frocks and frilled socks were presumably handed down to my baby sister, leaving me with a more limited wardrobe, and my parents were all done with having kids by their mid-twenties.

That was me then: Gordon Buchanan, the middle child. Now, back then, I'd probably get pretty short shrift, or accused of being a 'softie', if I'd ever raised the theory of how being born in the middle might have affected my personality in the long run. In essence though, the hypothesis of 'middle-child syndrome' runs that the oldest sibling gets attention by being the trailblazer – the first to experience all the new things and the responsibility of being the eldest – whereas the youngest will forever get attention as they are always going to be the baby of the family. The middle child (or children – I'm not forgetting my brother Stewart here) can wind up feeling like they are a bit of an outcast and a little overlooked.

I never felt like an outcast but there were definitely times when I felt overlooked. And it kind of suited me – there's real benefit to not being in the main gaze of attention. At school and at home I got away with so many things when others paid the price for the same conduct. Never underrate invisibility!

We were in no doubt that my mum absolutely loved all of us (when last I checked, she still does) but with four of us now kicking about, it was always going to be the case that, although her love was limitless, there was only so much of her attention to go around. From very early on, I remember having to find ways to fit in with what was going on with everyone else – and when attention did come my way, *especially* from the people I cared about, I loved being 'the one' in that moment.

I'm sure that's a big part of why 'There's a Worm at the Bottom of the Garden' was my first memory – just having her there, watching me without any distractions, would've been quite amazing. After Maggie though, when I turned three, Stewart and I both went to nursery school in Brucehill. Stu was of age but I started a year early.

It definitely wasn't because I was demonstrating any advanced academic potential – Stewart was struggling to settle in, so I guess my mum had thought it was a case of killing two birds with one stone: *Send Gordon in early to keep Stewart company, and get Gordon in with his bigger brother to keep an eye on him, so I can concentrate on everything else that I've got going on at home with the new baby.*

When primary school did come along it was actually just down the road, but that walk to school felt like the equivalent of a ten-kilometre trek. My mum came with me for the first day, but after that, although I was presumably supposed to be under the watchful eyes of my brothers, I can only ever remember walking in on my own. I can't actually recall ever seeing Stewart in school, and I can only remember seeing Sandy once. You may think I had to develop a degree of self-sufficiency and independence very early on, but the start of school saw the start of my lifelong predisposition for chronic daydreaming. Self-sufficiency and independence came with the turf! I never remember not being comfortable in my own company. I don't think I was ever one of those kids desperate to be in a group, or that felt the need to constantly have friends around me.

Not to toot my own trumpet but I reckon that daydreaming is one thing I can do better than anyone. I wish that weren't the case as a man now in his fifties but, from day one at school, I loved getting lost in my own mind: in my wild imaginings there was no reading, writing, adding or subtracting. Those things were for the classroom and although I was there in body, my mind was always somewhere else. A bit like the soldier bloke in *Avatar* but Scottish and five years old.

I'd say it probably was the first inkling that I had a natural ability to spend long periods working independently of others. It was a skill that would ultimately be useful – goodness only knows how many years I've since spent waiting for wildlife alone – but back then, the main motivation was just to get some peace and quiet, some 'me time', way before people used that phrase. I definitely wasn't going to be getting any quiet time at home and, pretty soon, there would be even less parental attention to go around.

Son of the Rock

In the late 1960s, one of my mum's best friends was dating some-one in this cool up-and-coming local band. She was working and living on her family's farm when her friend had asked her if she'd like to come to one of the band's parties. My mum turned up and the band were all there with loads of other young people, drinking and dancing, and there, right in the middle of it all, was one lad who was infinitely more pissed than everyone else.

That was our dad.

'There was something about your dad,' my mum said, recall-ing that night. 'Even at that party, I could see he was a nice person, a good man, but also someone who was probably a bit lost and in need of looking after. I felt sorry for him and then I quickly fell in love with him.'

By all accounts, my dad's parents were praising the Lord on High that he'd met this bright local farmgirl. *Finally, a good influ-ence,* they were probably thinking. I imagine they'd hoped that this turn of events might've seen their son settle down and begin to act with a bit more responsibility too, but I very much doubt anyone could've predicted my mum would be married and pregnant within a year of them meeting. My mum was soon off the farm and moving in with our dad. They got married and Sandy arrived very soon after. Real adult life arrived at breakneck speed.

Before us, our dad had been a 'son of the rock' and a 'son of the roll'. A Dumbarton boy experiencing all the freedoms of the 1960s – no kids, no responsibilities, a drummer in a cool local band, almost totally free to do whatever he felt like. Then all of a sudden there he was, still a very young man, only just into his mid-twenties, but now with four kids and very real adult responsibilities as a father and a husband. The band, his teenage years, and maybe some of his dreams, were left behind in the 1960s.

In the 1970s my dad was still a *very* 'sociable' young man. He loved a drink as much as the drums and, according to our mum, he'd often finish up his work for the day, head off for a 'social engagement' and that was him. He often wouldn't come back till we were all in bed, and I'm sure there were more than a few times that he didn't come home at all.

A few years ago, I said to my mum that I only have two memories of my dad at home before they split, to which she replied: 'I'm surprised you've even got that. He was never there!' She spoke of walking through the park with the four of us, seeing other families with their dads and wondering why ours wasn't with us too. One of the nicest afternoons she recalled where we were all together was an afternoon walk along the river at Balloch – ironically though, that was just before everything blew up.

Maybe my two home memories of him have stayed with me because they were such a rarity. I can remember him giving me a bath, and then the second memory was less of a memory and more of an atmosphere. He was at home and there was some sort of stooshie going on. I imagine that was right when they were breaking up and my mum and dad had just been arguing. My dad was never a screamer or a shouter – he doesn't have an aggressive bone in his body – but I do remember a feeling that whatever was happening was bad.

So, I have one happy hands-on moment with him as my father, and one sad memory with him right before he left our home for good. In my childish mind though, I squared away him 'going off' as him just being too important and too busy to have time for any of us. Somehow, I was able to take this really sad thing – him leaving and my parents divorcing – and twist it into something positive. *Good for him*, I'd think to myself, *out there now, free to do big exciting things, stuff way more important than being a dad.*

My dad is a remarkably talented man. He was a genuinely skilled musician and at one point, he was even among the very best rifle marksmen in Scotland too. He won loads of national competitions and the European championships. He was even tipped for the Commonwealth Games, but just missed out on a place in a head-to-head shoot-out with his closest rival. My dad's band the Big Six must have been a big deal in Dumbarton. All handsome young men, suited and booted – in photos indistinguishable from the Kinks or Rolling Stones.

They'd cut a record, had a Big Six tour van and did a couple of world tours (of the Scottish Highlands …). Plus, his family ran Dumbarton's first taxi firm, and owned the only garage and petrol pumps in our area too. Everyone knew Walter and Nell Buchanan's boy, so really, in my mind our dad was something of a local celebrity, and I totally hero-worshipped him.

My mum's grandfather *and* my dad's grandfather were both undertakers. My mum's side split from the trade and went into farming, and my dad's side also split but in quite an interesting way. My dad's grandfather Thomas Turner Buchanan had quite the career trajectory: he had trained as a joiner, his joinery led to making coffins, the coffin-making led to undertaking, the undertaking led to cars, then to taxis, and on to the garage and petrol pumps.

John Buchanan & Son was the first and, for quite some time, the only garage and petrol station in our area. Standing proud at the bottom of Comelybank Lane, with our family name emblazoned over the door. As cars became increasingly more available for people, that garage flourished and the undertaking business fell by the wayside. The garage was the family business. My dad's grandad passed it down to his son, and my dad, an only child, was poised to take it over from his father when the time eventually came.

As kids, we saw that garage as our own little family empire. John Buchanan & Son: established in 1880! A place that *everyone* knew and successive generations of Buchanans would keep going forever. Our dad had grown up in a middle-class family. I never once heard him speak negatively about either of his parents.

Walter and Nell, our grandparents, were really lovely people. He'd had a fortunate, even privileged upbringing, the first of his friends to own a car, but I do recall him once saying that he felt that his life had been mapped out by Walter. There was the expectation that the business would become my dad's life, just as it had been Walter's, and all the Buchanan men that had come before him. Possibly, in a very different life, my brothers and I could've been working together in there today.

My dad was working in the garage with my nana and grandad when I was born, and we were living a middle-class life back then too. When it eventually came to the time for my nana and grandad to retire, my dad wound up leaving the family business behind. I'd speculate that his heart wasn't really in it; I think it's fair to say that his heart wasn't really in other areas of his life either. My mum and dad split up in 1976, not long after I'd turned four. Some of my earliest memories are as vivid as Technicolor, but I have a total blank when it comes to that ground-shifting change. Suddenly our dad was gone and we were living in Bellsmyre council estate. There are no scenes in my mind to join together the different parts of the story.

After John Buchanan & Son was sold, our dad was a roving mechanic for Home Counties Van Hire. He drove a huge Mercedes mobile workshop and repaired the vans and lorries in their fleet. He became the service manager for Scotland and spent time in Aberdeen, responding to cries for help, rescuing truckers and van drivers in distress across the land. No need for a mobile mechanic's equivalent of the Bat-Signal, he had a CB radio; so, my hero-worship carried on: *My dad is out mending massive trucks,* I'd think to myself, *swooping in like a spanner-wielding Superman to save the day!* Next, he moved into the pub trade, managing and running hotels and pubs, which I still thought was pretty cool and very important – people needed rooms, people needed beer, my dad was the still the guy saving the day.

There were good times spent in the pubs and hotels he managed, and fond memories of him taking us to the Woodvale Airshow for a long weekend of camping and model aircraft rallies, which he was hugely passionate about. He even took me to my first zoo, my abiding memory of which was the plastic gorilla he bought for me to play with. We must have seen my dad often enough after the split, but I have precious few memories until he was living with Anne. Anne was on the scene at the time of the split and would eventually become our stepmum, not once but twice. They married in 1980, then divorced, and remarried in 2014, staying together until she passed away a couple of years ago.

Anne was kind and warm – someone who could really look after us in a motherly way, whenever we did go to stay with them. We were made to feel like we were an added bonus to being with our dad. Being a stepparent may be complicated, but with Anne it never was. We felt loved by her and that's all a child needs.

In time though, there was an inevitable physical distance between the four of us kids and our dad. Separated by more than 100 miles of highland roads and a stretch of water. And the longer we didn't share the same roof, the same home and experiences of daily life, then inevitably other distances would grow. Looking back, it's hard not to think about what he missed out on by not being there. I don't believe there was any reason to it all. I've never asked for a reason – some people, purely by the way they are put together, just struggle with stuff. Try as I might, I cannot hula-hoop. I'm just not built for hula. My dad, in the way he is put together, even with all his talent and intellect, was always going to struggle with being a conventional father.

My mum randomly said to me one day: 'You know, Gordon, the sixties have got a lot to answer for.' I asked her what she meant exactly and she replied: 'All these young men who were growing up with the world telling them that they could do whatever they wanted and that they never had to grow up.'

Eventually, he got out of the pub trade and found himself a job working in a quarry near Oban. He was off driving these enormous haul trucks with giant 12-foot wheels and that was when it seemed to dawn on him that somehow, somewhere along the line, 'Peter Pan' was actually getting older now, and that he might even need to wear glasses too.

My dad is a good person with a huge heart, and he is still hanging in there. We all see him as regularly as we can, but, by his own admission, he's falling apart at the seams. Some of his decisions and lifestyle choices have been questionable. I've never seen him eat a piece of fruit (tinned peaches aside) and as a kid I wondered whether I'd also be partial to an 11.30am vodka and lemonade when I grew up.

In spite of everything my dad put my mum through when he left us, she's never really had a bad word to say about him. She's never been hard on him at all, and certainly never was in front of us growing up. My mum always somehow seemed able to see my dad as that lost young lad still stuck at the party.

The Boy with the Bucket on His Head

There were three floors on our block in Bellsmyre and we were housed in a little flat at the top. I shared a room with Stewart, Maggie was in with our mum, and Sandy must've had his own space in there somewhere. The couple directly below us had five kids and I can still remember how lovely they were. Like so many people on Bellsmyre, they were always looking for work, but never really gainfully employed. People had very little but, thinking back to that early time in my childhood, I can remember lots of love and many happy times.

Within the estate, the kids had a few courtyards and a bit of grass to roam around on. You'd see big gangs of kids playing games together – climbing what trees there were, or just climbing up onto the flat roof of the local shop and jumping around. It wasn't bad by any stretch. I know how this is going to sound, but I also recall how we used to get an awful lot of entertainment from chasing around after emergency vehicles.

There seemed to be a disproportionate amount of house fires on the estate – from small chip-pan fires (the most common) to full-on infernos. We'd hear the fire engine sirens coming from a distance and that would be like the starting pistol going off for some mad kids' race. Off we'd all go, a sea of Bellsmyre children sprinting across the estate to gawp at some poor family's flat, with the roof going up in smoke and flames spilling out from the windows.

A far gentler memory was of the 'rag and bone' man. His 'rag and bone' shout was the equivalent of an ice cream van's tinkling tune. I'm not sure what we would have had to give away but my mum would always find something to trade. We'd rush down and hand over whatever we had, then he'd survey it with his beady eye and meticulous fingers before giving us one of his balloons, or maybe, if we were *really* lucky, a whistle.

I'm not sure of the divorce rates in our area at that time, but there was certainly a common theme of people marrying and having kids young – well before they'd matured into who they really were and knew what they wanted to be as adults. Inevitably, couples would either slog it out in an unhappy marriage, or realise they'd made a mistake, and the husband would leave the wife and kids.

A lot of dads were absent on our estate, regardless of whether they had split from their wives or not. There would invariably be the dads working very long hours in hard, low-paid jobs, but then they'd also be off down the pubs and clubs, spending whatever little money they had. Not seeing much of our dad hardly singled us out; it would've been more noteworthy if he'd been with us the whole time. To be fair, I might have a slightly exaggerated take on the proportion of couples who were calling time on their marriages given most of my parents' friends were either in our dad's band or closely associated with them and their lifestyle, but it just didn't feel like there was anything remotely unusual about growing up in a single-parent household on the Bellsmyre estate.

What it did mean, though, was that invariably we kids were left to our own devices – and what that meant in reality was play, followed by play fighting, *actual* fighting and then tears – usually mine.

You can take the grand sum of all the crackling, hair-raising tension before an extraordinary wildlife encounter, add to it the anticipatory feeling of stepping into a fresh wilderness for the very first time, and you will still never quite match the thrill of having a tin bucket placed over your head while your eldest brother lines up an air rifle to shoot you square in the face.

Sandy was probably only about 12, so I can't have been much older than nine, and Stewart, Sandy and I were all staying away with our dad. He was off at work and, quite incredibly, Sandy had been given an air rifle as a present, possibly for his birthday. So, naturally, having exhausted the fun to be had from randomly firing the gun into the sky, firing the gun at a can and firing the gun at a moving can, it was pretty obvious what the next logical step had to be.

'Right, Gordy,' said Sandy. 'I've got a good idea, sit down the bottom of the garden with that bucket on your head.'

I was absolutely thrilled and honoured to be involved with my biggest brother's plans. A starring central role too! I scooped up the old bucket without even thinking twice.

Like the celebrated Scots cartoon hero Oor Wullie, there I was, proudly swinging my tin bucket in my hand as I made my way down the grass to gratefully take up position for the firing squad of one. Not at any point did I or my brother stop to consider that what we were doing might have been in any way dangerous – or, for that matter, why the fuck Sandy couldn't have just put the bucket down at the end of the garden and shot at it without my head inside. But I was with him: in our minds, it was a much better plan if I was wearing the bucket.

I sat down, plunged my head into the darkness and readied myself for the metallic 'ping' of an air-rifle pellet striking the metal, mere millimetres from my face. I waited, but it didn't come. So, I waited some more.

The bucket had that strange aural quality you get when you put your ear over a large seashell. That *whooshing* sound that resembles a small wave breaking out over a pebbly beach. I could smell the metal sides too. A rusty old tinny odour mixed with something agricultural – probably, or at least hopefully, soil rather than shit.

He's taking his time, I thought to myself as I shuffled nervously inside the pitch darkness of my self-inflicted bucket cave. That heady mix of scent, sound and darkness somehow sharpened my focus on the gradually growing discontent that was rising up from within. In sum, it said: *I am about to be shot in the head by my brother and an awful lot of my body is not encased in this protective metal shield.*

I tried to wait some more, but by this point the tension was unbearable, so I reached up, grasped the thick rim of the bucket, lifted my face back out into the light – and got shot squarely between the eyes.

Jesus Christ. Had it been a more powerful air rifle, or if Sandy had been any closer, or, god forbid, he'd actually hit me in one of my eyes – then I would either have been Scotland's first cycloptic wildlife cameraman, or, much more likely, my life's journey would've been abruptly curtailed and you most certainly wouldn't be reading this book.

In all honesty, that memory still makes me laugh. It is definitely one of my favourite anecdotes involving Sandy and me, and, in the event, the metal pellet bounced harmlessly off my thick forehead anyway. Painful enough, but it didn't even split the skin.

It didn't beat any real sense into any of us either, but at least we weren't daft enough to think that particular game was worth attempting again. Whenever we did things together as siblings, there was always an omnipresent element of jeopardy and danger. Not least because young kids, and especially boys, are always pushing boundaries and egging each other on to do foolish things. With us though, there was also always that feeling that just one wrong word (or two, or three) could descend into fighting.

There were rare times when we would all hang out peacefully together, but we each had our own sets of friends and, as we grew, our interactions were often punctuated by clouts, dead arms or dead legs.

I should say, we are not talking all-out bar-room brawls or street fights here. I can remember one occasion where I really pushed Stewart too far and he wound up head-butting me properly hard – but that was the only time anyone was ever really hurt (and I probably deserved it). These 'fights' were just incessant kids' scraps. You probably know the kind: windmilling arms and whirling knees and feet. A roll about the floor with shoving, headlocks and elbows thrown in, but the biggest conflicts that caused most tears had psychological origins. We were perpetual wind-up merchants and piss takers. It seemed the best part about having siblings was intimately knowing each other's weak spots and when to push those buttons to maximum effect.

Unquestionably, boredom and proximity were the biggest factors in all of our scraps. It would start quietly – perhaps we would be playing together, quite calmly, or, in the case of my older brothers, just hanging out. Then someone would start gently ribbing someone else for a bit of fun. If our mum was within earshot she would always say, 'This'll end in tears', which would be roundly ignored, as the piss-taking and back-and-forth escalated till eventually one party either had no decent verbal comeback, or someone said something that really struck a nerve, and then it would, just as our mum predicted, end in tears.

I'm not sure if my memory of that time is exaggerated, but it seemed to me that we were having scraps nearly all of the time. This was *very* problematic for me, as my two older brothers were far bigger, far stronger and much tougher than I was. I was never going to come out on top during a tussle with either of them, no matter how hard I tried – and believe me, I did try, *a lot*. As Sandy was over three years older you'd expect him to easily overpower his younger brother, but you might think I could maybe get one over on Stu, who was just 368 days older than me. Very regrettably, Stewart was just a very hard bastard. A fair match would maybe be the 16-year-old me against the 12-year-old Stewart – but I imagine it would still have to be a very good day with a fair wind.

Sandy was older and, I thought, the coolest kid on the block. If I'm going to be completely honest, I craved his attention more than anyone else's. I looked up to him hugely and wanted to be just like him as I grew up. On the few occasions he did allow me to tag along on a ramble or adventure, life for me did not get any better. I'd go to great lengths to get in his good books, to bathe in the effortless 'cool' of his presence, even if it meant allowing him to shoot me in the head.

Sandy did get into a bit of trouble as a kid. As the eldest he was more in the spotlight, and – sorry, Sandy – the biggest wind-up merchant of the four of us. He would insist that he wasn't responsible for whatever had brought the fire down on him, he just 'happened to be there', to which my mum always piped up with my favourite saying of hers: 'Well, Sandy, if you fly with the crows, you get shot with the crows'.

Some of Sandy's edgier adventures just made me want to hang out with him even more. Lamentably, I was never offered an invitation to accompany him and his friends to play 'mad wanker', a high-risk game that involved jumping from roof to roof at the mostly deserted telephone exchange buildings. He probably realised that his idolising wee brother could become one of the crows that got shot.

Stewart was very physically strong and a great fighter. We all used to go to jujitsu classes – which we just short-handed to 'karate' – no doubt encouraged by our mum to blow off a bit of that extra steam on something other than each other. Stewart, it quickly transpired, was particularly talented at martial arts. He was so good, in fact, that the instructor would regularly have to match him up with much older lads, just to give him a bit more of a challenge. Even at 14, he could comfortably handle 18-year-old boys who were on the verge of adulthood. Stewart maintained that powerful air of an intrinsically hard bastard. He had, and still has, a wide, ready smile, but in his younger years he was just one of those boys that people knew not to mess with. Not that he is in any way aggressive, at all. That one head-butt aside, Stewart was always much more inclined to be a peacekeeper than an enforcer, but naturally, that would only last for as long as his patience held.

As I got older, I was convinced that I must be giving off the same latent menace as Stewart, and that people knew that I was also tough. I was never bullied or picked on at school. Even when my pals were targets, I was always left well alone, therefore, I reasoned, I was a hard and very intimidating fella. It actually took me till I was an adult before I was able to very quietly rationalise that maybe, *just maybe*, the real reason I had something of a shield around me was because of the simple fact that I had two big brothers. Despite the in-house quarrels, I must have known that any aggro from others could be dealt with in mafia style by 'the family'. As a teenager I certainly would have preferred to believe that I just had that 'hard' look about me – though I struggle to think of any hard man in history with a big mop of curly hair. It's just not the tough-guy look. But I guess we will never really know for sure …

Regrettably, I'd fight with Maggie as well. We could play happily together for hours, but on occasions the niggling would start. Though Maggie had the shield of not two but *three* older brothers, it transpired that she was not living under the *illusion* of being tough – she really was tough. Physically strong and as squirmy as a giant otter, for years she could dish it back to me as hard as I dished it out to her, and it took me until I was in my mid-teens before I realised that we were an even match and that 15 seemed the right age for retirement from wrestle-fighting your sister. Other than for a considerable purse, I'm not tempted to come out of retirement. The three-year age gap may not be in my favour these days.

Dandelion and Burdock

There was another air-rifle-related scrape from my childhood that was fairly typical of how quickly things could get out of hand. Back in the day, if there was ever a film on television, it was invariably themed around war, and, more often than not, it was the Second World War – so war games and 'soldiers' were just a natural progression from that.

If you had a stick, you had a gun, and games like 'Dead Man's Fall' were a staple for us kids. You'd all line up with one person acting as the 'shooter', who would then shoot everyone in turn, with the person who could affect the most dramatic performance of 'dead fella falling through the air' receiving the honour of being the shooter next time around. All standard macabre fun for a gang of children growing up in the 1970s and 80s.

Pretty quickly, sticks progressed to air rifles, and not the weak .177 rifle of the 'bucket on the head' episode. The superior fire power of the .22 made it the gun to have. Obviously, the .22 fired pellets, and not bullets, but it was still a gun, and dangerous in the wrong hands – which we, unquestionably, all possessed.

Of course, our mum didn't know that we all had guns. I'd secretly saved up my birthday money and bought an air rifle off a lad at school for a couple of quid, Sandy had the .22 upgrade and Stewart had a very cool and easily concealable air pistol – so, on the occasions when our mum wasn't about we were able to engage in a bit of movie roleplay in the concealment of our back garden. We shot at each other in short skirmishes rather than prolonged battles, with absolutely zero protective equipment in sight – not even a tin bucket.

One evening our mum had gone to work and Sandy, through seniority of age, had assumed he held some sort of 'staff sergeant' authority over the rest of us – I suppose he sort of did. Anyway, he walked into the living room and, just as I sat down with a can of 1980s favourite Dandelion and Burdock, he went into a little preamble along the lines of 'I'm going to shoot you'. I gave a complacent 'no you're not' kind of shrug. Sandy's response was a squeeze of the trigger and the *thwack* of the rifle, and the only thing I could fire back at him was: 'Sandy, you fucking arsehole.'

I felt the pain and, worse still, looked down to see a neat, pellet-shaped hole right through my only pair of jeans. It transpired it wasn't even a pellet that he'd shot me with – he'd actually managed to rip a hole in both my jeans and me with a piece of chewed up tinfoil. *I wasn't even worth a pellet!* The cheap bastard!

I was absolutely apoplectic and launched my 'grenade' – my, as yet unopened, can of Dandelion and Burdock. It struck him dramatically before spiralling away, colliding with the living room doorframe, rupturing and showering a fountain of liquorice and aniseed liquid across the living room.

Often, when we observe dramatic violence in nature, everything slows right down. If you are aware enough, it might even afford you a pre-emptive instinctual ability to frame a shot, as if you know precisely what's coming up before it has even happened, all in the tiniest fraction of a second. It's a hyper-evolved hyper-aware state, where you can see everything unfolding all at once: the gazelle's stumble, the lioness's turn, her claws, the jaws, the entire living room coated in a sickly black foam, my brother roaring forward in pure purple rage. React, Gordon. React.

I sprang to my feet, somehow managed to duck beneath his tentacular swinging arms and fists, and fled out of the house without any shoes on my feet. It was a rainy and cold winter's night but I ran as if I was on burning hot coals. Sandy was right on my heels, having lobbed down his gun. He may well have been in trainers too, but I had the motivational advantage of knowing precisely how this would end if I stopped running now – truly, I felt I was running for my life.

I charged through dark puddles on the tarmacked streets, rainwater soaking my socks through to their fibres and pulling them down as leaden weights hanging round my ankles. It was like being in one of those recurrent fever dreams where you are being chased by an unseen yet deadly force, and then you suddenly forget how to run. I sensed I was slowing down in the dank wet, so it was time for death or glory (or total cowardice, depending on your perspective). Through pure fear, I had put a bit of distance between myself and Sandy, at least enough to pull off a move direct from the cartoons. I rounded the next corner and dived for the cover of a roadside bush, leaving Sandy screaming past in hot pursuit of my shadow – a great black cloud of wet spray and brotherly rage.

I held my breath as Sandy suddenly stopped on the dim horizon. He had realised that I was gone and likely hiding somewhere close by. For a moment, he caught his breath. This shuddering silhouette in the darkness, a teenage werewolf rocking back his terrible mane before howling out at the moon: 'Gordon! When you come home, I'm gonna fucking kill you!'

I froze in shock and awe with just one logical thought puncturing the purity of my moonlit terror: *But … you shot me, Sandy. And that Dandelion and Burdock cost me 20p.*

Sandy sloped off but I knew I couldn't go home, at least not till our mum was back, but neither could I sit barefoot in a bush, holed out in the mid-winter Scottish rain. Very carefully, I crept back to our house and snuck into our back garden. Obviously I couldn't risk going back into the actual house. Sandy may have gone off the idea of killing me but I wasn't expecting a cuddle and apology from my eldest brother. Hypothermia didn't seem like a pleasant way to go out either though, so I climbed inside the only available shelter: our small garden rabbit hutch.

Sat tight with the bunnies snuffling at my toes, it was some hours before I spied the outline of my mum in the kitchen. She flicked on the light switch and filled the kettle, like a lighthouse casting a flood of homely light out to a little wee ship lost in giant stormy seas. A palpable sense of relief flooded through me, but I still needed to play the next bit very carefully. As much as I felt Sandy's reaction had been unjust, and well over the top, if our mum found out about the guns then we would lose them all – and the restorative justice that would then come my way from both of my brothers did not bear thinking about.

As casual as I could act then (given I was shaking with cold and fear, completely soaked to the skin with a holed trouser leg and rabbit pellets bobbling my socks), I strolled out into the kitchen. 'Oh, hi Mum,' I said, I think, rather coolly, while scanning behind her for any sign of Sandy and also noting that the Dandelion and Burdock disaster had been mysteriously, yet meticulously, cleaned.

'Where on earth have you been, Gordon?!' she answered, eyes wide with surprise at my dishevelled state. 'Oh erm,' I stammered. 'Just out playing with the rabbits.' I gestured airily with my hand to the ink-black rain-whipped darkness of the back garden. Incredibly, likely due to a heady mix of exhaustion and exasperation, she accepted that excuse with nothing more than a heavy tut and an eyeroll.

We had got away with it, *again*.

• • •

Despite appearances, I still don't think things ever really got that out of hand, but growing up there were always going to be those times when we all needed our own space. I was probably subconsciously searching for something to take me away from it all.

It was back in our Dumbarton days that the idea of escaping into the wild first tugged at the shirt sleeve of my soul.

The Bellsmyre estate had been built on land reclaimed from fields – but we were still at the foot of those rolling Kilpatrick Hills and, just peeping over the roof of the school, you could sense more freedom was to be had in the great green fields and woods that were even closer still.

There was a physical barrier between them and me, provided by the rest of the estate and the school, but I always felt grateful to be on the edge of all that countryside. Just looking at it, even from a very young age, I could feel this magnetic pull towards those places. My grampa still ran his dairy farm near the southern end of Loch Lomond, and visits to the farm were blissful. I knew, as far back as I could remember, that the fields, the hills and the woods represented something intrinsically good, especially for a boy like me.

Away from the farm, I was drawn to the greenest places closest to home. *One day, I'm going to walk to those hills and woods*, I'd often think to myself as I walked to school or came back through the estate. They were probably less than half a mile away – so hardly an epic expedition – but the idea of vanishing up there started to take root long before I'd had the opportunity to first venture their way.

Pretty soon it would become more than just adventure, or a chance to see something new: I wanted to become a real part of that type of wild too. More than anything, I wanted to go in there, and just for a short while, blend into the background and become invisible.

A Glasgow Kiss

It was the early 2000s and I was deep within the Abernethy forest. Creeping among statuesque pines and crunching my boot prints into thick snow, with my camera kit slung over one shoulder.

There's a rare sense of isolation to be had within that particular set of regal Scottish trees. The Abernethy sits within a National Nature Reserve that extends some 13,000 hectares from the river Nethy to the grand summit of Ben Macdui within the Cairngorm plateau. It contains a rich mosaic of wild habitats: heather moorlands, dense bogs and, most notably of all, the largest tract of ancient Caledonian pinewoods left in Scotland. This once great forest has its origins some 11,000 years ago, right at the end of the last Ice Age, when much of Scotland would've been wide-open tundra. As the glaciers retreated, pinewoods went on to blanket the nation, but with historical land clearance, the spread of non-native tree species and subsequent over-grazing by deer (who no longer have any natural predators), those indigenous pinewoods only exist in small disconnected fragments today.

Somehow though, when the conditions are right, and you are all alone in the Abernethy forest, you do feel like you can stretch out your imagination and tap into something of what ancient natural Scotland once was. Those trees still provide a harbour for many of our most threatened wildlife species: the dainty red squirrel, the Scottish crossbill, crested tits, pine martens, even the whiff of a rumour of one of the rarest creatures of all – the Scottish wildcat. For much of our congested and highly managed land, it still feels like a place lost to time. A quiet oasis where secret wonders may yet hide out and hold on.

It was getting towards winter's end, but still these lumpen snowflakes drifted down through the arms of the pine trees, covering my tracks and throwing out an ice-white shroud across an open forest floor.

I knew what I was looking for, what to expect and roughly where to head, but it still took me aback when I found it. Granted, the male capercaillie is a most striking bird. A huge woodland grouse, as large as a turkey with a shimmering black body, dark green breast and a blazing red streak above each of its eyes, but what truly marked this *particular* bird out was its fearlessness.

I quickly readied my camera, focused and began to shoot. There he stood, puffing out his chest defiantly as I swapped angles to get a range of shots and coverage. We could clearly see each other and, as I crept a little closer, I assumed that at some point, it would either back away or fly off – but it did neither. It carried on eyeballing me, almost advancing slightly, like a bouncer in a great black bomber jacket trying to gently shepherd a drunkard out from his nightclub's door.

I got to the point that I felt I was quite close enough – crouching down into the snow to make myself as small as possible, while angling my camera right up at this grand capper's eye.

And *that* was when it attacked.

. . .

A study in southern Finland found that around one per cent of the capercaillie population were observed to behave 'abnormally'. These so-called 'deviant males', presenting the very highest levels of aggression, were seen to attack stuffed male capercaillies and even the human researchers themselves. They would, apparently 'without hesitation', mate with a stuffed female capercaillie too. To this small clutch of angry, sexually charged outliers, it wouldn't matter what you were – a deer, a person on a quadbike, in a car or in a tank – if you were *not* a female capercaillie looking to mate, then they would be coming for you with maximum violence.

Perhaps unsurprisingly, the study also found that these ultra-alpha-cock birds were carrying around five times the testosterone of the average capercaillie male. It's probably fair to assume, then, that these exceptional males were very successful at defending the territory they carve out for their breeding season in spring. Indeed, a simple search on the internet turns up reams of other examples of these rogue birds attacking people from right across their northern European range, with some places even having to take steps to actively stop people from entering the areas where just one of these bruising birds was working its home patch.

Apparently, rogue capper attacks in Europe are on the increase – but this is more than likely connected to the tragic decline of the capper's natural habitat, and a resultant increase in their contact with humans, rather than some anomalous spike in the number of birds actually carrying around some serious beef within their systems. That same fractured Caledonian forest in which I had just encountered my very own angry capper was their preferred place to be – and the health of both that forest type and the bird itself went hand in glove. Or, in my current predicament, finger in beak.

Back in 1785, both forest clearance and hunting saw Scottish capper numbers collapse to such an extent that the native population were effectively extinct. Come the nineteenth century, capercaillie were reintroduced to Scotland from Scandinavia and, for a time at least, things were looking okay, but recent years have seen yet another massive collapse in capper numbers. This time, alongside the fundamental scarcity of suitable forest habitat, much wetter springs and summers have also likely impacted the fitness of both chicks and breeding females. Shockingly, the most recent estimates have placed Scottish capercaillie numbers down to as few as 532 birds, a fall of over half the population since the last survey in the winter of 2015. It places them firmly on the UK's 'red list' and leaves the future of this iconic Scottish species in real doubt.

When I had my encounter in Abernethy, a couple of decades ago now, there were no real restrictions for viewing capercaillies

– but today they are considered to be so vulnerable that the public advice from the RSPB is not to go looking for the bird at all, and it is now a criminal offence to disturb them during breeding. According to their guidelines, if you are lucky enough to come across one, the responsible course of action is to keep your distance, not share its location on a public forum, and carefully withdraw from the area – which might not be too hard if you, like me, had unfortunately bumped into one of those one per cent.

. . .

Before I could do anything, my finger was gripped firmly within this bird's powerful yellow beak. A bad enough outcome in itself – but you'll notice when males attack each other in the wild they will leap forward and grab hold of whatever part of their enemy that they can – whether that be the head, or neck, or wing – and then they'll just start to twist.

In terms of birds they are big, about the size of your average pumpkin, and they are incredibly strong too – but I must've been pretty submissive, as that capper's crocodilian death-roll didn't last too long before it let go and disappeared off into the trees.

His point had, very much, been made.

The capercaillie had sliced open my finger though, and with my crimson blood dribbling down onto the white snow, I had to wrap a sock around the wound to stem the flow. Admittedly, I had to laugh at how bizarre the whole thing was. Let's be honest, a very mild beak wound from a fat lump of a wood grouse doesn't quite have the same kudos as surviving a shark bite or a grizzly bear attack, does it? I probably should've known I had a high chance of getting my arse kicked too. Incredibly, this very bird had previous offences on its record. Just five years earlier, it had leapt onto the great Sir David Attenborough too. Bowling him onto the seat of his trousers in a fit of laughter, and flurry of heather, in what would later become a classic scene for his 1998 *Life of Birds* series. Clearly, this capercaillie hadn't mellowed out much since.

It would become one of my all-time favourite wildlife moments, but that day wasn't just about an isolated encounter with a magnificently bullish bird. It was about the sum of all its parts: wandering alone through a forest I dearly love, the Cairngorms peeping in through the gaps of this magical snow-covered scene and the animal I'd hoped to meet captured in all its pomp and glory (even leaving me with its own version of the Glasgow kiss). But the day was not yet done.

I remember what came next so vividly. Maybe pain somehow enhances the senses, making everything seem so much sharper and shocking a scene into your mind like a branding iron to the brain? Even now, I can speak that forest day right back into existence – reaching back in time and placing myself back between those Narnian pine trees, in deep snow and with one very sore finger.

I was walking away from where that capper was, through the pines, past the odd birch and the occasional granny pine – these grand solo trees that are in excess of 200 years old – when I heard a great noise rumbling off to my left. It was building towards a thunderous turning of snow and I ducked down once more –

hunkering among the juniper and holly, as a stupendous herd of red deer bore down on me.

Extraordinary rust-coloured coats and rippling muscle ploughed through deep white snow that was reaching fully up to my thighs. Those deer leapt above the juniper bushes, exerting their energy and soaring high, almost as ethereal beings. I was in full camouflage, completely at one with that ancient forest floor and its snow – somehow undetectable to those incredible animals – who were now close enough for me to see the steam pluming off their snouts and bodies. Away I melted into the scene. Momentarily, but wholly, swallowed by both time and nature.

That feeling of pure transcendence has an arcane and primal quality. I can't say for sure if I've ever really been moved in quite the same way since. Those are the moments that really raise the hairs on your body. The scenes that pull you into such a heightened sense of awareness that you lose all sense of yourself. Yet they are as rare as they are fleeting – a whole sweep of wonderful conditions and pure circumstance flowing together in a run of perfect natural events. A bit like if you were to pick out a series of purely random notes, place them on some sheet music and then discover that together they formed the most beautiful symphony you've ever heard – before the page whips away on the wind and it is all gone for good.

That is the majesty of experiencing something that is truly wild. I didn't even think to lift my camera – not that I could've adequately captured anything close to what it felt like to be there, in that moment – and I'm glad I didn't. It exists so vibrantly in the core of all my collected memories of a life spent working among wildlife, I almost wouldn't want a bit of film or a photo to shift or warp what I *know* to be the deeper truth of that experience.

That, though, is one of the biggest challenges in the job of capturing honest images of wildlife. You can try as hard as you want: arming yourself with the greatest technology of human invention, the best cameras twinned with the finest lenses, operators and editors, but you just can't quite do it true justice. You can't replicate the sense of being there in person.

Maybe that's the thing that keeps so many of us in this game – chasing the successful capture of a vision of a perfection that will sit forever out of reach.

Part of me does wish that I could capture it adequately, maybe just once. A piece that really did show exactly what it was like to be there. To bear witness to such a scene. Maybe if you could somehow store all those feelings in an image, you could carry it around and show it to others who might not yet feel the same way about wildlife as you do. Maybe, too, you could go some way towards persuading more people of nature's true brilliance.

For now, we are left with only the memories of those most remarkable moments, and the sheer rarefied privilege of just having *been there* must be enough.

The Gully

I am a proud Scot and it was the Scottish glens, forests and crea-tures that first sparked my earliest interests in the natural world – but before all that could be put into words, back when I was still a child of Bellsmyre, I was aware that nature was a place where I instinctively felt at home. Somewhere I was secure, where I could be left alone and momentarily hide from the world outside, and all that began with the Gully.

I'm not too sure how old I was when I first spent serious time in the Gully, but I could probably still do the walk from our flat on the Bellsmyre estate, down to that magical place, with my eyes closed.

You'd come out of our close and down to the right was all of the estate stretching out, but if you turned left you'd see the green fields and hills in the near distance. Out of the foothills a small burn weaved and tumbled its way towards our estate's edges, and, as it went, that little natural waterway scoured out a deeper course down into the earth. Eventually, it had funnelled out something of a tight ravine in rock and soil, leaving these very steep banks and an environment that stood unlike anything else to be found within our half-mile-square stomping ground.

The estate was hard up against the left side of the gully hidden by trees; to the right were fields set aside for grazing, though I never saw any cattle or sheep. Those fields were fairly uniform and devoid of trees – but step into that ravine and it was like you had entered a whole new world. Ancient tangled trees, roots and shrubs met thick grasses on super steep banks leading to the gin-clear waters of that burn. This was an old and untouched place where no agricultural ungulate could safely go to graze. It was plenty deep and steep enough to close out the adult world too.

In the Gully, there was no school or Bellsmyre estate. No teachers, parents or anyone else telling us what to do. You couldn't see the buildings, nor could you hear anything that was going on from outside those dense green walls. It represented an enormous labyrinthine maze of exploratory possibilities for curious children, while still being narrow enough to toss a rock from one side to the other. It might've only been ten feet deep in places, but for us kids, that Gully was our Grand Canyon.

It was also the first 'wild' place I'd ever been to. Sometimes I'd go in there with a little gang of kids and we'd soon lose track of time playing our games together: building dams across the stream, climbing in the trees and making spears or very rudimentary bows and arrows. But I'd often just go there by myself.

I loved the Gully. It was a sanctuary. Somewhere I could be alone, playing my own games in my own time, without any interruptions or rules. A place where I could explore this all-new wondrous natural world by myself, and for myself too.

It was the first time I'd had the feeling that nature really meant something to me. That it had this intrinsic value to me as a person. There were other places on the estate where kids could go – a bit of grass to have a kick about on, hide-and-seek in the local graveyard, chasing those sirens or jumping onto a flat roof – but the Gully was a place that stood out above the rest. There is a special chaos to nature that can't be replicated by whatever we build in its stead. No matter how good the playpark is that you build for children, kids instinctively know that the wild possesses the real magic.

I say I went there on my own a lot – but I wasn't ever completely alone, I nearly always had my Action Man down there with me. I loved that guy, and this was his world too – a place where no end of military operations, daring rescues and fraught battles occurred.

And we Buchanan siblings weren't *always* fighting. I also remember us going down to the Gully to play together (without anyone ever taking an angry spear to the head) and I have many happy memories of taking my Action Man back from his day out in the Gully for a long afternoon of domestic bliss at the hands of a Sindy doll controlled by my sister, Maggie.

Together we would play in Sindy's well-maintained house, where she'd have all the stuff required for a good wash, a meal or a nice cup of tea – but Action Man would always be ready in case he needed to leap into his jeep and nullify any enemy activities around our imagined white picket fence.

Maggie and I spent many peaceful days playing together with her dolls and my military figurines. In fact, I can go so far as to admit that there were many times when Action Man would luxuriate in his civilian time in Sindy's house, even when Maggie wasn't around. But for all that the Gully had meant to me as a child on that estate, a change was coming that would radically alter my perspective of what the 'wild' could be. Our next move as a family would bring me to an island whose possibilities for exploration were as wide as the skies above the seas.

Mull & Calve

My mum had grown up on a farm in the village of Gartocharn. Nestled between the southern shores of Loch Lomond and a tree-covered hill known sweetly as 'The Dumpling', Gartocharn is a quiet place with an idyllic atmosphere and a very simple way of life. It has a couple of churches, one shop and a primary school. It's the sort of place where you'd love to bring up your kids – and at one time, recollecting my own golden memories on the farm, I had notions of raising our own family there.

She left school at 16 and started work straight after her O levels as a research assistant with Vickers-Armstrongs engineering, down at the experimental tank in Dumbarton. She was working on submarines there, in the building that is now the maritime museum, before she found work as a clerkess for Yorkshire Insurance for a spell, before eventually returning home to work on the family farm. By her own admission she wasn't terribly good at the farm work, too busy enjoying herself at events put on by the Young Farmers club, where she served as the secretary for a year. She was working at the farm in August 1967, when she met my dad.

Quite suddenly, after my dad left, this country girl found herself living away in a town. Then her own mum passed away; she must've felt so alone.

A couple of years passed with us living in Bellsmyre and, as we all grew, so did my mum's desire to find somewhere similar to what she'd had growing up. A healthier, happier childhood, with space to roam out in fresh air and nature, but still a place that was new to her too. Somewhere she could make a completely fresh start.

There were fewer reasons to hang on in Bellsmyre. With us all getting bigger, the flat was feeling pokier with every passing year. My mum didn't have a well-paid job that was likely to change our living circumstances any time soon. My grampa had asked her if she wanted to come back home to the family farm with us kids, but my mum hadn't wanted to. Her friends had all left Gartocharn and moved on, so, as much as it would've been the safe and easy option, she felt like she needed to try and forge her own life's path.

It was time for another big life change, but this time it could at least be more on our mum's terms.

We had been to the island of Mull on family holidays. My grandparents owned an old 1950s-style caravan in the small town of Tobermory and, whenever we'd been over to stay, we had all completely loved the place.

When our mum raised the possibility of a full-time move there, we leapt at the opportunity. Tobermory was familiar to us, and it would, I anticipated, feel like we were on holiday all of the time. As far as I was concerned, there wasn't a single negative about it. Tobermory was a place I loved to be – and I wasn't going to miss the flat, the grey of the estate or my school – or any of my friends for that matter.

Any remotely good things about Bellsmyre were kicked miles into touch by the overwhelming positives from all those great holiday memories of big skies, fresh air, the sea, the beach and all the boats. Mentally, my bag was packed to go from the moment my mum mentioned it.

In the summer of 1979, we went over as a family for another holiday, but by this time our intention was that the next visit would be permanent; then our mum received the sort of news that would've removed any shreds of doubt in her mind.

While she'd been off looking for places for us to stay and sorting out school places, she got word that our council flat had been broken into. We got back to Bellsmyre and I remember seeing fingerprint dust everywhere, so I knew the cops had been in. It was the first time I'd seen fingerprint dust anywhere other than on the telly, so that all felt pretty novel, but it was also the first time that I'd ever really felt aware that Bellsmyre might not actually be that nice of a place to live.

The police had left the crime scene as they'd found it. I imagine the burglars were probably just youngsters on the hunt for booze. They must have known we were away and had broken in through the ceiling, having climbed in through a loft hatch on our close. They hadn't actually taken anything, but they had left some disturbing things behind. One of Maggie's dolls had been repeatedly stabbed and my cherished soft toy frog had been disembowelled, all its stuffing pulled out. It had then been tucked back up in bed for maximum horror when my blankets were pulled back.

I say they hadn't stolen anything, but they had actually taken a bag of frozen mince out of the freezer and tried to cook it on our stove.

I remember being so happy in the car as we left Bellsmyre, cheerily calling out in that innocent way that kids do as they leave any familiar place: 'Bye, signpost! Bye, street! Bye, hedge! Bye, Gully!'

We would periodically come back to Dumbarton to visit our beloved nana and grandad, Nell and Walter, and I would still see my dad wherever he was working, but to my child's eye, it felt like we were leaving the mainland for good. Truthfully, I was overjoyed to be going. I couldn't wait for our new life on Mull to begin.

• • •

Tobermory is located on the far north-eastern tip of Mull, right up at the northern opening of the Sound of Mull, which channels water between the island's east coast and the Scottish mainland. It is widely referred to as the 'capital of Mull' – a grand-sounding title maybe, but, with the very greatest of respect to Tobermory, there wasn't a huge amount of competition for that title elsewhere on Mull. I don't doubt that plenty of outsiders would struggle to see Tobermory as anything more than a largish village, but it was built in a truly beautiful corner of Scotland and very quickly became my happiest of very happy places.

Tobermory was originally founded in 1788 by the British Fisheries Society. They were looking to establish fishing communities in remote parts of western Scotland, with the aim of expanding their exploitation of the commercial shoals of herring in the Atlantic, but it was the harvesting of kelp for soap and glass that largely sustained the town over much of the next half-century. The harvest of that valuable seaweed would see the expansion of Tobermory's long curved pier, but, once the kelp trade collapsed in the mid-1800s, shellfish fishing really took over, and then came the tourists. With around 600,000 visitors a year, Mull is a big destination in Scotland, especially during our long summer days. Tourists will arrive in their droves to walk along our pretty harbourside and take in the colourful rows of houses that line our pristine waterfront, and then there's all the wonderful wildlife.

There I was, seven, almost eight, actually *living* in a place where people felt fortunate to just visit. Tobermory felt all at once colourful, exotic and very exciting. Never more so than when I ventured down to the bay. It may be a comparatively small port, but whenever I went down there, I felt like I was arriving at the gateway to the entire world.

Yachts, ships, cruise liners, naval vessels and fishing boats of all shapes and sizes would come and go – throwing out their crew, cargo and customers. Just thinking *that boat could go anywhere* was enchanting. I thought some really were sturdy enough to venture north towards the frozen seas of the Arctic Circle, or perhaps even down towards the ice masses of Antarctica. The biggest might be able to journey across the Atlantic Ocean, far away to our west and over to the American shoreline, or they might just cut a course through the Suez Canal, or round the African coast at the Cape, and head east across the grand Pacific towards Asia.

Colourful flags and dirt-brown rust. Flaking paint and salt-crusted ropes with often even crustier sailors. I felt they all carried the mark of some deep expansive experiences of far-off foreign places, and yet here they all were, right in front of me. Close enough to touch and smell. Like a small wave breaking onto a pebbly beach, an idea gently arrived in my own mind: I wanted in on that adventure too. Those boats on Mull helped me to see that the maximum extent of my own horizons was no longer limited by whatever existed in the space between the Bellsmyre estate and the Kilpatrick Hills. There, beside those Mull seawaters, my wanderlust could stretch off to places that sat far beyond the limits of what I could see. In fact, I'm sure it was in Tobermory where the very earliest feelings that I could do something bigger with my life first started to take root. That something *else* was waiting for me all the way over *there*, and, if these boats, right here, could go there – then why couldn't I go there too?

It wasn't just the bay that was filling me with all these unexpected new feelings. The shoreline was unexpected too, beaten by weather that felt often unpredictable, wild and raw, in a way that I'd just never experienced while living in Bellsmyre. Occasionally the storms would throw up new discoveries onto the rugged coast for me to comb over and collect, and the tides were always bringing brilliant things into my hands too.

On Mull's shores, I'd explore the desolate wrecks of boats, old abandoned sheds and stone buildings. They were long since stripped bare of anything of value to the adult world, but still filled with fascination for a young boy who was seeing it all for the very first time. Then there was the interior of the island itself – all these pristine pools and streams, endless gullies-on-gullies, cliffs on offshore islands harbouring impressive sea-bird colonies, craggy wind-whipped hills, dense patches of woods and all the new trees to climb. I loved going to those places within reach myself. That raw sense of excitement at being somewhere that was completely new to me, which I could then fill with my own ideas of what it all was, or what it once could have been.

There simply weren't enough hours in the day to fit all of the exploration in, but I soon realised that my Mull adventures were always going to be extremely limited for as long as I was restricted to the places I could walk or run to. A bike was the obvious first solution, but then I was still stuck with the places that any basic landlubber could get to.

As time passed, what I *really* wanted was to be able to get to the parts of Mull that were off-limits to your average young adventurer. The places where no one lived and people rarely, if ever, visited. 'Virgin' territory, where I could be something of a pioneer, while still being able to make it back home in time for my mince and tatties.

I didn't need to jump on a boat to the other side of the world, not yet anyway; I just needed one to get me away to those secret corners of Mull. It sounded simple enough, but I didn't *have* a boat, did I? And I didn't have any boat-owning mates either.

In fact, I didn't have *any* mates whatsoever. But that was all about to change.

• • •

Norrie MacDonald was a one-off. A dark curly mop of hair capping a skinny but athletic-looking frame. The sort of *slight not scrawny* build that you might see on a flyweight boxer or middle-distance runner. He had more than a whiff of eccentricity about him. On hot summer days, he discarded his shoes and roamed barefoot around the town and I thought that was very, very cool. He chose to skip and play hopscotch instead of football too, but you could tell just by looking at the way he carried himself that he didn't give a single solitary shit what anyone thought of him.

Norrie exuded an absolute confidence and self-assuredness, without really seeming too cocky or aloof. His nonchalant swagger may have been in part down to his family connections. On an island of large families, his was the biggest. He was a Maclean on his mother's side. The Macleans, an ancient and powerful Highland clan, had once owned and ruled all of Mull alongside many other islands within the Inner Hebrides, and large tracts of Argyll too. Ever since those times, the Maclean name on Mull has been synonymous with the de facto indigenous ruling dynasty – I may have had the shield of two brothers but Norrie's extended family of uncles, cousins, second cousins, and on and on, may have accounted for at least some of his confidence.

Of course, I wouldn't have known about any of that on my very first day in a brand-new school. Typically, I wasn't that desperate to make friends with anyone, but just looking over at Norrie, I can remember clearly thinking, *I want to be* that *guy's pal.*

We became friends not long after I had settled in at school, and after a year of knocking about with each other, we were true best friends. On occasions, I still enjoyed a bit of solitude, but from that point forward, we were pretty much inseparable and most of our Mull adventures were undertaken together. The cement of our friendship was that we were similar enough, and different enough, to create a lifelong bond. But being 'that guy's pal' had another advantage – an advantage that would upscale our roaming range: Norrie's dad had a boat.

Tobermory Bay is well sheltered from the open seas and, in fair weather, it could scarcely be a more perfect place for a couple of young learners dipping their maiden paddles into sea, but Norrie, being Norrie, wasn't going to be satisfied with just that. His dad's boat was a pretty basic, but beautiful, clinker-built wooden rowing boat. He took us out a couple of times, even letting us take the oars to have a go ourselves, so, in Norrie's mind, we had served our apprenticeship and passed our advanced boat handling course with flying colours. We were ready for bigger tests, and that started with solo voyaging.

I am certain we never told his dad we were taking his boat out on our own. For Norrie, there was never any question of 'are we allowed to?' – it was just 'we are doing it'. Our earliest trips went pretty well though – rowing out from Tobermory's breast wall with one oar each, circumnavigating the bay and safely bring-ing the boat back again – but given the steep upwards trajectory of Norrie's self-created sea-faring course, we were soon looking for bigger things.

Calve Island lay only half a mile across the water of the bay, but here, truly, was a place where no one ever went. Despite the fact you could clearly see Calve from Tobermory's bustling Main Street, I think you'd struggle to find more than a handful of people who had ever set foot there. Getting to Calve was our equivalent of the lunar landing. It was 'Calve or bust'. We had the means (Norrie's dad's boat), we had the time (school was an irrelevance, homework a nonsense), we had the experience (well, we did according to Norrie) – so it was the obvious next step and really, if I was nervous at all, I'd just remind myself that this was *exactly* the sort of adventure I'd always hoped for. Just like all those boats that rolled into Tobermory Bay, we were finally heading off to our own far-flung and adventurous places.

For reasons that aren't completely clear to me now, we had Norrie's uncle's dog, Bess, with us on that first trip. Bess was a curly poodle-type hound of mixed ancestry, but she seemed keen, so out into the boat we all went. Steadily, we began to paddle across the bay, but this time we didn't stop. The boat drifted out across deep and dark waters frequented by porpoises and grey and common seals, heading towards the island.

At the time, we were huge fans of the *Scooby-Doo* cartoons (maybe that was why we had brought the dog?), the paranormal adventures and crime-busting investigations of four teenagers and their cowardly Great Dane, and in particular we liked the pugnacious Scrappy-Doo with his 'Puppy Power!' catchphrase. Whenever we felt we needed to put a bit of extra welly into our strokes, out would go the 'Puppy Power!' shout, and away we'd pump – whirling our oars, pulling and pushing our way right out across the bay and off into virgin waters.

Slowly, we drew up to the island's shoreline. A dense and dark floating mat of bladder wrack seaweed ringed the coast, and the dog, who was clearly ready to get her paws onto dry land, leapt clear of the boat. Clearly, our hairy shipmate had thought the bladder wrack was all solid, and, as she disappeared in a panicked splash of water and weed, Norrie and I both fell about laughing. We grasped down into the weed's thick twisting arms and pulled up our daft friend, before we stepped out onto Calve proper for the very first time.

Curving, dark shoreline rock, all creased and weathered through waves, storms and time, gave way to what looked like a near-impenetrable interior, all choked up with bracken and dense grasses. For a moment, I stood on that shoreline, caught my breath and tried to take it all in. Calve felt like a place that sat some way beyond human habitation, yet when I looked back across the bay towards our home, I could still make out the rainbow line of Tobermory's main street with its piers, trees and boats.

They looked so small and distant now. Everyone I knew was over there, getting on with their normal lives while Norrie and I were landed here, somewhere utterly new and extremely exciting. I took a deep breath and just thought, *Not a single person has the faintest idea that we are here.*

I hadn't ever felt like that before – it was an intoxicating and, quite honestly, pretty addictive feeling. It was one that I've probably chased for most of my life since that moment, but nothing was ever really going to live up to that first time. We might not have got a flight anywhere, or even come close to slipping over the seaward horizon; in fact, if anyone'd had a pair of binoculars, they'd clearly have seen us both stood there gawping back across the bay, but it still felt like we'd landed on the moon. Ready to make our own 'small steps' while staring back at our tiny home planet, fully able to compress Tobermory in its entirety just in the gap between our thumbs and forefingers.

So what, Norrie, are we going to do now?

Calve is a little over a mile across, so plenty big enough for two little lads on their first major expedition. Pretty quickly, we discovered that the island's dense interior was very hard going. There was one obvious hill and a few wetter areas where bog myrtle grew, bearing its yellow catkins in the spring and sending out a fresh citrus scent if you rubbed its leaves in your palms. There was also a prolific number of nesting birds, including terns, swans, ducks and, especially, herring gulls, but barring a single white cottage on the south-facing coast (okay, so we knew that Mrs Cotton lived there in the summer), we found no real evidence of any human activities whatsoever. No proper pathways or management, no visiting boats, wildlife tours or other semi-feral kids. It felt fundamentally untamed, just as nature had intended, and above all, it felt like it was *all ours*.

Years later, I came to learn of the long history of land use on Calve. As a teenager, I worked at a pony-trekking centre run out of a croft by a family called the MacDougalls. Their extended family included a pair of brothers who held the traditional grazing rights to Calve and, periodically, I'd row out and help them dip and inoculate the sheep they'd been grazing there. The truth was, Calve had long since been shaped by the hands of humans and their agricultural ambitions, but I was blind to that as a child, and I doubt I would've cared if I'd known anyway. Especially given that my main focus was always going to be the island's coast.

Living on Mull, it became immediately apparent that I was magnetically drawn a magnetic draw towards the shore. I would spend hours scouring rockpools and the tideline for anything of interest. Shells, driftwood, shiny pieces of sea-glass, brilliant white cuttlefish bones, bashed-up crates or mermaid's purses. My prize find was a stranded and sadly deceased porpoise; I didn't discriminate, *all* the artefacts belched onto a beach could tell a story of sorts and *everything* was a potential treasure, however broken, sharp or smelly.

Even an old tin can could take on a special quality once it had spent time drifting around the saltwater. New life would grow on its sea-weathered body, populating its original metal form with fine weeds, shells, barnacles, even tiny crustaceans and shrimps, and that was before you'd poured out its innards to find out what had long since slipped inside to call it home.

In some of Mull's more sheltered bays and coves, you could even discover something of the history of that little patch of water too. Those little areas once provided a sanctuary for the boats that worked our seas and, if something had broken on board, you could very well imagine a sailor just lobbing it overboard. I'd find it amazing that the very next hand those broken pieces would meet could be mine. These little historical echoes from the sea – shattered plates and cracked cups, some of which were delicately decorated with Chinese symbols or drawings, all of them carrying their own stories out to the ocean, and sometimes over extreme distances too.

Things haven't changed. I still love the shore and, quite honestly, if I didn't have any responsibilities, or all my dearly loved ones at home, I'd probably become a full-time hermit living in some remote hut on a beach somewhere. Is there even such a thing as a professional beachcomber? That's what I'd be, anyway. I'd never get bored of raking about between the rocks looking for stuff. Pretty soon on Mull, the primary motivation for any coastal adventure was looking for treasure. Bits of pottery aside, there was actually good reason to believe you had an outside chance of finding something truly valuable too.

Legend had it that lying somewhere on the bottom of Tobermory Bay was the wreck of a great Spanish galleon. Allegedly, it had fled the English fleet in 1588 before anchoring in Tobermory for supplies. There, it had found its watery grave not at the barrel of the English naval cannons, but rather at the hands of the locals. Now, depending on your capacity for fantasy and fable, one branch of local folklore spins the yarn that it was the local clan chief, Donald Maclean (yes, that *is* the very same Maclean ancestral line shared by Norrie), who bravely boarded the galleon to get the money, only to be locked deep within the bowels of the ship's munitions store. In a move straight out of the James Bond handbook, Maclean then managed not only to escape his prison cell, but also to set fire to the munitions store as he went, thus sending the ship explosively into Davy Jones's famous locker – a story that would've probably pleased a young Norrie no end. By far the most important piece of all the various galleon legends, though, was the rumour that it was carrying an immense hoard of gold bullion. All of which had sunk to the depths of Tobermory Bay alongside the wreck itself.

The whole story isn't quite as daft as it sounds. Throughout the mid-1600s, cannons and guns from Spanish wrecks foundered near Tobermory were actually recovered by crews using primitive diving bells. Even as late as the 1950s, the Duke of Argyll signed a contract with the British Admiralty to locate the Spanish galleon of legend. They recovered cannons and cannon balls, and even a human skull, but no gold.

One day, Norrie and I did find something really special on Calve. There we were, just doing what we always did: picking our way along the high-tide line looking for interesting things, when, on one of the island's sand flats, nestled among the kelp and some old broken bits of tangled net and rope, we discovered a small brown canister with something trapped inside.

Quickly, we pulled off the lid and found a completely dry piece of paper rolled up, which asked for our names, addresses, the date and precisely where we had found this utterly authentic 'message in a bottle'. That was incredibly exciting in itself. Goodness knows how many messages in a bottle we had sent out ourselves, without *ever* getting any replies – but I remember that the top of this message had, quite sensationally, declared that this little bottle had first been released into the ocean by research scientists based all the way over in Nova Scotia, 2,500 miles away, on the eastern coast of Canada!

We rushed home, immediately filled out the form and posted it straight back to Nova Scotia – and never heard anything from them ever again. Still, neither Norrie nor I could quite get over what we'd found on Calve that day. This wasn't just some crap that had broken off a boat or been idly tossed out into the sea; whoever had placed that bottle in the Nova Scotian ocean had hoped that it would be found by *someone* – and that *someone* just happened to be us. I guess it did make us feel pretty special to be the people who'd ended that bottle's transatlantic journey, but more than that, it felt incredible that something so small had made such a giant crossing. Through storms, along currents, and with an almost infinite number of variables that could've sent it off in any given direction, only for it to come into our hands that day. The odds against us finding it felt truly astronomical and it left a deep impression. Really cool things could happen, if you keep looking out for them.*

---

* I recently asked Norrie about that wondrous find – and was stunned when he replied that the bottle hadn't, in fact, floated 2,500 miles from Nova Scotia. It was actually from an oceanography department in Cork University, on the southeast coast of Ireland. Still, pretty amazing that it had come into our hands that day – but it does say a lot about how, as a child, I'd been so desperate for this message to have been from the absolute furthest place I could conjure up in my imagination, that I'd then fully believed it really had come from Nova Scotia for the next four decades!

After that very first visit to Calve, I imagine we would've employed some serious 'Puppy Power' to pump us back to Tobermory before darkness fell. However, no sooner had we set foot back on home shores, I am sure we would've made immediate plans to return to Calve as soon as possible. And return we did, time and again, to our own patch of paradise, cast away in Tobermory Bay.

Inevitably, Norrie's parents discovered that we'd been taking their rowing boat out to Calve on our own – but by that point, we really were demonstrably capable of rowing and staying safe, so it wasn't going to be a problem. In those days, in those remote and rural parts of Scotland, if you were proven capable of doing something, then your age didn't hugely matter. Kids would go off all day and learn how to look after themselves while climbing, fishing, swimming or playing endless expansive outdoor games on their own. Realistically, Norrie's mum and dad would have known that they couldn't have stopped us even if they had tried, and besides, it was better that than having us getting in their way kicking about the house all day long.

Norrie's maternal grandmother had grown up on the island of Tiree, over on the far western edge of the Inner Hebrides. Twelve miles long and just three miles wide, with a population numbering only in the hundreds, Tiree made Mull look like Manhattan. Locals there maintained crofts, small farms on the fertile land, and fished. These were tough, practical people, so really, Norrie's mum wasn't going to be remotely bothered that we were taking these, now quite regular, expeditions across to Calve. In fact, once she'd realised what we were doing, she asked us to collect some herring gull eggs for her to cook up.

In one fell swoop, Norrie and I had officially graduated from secretive 'island pioneers' to established hunter-gatherers and providers – and Norrie's mum always rewarded our endeavours with the most delicious, buttery-yellow gull's egg pancakes known to mankind.

Calve Island still feels like *my* place, somewhere I feel a real sense of deep belonging and peace. It would probably be my choice for going full-time 'beach-combing hermit' and periodically, I'll still go back to Mull and make my pilgrimage. Standing on that desolate Calve shoreline again, just as I once did as a boy, I'll look back over the bay towards Tobermory and am somehow still able to think, *You're all over there and I'm all alone over here.*

Must Try Harder

For me, school on Mull was torturous.

Away from school, as long as we were back home for nightfall (a rule we *mostly* stuck to) and didn't do anything considered to be too life-shortening (another rule we *mostly* stuck to), we were free to roam wherever we pleased. School though, was enforced captivity.

Breaktimes were great, but that aside, it is fair to say that whenever I was inside that place, I always wanted to escape outside. No matter how hard I might've tried, I just couldn't seem to focus on anything – quite ironic given the importance of 'focus' and concentration as a wildlife cameraman. I *hated* being forced to sit still in a chair and listen to the teacher, and I really struggled with the subject material too. Reading, or at least absorbing what I was reading, was a big problem, as was basic maths.

I'm pretty sure I'm dyslexic. I haven't ever been formally tested, but whenever I've taken those free 'Hey! So, you think you're dyslexic?' tests online, it's always confirmed my strong suspicions.

As an adult, I've found my own ways to work around it, but reading still exhausts my brain. I have to start slowly, in my own time and at my own pace, and piece the words together in line with the unique way my own mind interprets words on a page.

That said, I read a lot of books and love listening to audiobooks too. I now know that if I can place words on a page with the right font and spacing, I can get it all to make sense to me – but that took many years to hone and perfect and was never the case at school. Maths can still sometimes be a problem, especially if a maths question comes my way without warning. It used to be like someone had lobbed a bucket of iced water in my face, but as a grown man, now in a very different time and place, I do find it a lot easier to simply say, 'I sometimes have trouble with maths.'

Dyslexia recognition wasn't too widespread when I was growing up – at least, it certainly wasn't on Mull. There were twins in our class that were 'diagnosed' as dyslexic, and they got extra help, support and more time to complete the tasks set in school. It just never occurred to me that that was my problem. In my mind, and probably my teacher's too, my issue was daydreaming and not dyslexia. Generally, the feeling was if you fell behind, it wasn't because you had additional learning needs, you were pretty much always dismissed as being a bit slow or thick, and that was that. The attitude among my teachers was 'but, this is *easy*' – they never stepped back to reflect on *why* I might have been really struggling to get it.

It was *always* embarrassing and meant that I largely spent my school days avoiding the things I found the hardest to do. You'd think that would be pretty much impossible, but believe me, if I'd put half the effort into finding some ways to learn that suited me better, as opposed to the energy I put into cheating, then I certainly would've finished school with better grades than I did.

Norrie always did well at school, so that helped an awful lot as I could sit next to him and copy his answers. That's entry-level cheating of course, anyone could do that, but there were times when a more sophisticated strategy *had* to be employed.

In my later primary years, on Friday afternoons, we would have tests called 'Twenty Mental'. It went a bit like this: we would all be sent to the 'noisy quiet room' and the teacher would call out 20 'simple' arithmetic questions: adding, subtracting, basic division and multiplication.

At first, getting around the basic fact that I knew virtually none of the answers was really easy. I'd leave the answer blank and then I'd just sneakily fill it in when the rest of the class called out their answers in unison. I wasn't foolish enough to get 20 out of 20 on the 'Twenty Mental' – oh no, that was a classic rookie error; *always* aim for 'bang average' and you'll never be questioned.

For a time, I coasted, only really grasping the most basic addition and subtraction, and avoiding the times tables (my nemesis) like the plague – my palms still get sweaty at the thought – but then things got quite a lot harder.

The teacher must've cottoned on to the sheer amount of cheating that was happening during 'Twenty Mental' and so we were made to mark our work using a different coloured pencil than the one we had just written our answers with. She even made us give up the answer pencils to make sure there could be no skullduggery whatsoever. It took an extra bit of sleight of hand, and a hell of a lot more anxiety, but I did mostly get away with it by smuggling an extra 'answer' pencil up my sleeve. The rest of the time, I employed a charm offensive. Cause no trouble, be polite, say 'please' and 'thank you', and you'll be afforded a stunning amount of leeway.

There wasn't any real Machiavellian intention behind me being polite. I wasn't actually doing it to get away with cheating in my tests; I was a basically nice wee fella at heart, and wanted my teachers to see that in me too. Especially my first teacher on Mull, Miss Annie Shepherd.

Miss Shepherd was a beautiful, deeply loving and caring lady. She really swept me up from day one and made sure I was always okay. It was probably just that I was the new kid, so she felt a duty of care to help me settle in, but I genuinely felt like I was her special little guy too, and I'd have done anything to keep her happy.

That wasn't too hard, I really *was* always very polite and well-mannered – and would cling to those specific phrases turning up in my report card as the one real positive alongside 'must try harder', or – worse – 'Gordon tries hard' appearing next to a shockingly bad grade. The only really annoying thing I ever used to do was lob pebbles into the backs of the other kid's wellies when they weren't looking. A real little dick way to be carrying on, especially if they were doing hopscotch and were mid-jump. I was elite-level world-class at 'welly pebble' though, and I took real delight in watching my victims have to sit down and shake my pebble free.

Then there was the fox. Oh, good god, the fox. Miss Shepherd had set up a workshop around 'old things' and asked us if we had any 'old things' at home that we would like to bring in and display. Fiona, one of the girls in our class, brought in a fox fur stole from her grandparents. (That's a 'fox fur stole', *not a fox fur she'd stolen!*) Fox stoles are essentially, and quite macabrely, a completely skinned fox from nose to tail, which served as popular scarves among women of a certain class in the first half of the twentieth century. Miss Shepherd thanked Fiona for bringing in the stole and explained to everyone, very clearly, that under absolutely no circumstances was it ever to be touched.

It went onto the 'show and tell' table alongside the rest of the old things, for us all to look at, but I only ever had eyes for that fox. I found it fascinating. Its pointed snout and lithe auburn body, and then the tail. Goodness. The tail. This heavy-looking voluminous furry mass that extended for half that fox's body. The poor thing must've been killed in its full winter coat, and not only was it beautiful, but it was also the oldest thing I'd ever seen. It was the closest I'd been to a fox too. (There aren't any foxes left on Mull, or badgers or squirrels for that matter. Despite a common misconception that those species have never been on the island, I have actually seen deeds from a Victorian-era estate which detailed the gamekeeper's fees for removing all of those animals – so it was a culling and trapping effort that saw them off, rather than them never having been present in the wild.)

I knew I was about to do a very bad thing, but my urge to examine this new creature was far too overpowering. Everyone else had gone to break. The teachers were off in the staff room having a smoke, most of the boys were running around as footy champs and Norrie was presumably chalking up a hopscotch grid. So I sloped off back into class, purely to get my illicit paws on that illustrious animal.

I double-checked no one was around and quickly picked it up, only for, horror of all horrors, the tail to snap clean off.

It lay on the ground as a big furry mess, and, in that moment, it felt as if the fiery gates of hell had yawned open directly beneath me. *This*, I thought to myself, *is the single worst thing I have ever done in my life.*

With panic building, I darted my eyes around the room like a meerkat on lookout. *No one is here*, I deduced, correctly; so, very slowly and carefully, I replaced the fox on the table and gently slid the two severed parts of its body back together. Like a substandard magician ham-fistedly conjoining two halves of his severed assistant, I prayed no one in the audience would spot my own metaphorical mirrors. As long as there was no gap in the animal, I thought I might just get away with this for days, by which time, no one would be able to guess it was me.

Everyone came back from break and Miss Shepherd noticed it instantly. Her embarrassment was profound. Having apologised profusely to Fiona, and asked her to pass on all her apologies to her grandparents too, she rounded on the class. 'Who has done this?' she asked. I felt every inch of me tighten. I was compelled to tell her the truth, to show her that I wasn't a liar, but also, I dearly wanted to just take my deception to the grave. I had a deeply held belief that I was her 'special wee guy', and honestly thought that if Miss Shepherd could pick the person she least wanted to be the 'great fox breaker', then I would be at the very top of her list. I had *hugely* let her down.

It was horrendous. I sat there in silence, sensing that I absolutely reeked of suspicion and shame. Everyone must've known it was me, *I was the only person who didn't go out for break!* But still, I said nothing, and it is no exaggeration to say that for many weeks afterwards, I still assumed I was going to get caught, and it took years before I privately fessed up to my friends, who could all still remember the fateful day that Fiona's fox was broken in half.

It is fair to say that the pressure of things like cheating at 'Twenty Mental', the guilt I felt over lying about the fox and also a weird, pervasive feeling that I was going to be randomly arrested at some point (despite never actually committing a real crime) and then spend some time in prison, all pretty much point towards my school days having often been fraught with anxiety.

'Twenty Mental.' Even now those two words can give me the chills. And I still haven't told Fiona that it was me who broke her grandparents' fox. Fiona, if you are reading this, I am profoundly sorry!

In the end, every single member of my 'B' class (you couldn't get lower than 'B' class) failed their O-grade (the Scottish GCSE or O level equivalent) arithmetic exams. We were a collection of truly *terrible* students, so none of that was any good for my learning, but then it turned out I was colour-blind as well.

I know. A colour-blind and dyslexic wildlife cameraman. It sounds like a comedy sketch from the 1970s. That all became very clear (or very unclear) on the day a teacher looked over my shoulder and simply asked: 'Gordon, why do you always colour in old people's hair that colour?' I looked down at my drawing. 'Erm.' Feeling more than a little bit confused, I proffered, 'Because that's the colour of old people's hair?' It turned out I hadn't been able to tell the difference between grey and green.

One day, an external assessor arrived from the mainland: a brusque, sour-faced lady armed with a bunch of colour-blindness test sheets. Fortunately for me, I'd been forewarned about her investigations by my brothers.

'D'ya know what she's here for, Gordy?'

'Nope,' I'd innocently replied.

'She's gonna feel yer balls.'

Brilliant. So regardless of the fact she was actually setting me a colour test that I had zero hope of passing, I went into her little testing room with the awful feeling that I was actually about to be forced to drop my underpants.

'Well?' she said sharply. 'What can you see?' Soon, rather than me showing her my bollocks, I was staring at a sheet of paper covered in lots of little dots and bubbles. I now know that they were all different colours, and that, right in the middle of it all, you were supposed to clearly see one massive number. Well, with that first sheet, I couldn't see anything, and told her so. To be honest, I had assumed it was a trick question.

'What?' she replied sternly, looking at me as if I was the biggest of our village's idiots. 'In the middle, boy! What's the number?'

I looked again. Nothing. She tried another one, and I could sort of make out the number, but then, as we cycled through the next few sheets, it all went blank again. By this point, I knew that this was definitely not a trick and there really was a number on every page. Given how annoyed she was already, I thought it was best to just guess. Which, obviously, made her even more angry.

I might've been able to cheat on some of my tests, but there was to be no getting around my colour-blindness. As a teenager, I'd dreamt of being a light-aircraft pilot. I'd seen a documentary in which a pilot in East Africa flew around in a Cessna plane, spotting animals so a ground team could move in and round up the species to translocate them elsewhere. All pretty niche, but that was a lightbulb moment. *I'd love to do that*, I'd thought, *to be out there with all those big elephants and rhinos, flying a plane right over the top*. Incredible. The ultimate freedom.

I turned 15 and the careers guidance counsellor was ushered into school from the mainland. Whenever it was time for 'real talk' they seemed to float these serious people over from the west coast. 'No, son. You can't be a pilot if you're colour-blind,' he'd said, instantly killing that one off. 'In fact, you can't join the RAF, the police, the fire service, or be an electrician ...' He went on and on, thumbing through his big book of jobs that I could no longer do.

I wasn't bothered about the rest of those careers, but part of me wondered if I could find some sort of 'spare pencil' loophole around my colour-blindness, and somehow still become a pilot. There was no time to think about any of that though; the bloke was already ushering me through a different thermocline. 'We've studied the results of your tests,' he continued. 'According to this, you'd be best suited to being a nanny. Is that something you'd be interested in, Gordon?'

I mean no offence whatsoever to anyone who is a nanny, but it wasn't something that felt like my one true calling. Not long after that, a twist of fate would set me on the path to becoming a wildlife cameraman but, before I'd left school to pursue that, the careers officer was back again.

This time, he went to great lengths to tell me that 'wildlife cameraman' wasn't in his big book of jobs either, and was therefore not a viable career option. I told him all the reasons that it actually was, not least because I'd met one on the island and he'd offered me a job. He harrumphed and went back to the book for help.

'Zookeeper!' he eventually declared. 'You could be a zookeeper!'

Monkey See, Monkey Do

We see ourselves as by far the best, the most successful and the smartest animal on earth, by virtue of the fact that we will score top marks in any of the intelligence tests we set for both ourselves and the other animals. But the idea of 'intelligence' is nearly always measured by our human standards – so the chimps that use rudimentary tools in a way that's similar to our Stone Age ancestors are 'intelligent', as are the orangutans who have learnt to make umbrellas out of leaves, the lab pigs that can operate a joystick, the rats in experiments that will play 'hide and seek' with people, or the ravens and parrots that exhibit complex problem-solving behaviour. All of them are graded by us, according to both what they have in common with us and how well they can execute that task compared to us.

But what is the purpose of the pig learning to use the joystick anyway? It no doubt learnt to use it to get a food reward, which is smart, but it's no real test of the actual applied intelligence of what pigs really do in the wild, is it? And therein lies the problem. If you're an animal with no obvious human attributes, for instance, an earthworm, then you're highly unlikely to meet any of our 'intelligence' standards, as there isn't a test we can 'set' to measure you. That's despite the fact the earthworm's physiological intelligence in its movements and make-up, which can reshape landscapes and change the entire consistency of soil, are quite clearly vastly superior to our own.

The truth is that every species on this planet, even the most marginal or endangered, has had to survive, adapt and evolve their way through an extraordinarily diverse range of 'tests' set by the habitats and deep time in which they have lived. The creatures around us are inherently 'intelligent' by virtue of the fact that they are still here with us – survivors of all those evolutionary twists and climatological curveballs. Yet, instead of crediting and valuing other species with, at the very least, an equivalent intelligence for the remarkable skills they must possess, we'd far rather dismiss them altogether by saying something like: 'Ah yeah, but they can't actually speak, can they? They haven't got any words.'

We also judge other animals on their ability to collaborate with each other. There can be no doubt that the success of the modern human species has hinged on our ability to get things done by working together. I don't just mean at the basest level, for instance, how a football team work together to pass a ball around a pitch, but the almost immeasurable levels of human collaboration that have occurred to make so many of the everyday things that we take for granted.

Chimpanzees, by human standards, are widely considered to be our most intelligent relative. Naturally, they have a proven ability to behave in ways that will feel familiar to us, and their ability to collaborate effectively with each other is also widely proven. Chimps have the largest average group size of any of the non-human great ape species (45–55 members, but it can be as large as 100-plus individuals). In fact, their levels of collaboration have even been seen to improve the *larger* the troop size becomes, especially if they are required to work together in the hunting of smaller primates, like colobus monkeys. However, there is also a critical mass of chimp troop membership, beyond which the entire collaborative effort falls apart and the whole society collapses into chaos. The precise number for that 'tipping point' varies between troops, but regardless, you will never see chimpanzees being able to collaborate on anything like the same mass scale as us. If required, we are demonstrably capable of collaborating in the collective order of tens of thousands of individuals, whereas chimps couldn't even come close to that number. A really basic example would be to imagine a big concert venue, let's say an arena that holds a few thousand people. We'll all file in there, watch and enjoy the gig, and leave in orderly streams right after the final encore. Substitute all those people for chimps and it is an all-out war. The chimps would be tearing each other limb from limb before the soundcheck had even started, and that's not just because they've seen the price of the beer.

However, if you were to place, let's say, 15 chimps in that very same arena situation, perhaps with people to model their behaviour, then they would likely be capable of toeing the line and even understanding when it was time to leave. Intelligent to a degree then, but still nowhere near our level. Right? Well, no. Not really.

One of the most incredible animal studies I've ever seen was testing the ability of a chimp to recognise a sequence. The chimp in question, Ayumu, was presented with a mixed spread of numbers across a screen from one to nine. Those nine numbers would then disappear, and Ayumu would have to point out, in ascending order, where each of the numbers had just been.

Superficially, this might all sound quite straightforward, and potentially very human too. Most of us would feel fairly confident that, given enough time, we could memorise the positions of the nine numbers on a screen, and then indicate the positions they were in when they vanish. Some of us could be pretty good at it too.

I might not have had any really obvious strengths within the academic arenas laid out at my school (and I'll leave any commentary on the quality of my camerawork and television presenting ability up to you, my dear reader) but one thing that came to light later in my life was that I am, in fact, a 'super recogniser'.

Super recognisers are people with the ability to memorise and recall thousands of faces, often having only ever seen them once. It wasn't something I was that conscious of – I just assumed everyone could do it – but when I did become aware that my ability to recognise faces was way above the average, I pretty quickly realised I'd also have to keep it a little quiet for the most part. There's a very fine line between really weirding people out in public, because you've just recognised them from the one time you saw them working in a shop on your high street, and making those same people feel noticed in a really positive way, because you recognise them from the one time you saw them working in a shop on your high street.

I'd always felt that it was mostly a nice thing to be recognised, that idea that we are not 'invisible' as regular people going about lives anonymously. I certainly don't mind when strangers come up to me to say hello because they've enjoyed one of my programmes. I think it jolts me out of my everyday meanderings and is, I hope, a pleasant interlude for us both. Although, I did laugh the other day when someone shouted out across the street: 'Ho! Gordon Buchanan! You're a wanker!'

Super recognisers have found employment within the intelligence services and police, with the real elite even capable of outscoring computer recognition software and (for now) artificial intelligence, when it comes to placing human faces. My powers of recognition were so good, I was even brought into a University of Greenwich study. That, though, was where things got quite a bit trickier. My ability to recognise human faces remained strong – so I was moved on to chimp faces, which was okay (chimps, facially, can still look quite different), but it all fell apart with dogs. I can remember being shown a photo of these three pugs, and then the test would move along and I had to punch a button if I could remember seeing the same pug again. What I learnt from that particular study is that pugs really *do* all look the same, and that my ability to 'super recognise' was limited to human facial recognition only. If you were going to commit a crime, I'd say, off the record, it's best if you train a pug to do it for you.

Regardless of the specifics of the various tests though, elementally, recognising and committing to memory certain patterns, sequences or 'faces' is something that some humans can really excel at – but that's only when compared to other humans.

Ayumu was exceptional at the number sequence test, even among chimps. He was able to correctly remember the sequence almost 90 per cent of the time – knocking out the numbers in seconds, having only actually seen them for a fraction of a second beforehand.

It was quite something to behold, and far in advance of anything humans could ever manage. Even the very best of the human participants at the research institute were never able to beat Ayumu. In fact, even your most bang average chimp was able to beat most humans more often than not.

Ayumu's skill isn't in tracking the position of each number with his eyes; the duration of time the numbers flash on the screen isn't even enough to scan the screen. It's that chimps have an 'eidetic' memory – this ability to see the entire pattern as an instant snapshot and then commit it straight to their memory. Researchers believe we lost that ability and replaced it with language; but it is humbling, to say the least, that when it comes to one of our very own tests of human intelligence, our skill in remembering stuff, there are animals that can batter us with real ease.

For the chimp, its eidetic talent makes perfect sense. Chimps need to very quickly evaluate snapshot patterns when they are deciding which tree might hold more fruit in the forest, or make decisions about what branches to cling to as they move through a jungle at speed. For us, the survival imperative to process a pattern or memory in that really urgent way just isn't there. If we tried to sprint across a busy four-lane motorway, we would probably die, and the chimp would probably make it.

It's not simply that chimps have a better memory than us, though, it's that they see the world in an entirely different way. We may share a common ancestor and we may have traits that feel very familiar, but fundamentally the chimpanzee has evolved along its own distinctive path; our real blind spot is our failure to recognise that other species interpret the world in ways that we can't even comprehend. Fundamentally chimps are *neither* more nor less intelligent than us – they are simply better at being what they are: chimps.

Trailer Teuchter

Teuchter (noun) – *Originally a term of*
disparagement adopted by Central Scottish and used
to describe Highlanders or Islanders, especially those who
are Gaelic speaking. More recently reclaimed locally as
a term of rural pride in a 'Teuchter' identity.

There were always going to be a few things that marked my family out as a little bit different when we first arrived on Mull. To begin with, we must have sounded different, having not yet adopted a Hebridean lilt. Given the overwhelming majority of full-time families on Mull were indigenous, long-term generational residents, who rarely seemed to move from the island, that made us pretty novel for a start. Of course, tourists arrived from outside – in their droves during the summer holidays – but at our little local school it was pretty clear that we were always going to be an unknown quantity. But the community of Mull is a very easy-going and welcoming one. Pretty soon, we went from being a curiosity to being accepted and well integrated. I certainly felt like I quickly slotted into my new island life – but I probably just retained a wee bit of that 'outsider' feeling in my subconscious.

There was one difference that was less surmountable though. Our dad wasn't with us. Unlike on the Bellsmyre estate, where single-parent families were typical, when we moved to Mull, I realised that we were now one of very few families who'd experienced a divorce.

Occasionally, I'd have these pretty awkward conversations with well-meaning people who didn't know us too well: 'So who are you and who are your people?' it would begin. 'Gordon Buchanan,' I'd politely reply, and watch as the mist descended on their face as they flicked through their mental version of Mull's *Yellow Pages*, searching for the local familial link.

Naturally, they'd draw a blank and out would come the searching: 'Oh, so who's your father then?' question. 'Oh, well, you wouldn't know him,' I'd fumble along, having already seen this whole conversation unfolding before it had even started. Soon, I'd be forced to admit that 'he doesn't actually live here'.

That was always a bit of a sting.

It wasn't like I was in any way embarrassed about being from a divorced family. It was more that I felt I'd almost have to try and explain it to them using their own terms of reference, maybe because I thought they might not understand that some families just didn't live with their dads. It was a second-hand embarrassment at their own awkwardness that the standard 'Mull solution' of twinning an unfamiliar face with a father figure just wasn't ever going to work with me.

In the early summer of 1979, my mum bought a modern-style caravan off a farmer on the mainland and we moved into it in the August of that year. I remember thinking it was pretty posh compared to my grandparents' old caravan that had stood on the same site. It had an instant gas water heater, a two-bar electric heater and a small Portaloo-type toilet with a shower cubicle. To get maximum water-to-cleansing benefit, the shower hole would be plugged to affect a shallow bath for us all to wash in, but, on a very occasional Sunday, Stewart, Maggie and I would wander up the lane to a guest house run by a lovely lady called Sheila. Our mum and Sheila were friends, and she would let us have an actual bath at her guest house (*what opulence!*) so we were clean as a whistle in time for school on Monday. Sandy didn't accompany us for that scrub down. The three of us would share the bath and, even if he could have fitted, I can't imagine Sandy fancied a communal wash with his siblings. He always preferred a sit-down shower in the caravan.

My mum was, and still is, a resourceful lady – always capable of finding a workaround if it saves time, money or hassle – but with five of us using just one portable toilet, it used to fill up pretty quickly. A full loo meant either borrowing a car from a friend or lugging it somewhere to dispose of the contents, so our mum came up with a toilet remedy to extend the fill time: 'Pee down the shower plughole, give it a quick rinse away and save the loo for the big jobbies.' I remember thinking that this not only made sense, but that my mum was a genius.

It all worked out alright as a system until I invited Alastair Campbell (no, not *that* one!) over to the caravan. My mum was relieved that I was making some more school friends and over he came for the very warmest of Buchanan welcomes. My mum offered Alastair some digestive biscuits and I gave him the grand tour, which, owing to logistics and caravan dimensions, couldn't have lasted more than 90 seconds. Then, quite reasonably, he asked to use the loo. 'Yeah, no problem,' I said, before adding, 'if it's a jobbie use the loo, but if it's a pee then send it down the plughole in the shower.'

That line fired off inside my mum as if one of us lads had urinated on an electric fence. 'Auch!' she burst in, red-faced and affecting a highly self-conscious and utterly unconvincing laugh. 'Gordon! Peeing down the plughole! I've never heard something so ridiculous!'

I stood there blankly, trying to work out if she had completely lost her marbles. 'What a ridiculous notion!' She was doubling down, trying to make me understand something I couldn't quite grasp, while my now distinctly cross-legged pal, Alastair Campbell, was directed *firmly* towards civilised society in the form of a very proper Portaloo pee.

• • •

Our mum's theory of us having more space on Mull was one that was carried by the great expansive wilds outside and not by our living space. The caravan was even smaller than the Bellsmyre council flat. It had a single communal living area-cum-kitchenette, where our mum

Sandy, my mum, me (on her lap) and Stewart at Butlins before our parents split

Me feeling under the weather and tucked up in our grandparents' garden

Bellsmyre Scallywags: Sandy back left, Stewart and I centre of middle row, and Maggie second from left front row.

The Buchanan Garage – our family business.

Me in a pirate outfit at the community Halloween party, circa 1980.

Outside the flat in Bellsmyre
housing estate. Maggie and I
are the two curly tops!

A rare family trip to
Butlins: I'm in the pram,
Stewart is in the middle,
Sandy on the left.

The timber wolves
sheltering from inclement
Scottish weather.

The timber wolves
outside our caravan,
circa 1979.

Stewart and I on
the Calmac Pier
in Tobermory,
circa 1979.

Me riding in a cross country event in Argyll.

Left to right: Stewart, me, Norrie & another local kid on Fisherman's Pier, Tobermory.

Our home on Tiwai Island
for a year and a half.

Me with friends from Kambama
village, Tiwai Island, Sierra Leone.

Nick and I in our Tiwai
bathing spot, 1990.

At the Tiwai
sunrise spot, 1990.

Me about 150 feet high in a tree opposite the scaffold tower on Tiwai, 1991.

Tiwai chimps.

In my hammock
at camp, 1990.

At Kambama village,
Sierra Leone, 1990.

Me with a palm civet on
shoulder on my 18th birthday.

Nick with Tum-Tum the otter.

cooked up the usual seventies fare for dinner: mince, spuds, stew, maybe a curry and rice, and then toast or cornflakes for breakfast.

Our bedrooms were just off the kitchen. Stewart and I shared one room with a set of 75cm wide bunk beds inside. I think there was a drawer underneath, but there wasn't really anywhere to put much of our stuff – to be fair, I think a grown man would've struggled to get in there, close the door and just stand square-on. There was another bedroom next door with a set of bunk beds for Sandy and Maggie, and then our mum would sleep on the little table in the living room, which you could neatly convert to a bed by dropping it to seat level and laying cushions on top.

It might all sound a bit threadbare and tight, but it was far from bleak. There was a housing shortage at the time, so lots of young families were living in caravans, and we weren't one bit bothered that ours was crowded. It always felt really homely and cosy to me. In fact, I honestly thought that living in a caravan was quite exotic and actually felt sorry for all those people stuck in their big boring houses. My mum worked incredibly hard to make sure we never went without – we certainly didn't consider ourselves to be poor, and we never felt dissimilar to anyone else either.

Our caravan was situated on the edge of Tobermory, tucked into a small wood and close to a workshop-cum-garage. Frankly, I felt like we had won the lottery. For an adventurous child, I had the best of all worlds. I could lark about the caravan with my brothers and sister, head off and build dens with school mates, or, when I needed to be alone, have my own exclusive set of trees to completely lose myself in. Then there was a whole load of half-disassembled cars and vans to play in too.

That first summer, I was absolutely living the dream. I'd run around those woods, climb trees and then muck about in all the old scrappy bangers in the workshop yard, jumping behind the wheel and playing endless games of cops and robbers. As far as we were all concerned, you slept in the caravan, you had a bit of brekkie and you were all out till tea and sleep. 'Home' was the rest of Mull, and we were all outside nearly all of the time. I loved it.

Looking back now, it's hard not to think about what it must've been like for our mum. On her own, sorting out all our teas, putting us to bed, then cleaning down and having to untuck her own duvet and cushions from beneath that little caravan table. It must've been tough at times, and completely exhausting, but she never once complained.

Things changed quite dramatically when it got cold. Late summer gave way to autumn and the chill blowing off the Western Isles soon began to sink its teeth into Mull. It was immediately obvious that our caravan was woefully ill-equipped for anything other than summer living, and by the time that first winter had properly arrived, it was absolutely freezing. I mean, ice-box cold, sub-zero from the whitened tips of your toes to the core of your shaking bones. Our mains water pipe froze solid.

As always, my mum did everything she could. Extra blankets and hot water bottles to take to bed with us every evening, but getting out of your sleeping bag in the morning was horrendous. I'm not sure how my mum navigated the provision of our copious cups of tea, but each morning we'd come into the living room area and she'd be there, holding our school clothes in front of that two-bar electric fire for us to slip on, each in turn.

Somehow, I still rationalised that winter was all part of the adventure. I can look back and see us huddled together on those winter mornings and feel that real sense of togetherness. It still wasn't all that bad, but I'm sure some residual feeling from that experience fed my lifelong hatred of being cold. Not cold places, I should say – I love those – just being really cold, especially if it was at all avoidable.

• • •

That bitter winter of 1979/80 aside, I have so many fond memories of living in the caravan. I can still see the many blessings they can bring. Living in ours taught me a lot about how little you actually need to crack on with life. How to cut back to the essentials and still be really happy and comfortable, and also, most importantly, how to happily work away in tight spaces.

I still prefer things that are simple and straightforward. Stripping away the clutter of our complex modern existence and just being able to know where everything is and exactly how it works. It's such a liberating feeling. Especially if you can fit everything into just one bag. Certainly, caravan living helped me adapt to working in wildlife hides, but I still really enjoy camping for pleasure too. When our kids were young, we had a couple of holidays in the south of France, staying in caravans that were the same dimensions as the one we'd all lived in on Mull. Sure, it was a lot warmer down there and caravans had improved in the thirty-odd years since I was first living on Mull, but I couldn't help but think that this was still a really great way to live. It's not even just the simplicity. There's something really fundamental about experiencing the sensation of rain and wind when you're safely ensconced inside a sturdy caravan or a good tent. Being deeply comfortable with the basics of life, with all that weather right there, raging away outside, while you're dry and warm, preferably with your loved ones and a solid dram in hand.

Yet, like most, I still choose to live in a nice normal house that is filled with way more things than I probably need, as well as all the clutter that I've picked up though a lifetime of working around the world.

I look around my study at all of the memories and know that I'd probably struggle to get rid of it all, but still, whether packing for work or holidays, I love the straightforward simplicity of having just one bag, and knowing that's going to be my entire world for the time being.

• • •

Island life suited me right down to the ground. I was settled into the 'teuchter' way – this slang word you'd occasionally hear thrown the way of Highlanders and Islanders by those from the south of the nation. It pretty much amounts to being called a country bumpkin or a hillbilly, but I quite like the idea of being a teuchter. As the months passed, I folded myself deep into Mull's island bays and crags. I orientated myself by nature, the trees, rocks and water, and soon felt that this place was where I was always meant to be. This was home.

Soon, Norrie and I were part of a little gang of Tobermory boys. Even though I would spend most of my time with Norrie, we also had McGuiness and Alan Malloy as the core of our wee tribe, and together we adventured all over our patch of the island and built dens in the trees.

Mull is a haven for nicknames. Pretty much everyone has one and they are used with such frequency that it is often quite hard to remember what someone's actual name is; that's if you ever knew it in the first place.

Norrie had the very much unwanted nickname of Twiggy and, as is often the way on the islands, he also inherited his common nickname from his dad: Tash, or wee Tash to give him his full title. McGuiness was actually Steven MacInnes, so that was pretty straightforward, and mine was Curly or Curly Bill. No prizes for figuring that one out! Curly, disappointingly, morphed into Shirley, and then I was called Beeve.

This was around the time that Citizen Band Radios (CBs) and walkie-talkies were at the peak of their popularity. Everyone knew someone who had one, and among young lads, calling each other, or bothering truckers, or just earwigging on other people's conversations, were just about the coolest things you could do. Everyone had to have a 'call-sign' or a 'handle' – their own unique name when they fired up their radio. Alan's was Soda Pop, I think McGuiness's was Bush Whacker, and mine was Beeve. Why? Well, periodically, I'd hear the football results read out over the CB airwaves, and, over in the small Fife town of Cowdenbeath, 'The Blue Brazil', Cowdenbeath FC, plied their trade in the

Scottish Lowland League. One day, I was listening to the results come in, still looking for a call-sign for myself, and mistakenly heard 'Gowden Beeve' instead of 'Cowdenbeath'. Realising that this mis-heard name spelt out my initials, GB, I drew the conclusion that 'Gowden Beeve' and I were a match made in CB heaven. Thus I adopted the call-sign Beeve in homage to the irresistible Gowden Beeve.

That was us: Malloy, McGuiness, Tash and Beeve. Looking back at some of the things we got up to together, it is quite something that no one was ever seriously hurt, or worse. Two really idiotic escapades immediately spring to mind – one involving Norrie's dad's boat and one involving cliffs, neither of which I could ever condone. To be frank, if I had ever caught my own children doing something as foolish as the things we did, I highly doubt I would have let them out of my sight ever again.

One day at school, there was a lot of excited playground chatter around the recent news reports. The tail-end of a hurricane was about to batter the west coast of Scotland, bringing huge winds and immense waves along with it. Norrie came over with a look of pure glee in his eye. 'Beeve, have you heard about the hurricane?' I looked at Norrie and then turned to McGuiness. Each of us was thinking the exact same thing: 'Let's go out in the boat!'

We can't have been much older than 12, but we had a fair few years' experience of punting Norrie's dad's boat about by then. It had been upgraded to fibreglass by now, and he'd even installed a little engine. 'Ah, this is going to be ace!' said McGuiness, as the afternoon's whistling winds announced the arrival of the heavy-duty weather. He was practically clapping his hands together in excitement – we all were; not for one second did anyone consider the stupendously stupid risk we were about to take. We didn't have life jackets and, obviously, our maritime expeditions were still largely taking place in secret – if any responsible person had known what we were up to, then clearly, despite the slightly lax attitude towards basic health and safety on Mull, we would've been stopped. *Immediately.*

I wish I could say that it did all go safely 'wrong'. That we were caught, rescued, soundly told off, or at the very least taught a very serious lesson – but I'm afraid we did, in fact, have an absolute ball.

The tail of the hurricane hit and the waves were whipped into a froth-capped frenzy. We hooped and hollered, driving the boat out into the swell, surging up and over the highest waters any of us had ever experienced. What a rush it was. He's a strapping man now, but back then, McGuiness was a titchy kid. I can still see him stood there, bouncing at the front of the boat and holding on to the rope for dear life, a miniature Horatio Nelson howling out in happiness. Norrie and I were at the back, driving the boat up the face and over the crest of enormous, towering waves before we slid down the backside of the breakers and went for it all over again, and again, and again.

We even slipped out from the shelter of Tobermory Bay and rode the massive dark and foaming seas that were pounding down the Sound of Mull. Screaming out into the salt and the spray, experiencing the most magnificent, magical, adrenalised high of our entire childhoods.

We pulled back into Tobermory, soaked through and still laughing, bonded forever by what we had all just felt. No one had even stopped to notice the three little boys and their boat, right out in the storm. Tobermory might be busy, exceptionally so at times, but the sea somehow sat in a realm all of its own. We had learnt from our illicit trips to Calve that when we were out there, in among the waves and shrouded by sea, you could make yourself invisible to all of Mull's civilian life. The very obvious dangers aside, the sense of liberation was absolute.

I say 'invisible', but I should caveat that with the word 'almost'. There was actually a previous occasion where Norrie and McGuiness weren't so lucky. They took the boat out far, right round towards the lighthouse, and got into a bit of trouble. They were spotted and subsequently rescued. I can't remember whose dad it was, Norrie's or McGuiness's, but he was there, ready to welcome them back into the harbour with not just a 'skelp', a slap round the head, but a thrashing.

My mum never once gave me as much as a clip round the ear. It just wasn't her style. Her look of disappointment stung far more than a belt buckle to the arse. But back then, getting a clout, a skelp or (for exceptionally bad behaviour) a full-scale thrashing was the norm. It didn't matter which parent dished it out, no one was going to be saying, 'How dare you lay a hand on my child?' – they were far more likely to buy you a pint as 'thanks' for dispensing the discipline before they'd had to do it for themselves. It wasn't good, looking back, especially when measured against modern parenting standards and sensibilities, but Norrie and McGuiness's boot up the arse, clip round the ear and clout up the rear combo was more than enough to dissuade us all from too many more really dangerous adventures in Norrie's dad's boat.

That was okay though … we still had the cliffs.

One day while out beachcombing, I discovered an old piece of rope above the high-tide line that truly was 'enough rope to hang ourselves'. It had been lying high and dry long enough for grass and moss to have grown over it, and, as I pulled it up from beneath the ground, it just felt like it got longer and longer. In sum, it was the longest piece of rope I had ever seen. It must've fallen off the deck of a big ship at some point, or been hurled from a fishing boat when it was no longer fit for purpose, but it was a real monster and we certainly had a purpose for it.

I hurried back to Norrie, McGuiness and Alan, and breathlessly announced my discovery: 'I have found *the rope*.'

The rope. Nothing more needed to be said. This was *the rope* of our very wildest imaginations and there could be only one course of action: we had to find a cliff as high as that rope was long. We all agreed, and then took to working out a way of moving this enormous heavy mass of cordage to the highest possible point.

It took some effort to drag the rope to the top of the nearest and biggest sea cliff we could. It was old, thick and very heavy – but we were extremely determined. Once we had managed to get it into position, we tied the rope to the trunk of a small tree and dropped the lot straight down the vertical cliff face.

What a lot of fun we then had that afternoon. Alan, Norrie, McGuiness and me, climbing up and down that massive cliff via an ancient, and quite possibly semi-decayed, length of rope. Our risk-taking was purely about seeking thrills in any way we could, and I think we were pretty impressive in our 'resourcefulness'. I can't think that any of us ever gave much thought to how easily it could've gone wrong.

I've retold the cliff story a few times and I was always left wondering if I had exaggerated the size of it in my memory. I was a little kid, after all, and I'm sure that if I returned to many of our adventurous arenas, I would find that their size and scale had been a bit inflated in my mind.

One day recently, though, I took a stroll over to that particular cliff on Mull only to discover that, nope, it really was absolutely massive. In all honesty, it was probably even worse than I'd remembered. I craned my neck to the very top and shuddered at the thought of someone slipping, losing their grip, the rope snapping or just coming loose from the tree. We had some courage and serious audacity back in the day.

I wonder, too, whether that early risk-taking did in fact help me later on in my adult life. When I enter potentially hazardous environments, where there is a reasonable degree of danger, I'm always able to maintain some sense of calm. Usually too, I see that a bit of risk-taking can lead to some really rewarding encounters, for as long as you could *safely* push yourself forward.

The Giants

'My goodness, that is like seeing … a mammoth come back to life.'

I bowed down behind my camera and lowered my voice to a deferential whisper. I might have been downwind, semi-concealed by a bush, and the opposite side of a watering hole, but the magisterial aura of the great Satao II transcended all space and time.

I was in the company of the King.

African savanna elephants are the largest land mammals on earth, but they are endangered, and these so-called 'super tuskers' could number as few as 20 individuals. They are the giants among the giants. Enormous elderly male elephants with tusks so long they virtually scrape the ground before them.

Satao II dwarfed the other bull elephants at the watering hole that day. His broad shoulders and thick head stood well clear, but his great ivory tusks, darkened through age and industry, extended some seven feet long and weighed over 50 kilograms each.

Even for a super tusker, Satao II was big.

I tracked him with my camera as he delicately pierced the watering hole with the tip of his trunk. Elephants have this amazing ability to both crush a tree and pluck a twig from the ground. Gradually, he moved around the watering hole's perimeter until he was just metres away from where I stood. He was close enough for me to see the individual creases in his trunk and how the hard-baked mud, completely covering his back, was flaking away in the African sun. It was inevitable that he would see me. And with that, he lifted his immense head and stared directly into my soul.

I have filmed hundreds of elephants during the course of my career, but none were quite like Satao II. My hands shook as adrenaline coursed through my body. 'He has literally taken my breath away,' I said to the camera behind me, after he had moved along. 'You can just tell you are in the presence of an incredibly special animal.'

Elephants will always be one of my favourite animals. They are African icons. As much a part of the landscape as they are creators and curators of it. They are ecosystem engineers who trim back the vegetation and widely disperse the seeds of plants and trees in their poo.

Their immense bulk and strength helps to open up the bush as they move, allowing new growth to spring up in the clearings they make and creating new pathways for smaller creatures to travel along in their wake. In the dry season their tusks and trunks dig deep into the river beds and open up new places to drink too, greatly benefitting all the other thirsty visitors.

Their size and scale can make them intimidating, but elephants are tender at heart. For them, their family is everything.

To better understand any animal, you have to inhabit their world. In 2016 I came to Kenya to film and present *Elephant Family & Me* and, over the course of two trips, I planned to follow a new mother and her baby on foot.

Tsavo National Park is loosely shaped like an elephant's tusk meeting its upper trunk. It is the largest national park in Kenya and home to more than 11,000 elephants. For this series, I was joined by my guide and mentor Benjamin Kyalo from the David Sheldrick Wildlife Trust. Benjamin had 16 years' experience with elephants, but he knew one herd intimately. 'As soon as I talk, they will be able to recognise my voice,' he announced, in his lilting local accent. 'And how do you think they'll be with me?' I enquired. 'I'll just tell them: "he is my friend",' he simply concluded.

It sounded straightforward enough, and I certainly felt safe with Benjamin, but I also had enough experience with elephants to know that I needed to be very wary of their power. They are one of the most dangerous animals on earth and have been known to trample and gore people to death. Benjamin showed me a harrowing video of an elephant charging and ramming a jeep with its skull.

It was hardly surprising behaviour. In the decade before my arrival, poachers had killed over a third of Africa's total elephant population. On average, 80 elephants die every day from snares, guns or poison. Mostly to supply the illegal trade in their ivory tusks.

The inconvenient truth is that the elephants of Africa are resident in some extremely impoverished communities, and the cash on offer for obtaining and smuggling ivory is an irresistible temptation for some. I had to accept, too, that my love for elephants was a luxury born from the privilege of being able to see them solely as these wondrous and majestic creatures.

As the local human population expands, they inevitably encroach on the elephant's traditional territories. Roads, railway lines and settlements all create potential new battlegrounds for human and elephant conflict. Elephants have trampled plenty of unwitting villagers, and, in their ceaseless search for food, they will enter farmlands and destroy all their precious crops too.

In sum, for many communities, elephants are a headache that they could dearly do without. For them, it is perhaps hard to shed a tear over another dead elephant at the hands of the poachers, especially if they have killed a family member or ruined their livelihood.

Some have taken matters into their own hands when it comes to defending their homes and farms, and even the National Park itself wasn't a wholly safe place for elephants. During the filming of *Elephant Family & Me*, we aided an elephant that had almost lost his foot to a snare. I have long since come to accept that saving endangered African wildlife requires real investment at a community level first, to help alleviate the terrible symptoms of a hard life lived below the poverty line.

Elephants are highly intelligent. Plenty clever enough to identify that all humans are a potential threat. Benjamin told me that the chances of being hurt by his herd were very small, and that they would always give a warning first, but if I ever saw them flaring their ears, trumpeting aggressively, coiling their trunks beneath their bodies or shaking their great heads, then I'd better back off sharpish.

That was easier said than done while on foot and well away from a vehicle.

'When walking on foot they can easily kill you,' Benjamin continued with his grim health and safety message. 'They have got a very powerful trunk combined with the tusks. When you fall onto the ground, they will pierce you. Then, after they have killed you, they will just cut branches and cover you.'

'Really?' I raised my eyebrows quizzically. 'At least you get a burial, of sorts.'

Benjamin did not laugh.

It was another example of the elephant's higher intellect. They have even been observed to bury their own dead, as well as mourn. On the second trip of the series, we were blessed to be present as the herd celebrated a newborn calf. We witnessed trumpeting, purring, tender trunk touching, secretions from the temporal glands and huddling – all sure signs of heightened emotion that looked very much like a collective joy. They will work together to help when a member of their herd is injured or trapped, and, as I was to discover, when it comes to their youngest members, child-rearing is seen as a collective responsibility among the mums. Nothing is more important than that little baby elephant.

I was following Wendy, a 13-year-old mum, and her seven-month-old calf, Wiva. Wendy was an orphan. She had been found alone in the bush, separated from her mother at just two days old. She was a miracle survivor, but it had left her with a natural mistrust and a wildly independent streak, which was clearly evident on our very first meeting.

'Wendy, stop! Don't try to do anything funny!' Benjamin called out urgently. I couldn't have seen her for anything more than 30 seconds before she had strolled over and guided her muscular trunk right into our vehicle. 'I'm not sure I like that …' I mumbled nervously, as her trunk slipped down my leg. 'Don't grab the camera!' cried Benjamin, leaping over the seat towards the elephant and me.

He implored her to back off, and, as she did, Benjamin crawled out of the open window and stood between us, hands on his hips, like an angry schoolmaster telling off his naughtiest pupil.

'That certainly got the heart racing … a little bit,' I admitted, as the immediate danger passed. Frankly, I hadn't liked it at all. If that had happened while I was still sat in the jeep, then how on earth was I going to be tolerated while walking around outside?

'Very naughty!' Benjamin scolded, as she sloped off to the bush. As for the precious Wiva, she was almost completely hidden away the entire time. Smuggled beneath another maternal elephant's belly and firmly concealed behind a forest of adult elephant legs.

Nearly all of the elephants in Wendy's herd had been rescued and some had been transported here from outside of the park. Their mistrust was evident and reasonable – many would have had terrible life experiences with humans. I knew this was going to take time, and, over the course of those two trips, small incremental steps forward were slowly taken.

The first big thing was to get away from the vehicle and establish me as a trustworthy person. Benjamin encouraged me to just talk, so the herd could get used to the sound of my voice. Later on, I spotted Wendy with her trunk up, curled over in my direction like the spout of an old teapot. She was smelling the area, working out if I was safe with the most sensitive of all her senses.

It wasn't simply that I needed to gain the trust of Wendy and the wider herd; I also needed to get my timing right on the days when I chose to walk among them. They needed to feel at their most relaxed and, through careful observation, it became clear that that time was when they were down by the watering holes or taking their dust baths, to coat their skin with a layer of dirt to protect them from the sun. It wasn't just that these were nice social activities. They happened in places where the ground was open, and being able to see exactly what was coming always helped put the elephant herd at ease.

It definitely helped if there were no bull elephants around too. Males leave the herd in their adolescence, but they will return again to breed. Whenever they were about, and *especially* if they arrived with other bulls during the breeding season, they destabilised the harmony of the whole herd. Their presence always made everyone nervous, especially those caring for Wiva, who could easily be crushed underfoot if a scrap were to break out.

The best day I had on that first trip came at a time when everything appeared perfect. The herd were relaxing by the watering hole and Wendy had already taken some strides towards accepting me. 'Having only got glimpses of Wiva,' I intoned, filming from the truck's side, 'the herd has come forward. Almost as if they want to show her to me.' They were really close to me now and I knew this was all a really good sign. Elephants have been seen to 'show off' their young, so, out into the open I stepped. Calling calmly to announce my presence.

Wendy came forward first. Visibly less agitated than before. I held out a hand and she placed her trunk tip in my palm. Very gently, I blew down her nostrils. Benjamin had told me to do this at the earliest opportunity. It was the final and most important piece of her accepting my scent.

She lifted her trunk as she took in my smell. And remained calm.

'No monkey business here,' commanded Benjamin firmly. Just minutes later, Wiva worked her way through the forest of legs and was now only her mother's length away from me.

It was a huge breakthrough. By far the closest I had ever been to the baby. I stroked tusks and looked into deep dark eyes, as the communal dust bath began in the dirt pile all around us.

Great plumes of brick-red dust clouded the skies and I eased my camera into the thick of it all. A window had very gradually creaked open to me. We were firmly moving towards a place where we felt much more comfortable with each other, and I was finally gaining a deeper understanding of the elephants' world.

But the wider world of nature has that element of perpetual chaos and things can always change in an instant.

The herd was led into the bush by a thoroughly red-looking

little Wiva, and I paused at the pathway to the thicker vegetation, just to deliver a closing piece to camera:

'I don't think I should go on any further. There's just the last few members of the herd …' I pointed them out as they shuffled away into the shrubbery, '… and it's just too dangerous to follow them, because not only could we bump into …'

I didn't even get a chance to finish the sentence.

I had become aware of a formidable presence behind me. It was as if I had manifested the very thing I was about to caution against: a huge dark and raging bull. It was on the road, within charging range, and the warning he gave could not have been more minimal. An aggressive flick of his head and a pair of huge flaring ears were all we got. Less than a second later he sent his three-ton bulk storming straight forward.

I was back behind the truck again. Catching my breath with, thankfully, only my feelings crushed. The bull had more than made his point and we had ceded the ground. 'It's a shame.' I rested my head on my camera's tripod, feeling despondent. 'You get lured into a false sense of security and then something like that sets you back a long way.'

Elephant Family & Me involved a degree of this curious little dance. I'd progressively establish a little trust, pull into the herd a little, before being pushed away to start all over again. In that, though, I had found something that we did all share. How much are any of us willing to completely trust an animal that could potentially cause us harm? As much as I wanted to be as close as possible to Wiva and Wendy, I felt I had to keep my wits about me and maintain a degree of wariness and, clearly, some members of the elephant family felt the same way about me too.

Benjamin was already as close to that herd as it was possible for a person to be. This, though, was how he had chosen to spend his life. He saw far more of his elephant family than he ever did his own, and to get anywhere near to the level of trust he had established would've taken me the same level of sacrifice and time. Sadly, that was time I did not have.

On it went into the second trip, four months later, in the middle of the Kenyan dry season. At one point, over by our favourite watering hole and dust bath, I was completely surrounded by the herd. All moving around me, seemingly without a care in the world. By then, I was confident enough to kneel down before Wendy. Gently, she caressed me with her trunk. I had pushed myself towards the very edge of my own sense of security in that moment, without ever quite shedding that feeling of vulnerability in front of a species that was, clearly, so much more physically dominant.

I may not have become a part of their herd then, but I had learnt a huge amount – certainly far more than I ever could have if I had not taken the chance of moving around them on foot. More than anything, we discovered a way to peacefully inhabit the same space for a time. Given the challenges that elephants face in the wild every single day, especially at the hands of humans, proving that a calm co-existence was possible had felt really important.

That deeper sense of striving to make a meaningful individual connection with animals, though, especially really large ones, was something that had started from a very young age.

Hold Your Horses

As a child on Mull, I might not have had a pair of binoculars, a long lens camera or a bird book, but I was outside actively engaging with the wild, in my own way, from the moment we arrived. Outdoors was where all the best fun was to be had. I'd often bring nature into my hands – crabs and small rockpool fish caught on the coast, slow worms and common lizards plucked from beneath rusting sheets of corrugated iron, frogspawn, newts, tadpoles, toads and frogs, gently scooped from Mull's small streams and ponds. I used to love collecting things from the wild. Little keepsakes such as interesting-looking leaves or nuts, pieces of egg shell or coloured rocks, or small living creatures that Norrie and I would care for in a tiny menagerie.

At one point, I even found a tiny fledgling wren abandoned on the ground and in some strife. I nursed it back to strength by handfeeding it worms, and, once it was strong enough to do so, it would actually sit on my bike's handlebars and ride around the island with me. Slowly, as birds do, it learnt how to funnel and shape the whistling wind around its wings; one day it took off from my handlebars and disappeared for good.

We experienced nature through instinct and feel, without any formal study or deep thought. I simply loved seeing things that I thought were fundamentally interesting and 'cool', and I would then invest more of my time into trying to understand them better. Often, by inching myself closer to their lives.

That fundamental curiosity has never left me and shares such an obvious parallel with what I do for work now, but back then, I wasn't armed with anything like the knowledge, or, frankly, the ethical sensibilities or sensitivities that I possess today. We certainly meant to do no harm but, basic ethics of taking from the wild aside, I can't say we ever really thought too long or hard about the daily responsibility that would come along with caring for animals. An awful lot of the larger creatures that came our way did so as a direct result of Norrie's cocksure confidence and our impulsiveness. If Norrie wanted something then he pretty much always got it; he was remarkably skilled at getting his own way with his parents.

His mum might've said 'no' to him getting a rabbit, but he went and bought one anyway. She might've said 'no' to him getting a dog, but – sensationally – on the way back from a trip to London for a Madonna concert, *when he was only 15*, he somehow managed to buy an Alsatian. 'Yeah, so I found this stray dog in a bin,' he confidently offered as an excuse to his mum. 'Did you buggery! I told you you weren't allowed to get a bloody dog!' He even got to keep it – well, for a little while at least – like Norrie himself, the rapidly growing Alsatian pup was more than a bit of a handful.

The most astonishing display of all of this came one morning when, roving the coves and beaches, we came across a seal pup. Norrie didn't think twice, and to be fair, nor did I. We very quickly, very rashly, deduced that the pup was on its own, not really moving much, and therefore was *quite obviously* in dire need of immediate rescue: by us.

These days, *of course*, I know that seeing seal pups on their own is not usually a cause for any concern. There are two seal species in Scotland: the 'common' or 'harbour' seal, which numbers around 50,000 in UK waters and prefers to make its home on sheltered beaches; and the larger 'grey' seal, which numbers more than 120,000 and is more often found in exposed open waters. The UK has over 50 per cent of the world's population of greys, with the Hebrides and, in particular, the Treshnish Isles to the west of Mull being really important breeding sites. Female greys will periodically leave their newborn pups on their own while they hunt for fish, and, after three or four weeks of suckling from their mother's milk, those pups are left to hunt, feed and fend for themselves anyway. That lactation period is among the briefest of all mammal species and it's not unusual for the young greys to spend another fortnight just hanging around on the beach on their own, before eventually slipping away to an independent life at sea. Common seal pups are hardier still. They can swim and dive from just a few hours old, and will very often follow their mums to learn how to hunt, before they are also weaned and expected to be fully independent from just three to five weeks old.

It was a common pup that we found that day. It was small, dark and incredibly cute, with a puppy-dog face and huge brown eyes. Not that grey seal pups aren't cute, of course. If anything, they might be *even cuter* than the commons. Greys are born with these lustrous snow-white furry coats, which researchers believe to be a relic from when the species bred in wholly ice-covered landscapes, but that common seal looked like a tiny little Labrador puppy, and we were almost falling over ourselves in our haste to help it out of the imaginary trouble we had assumed it definitely was in.

The pup had likely *not* been abandoned – nor was it injured or starving. It was far more likely to be either readying itself to head out to sea, or just waiting for its mum to return from a hunt. However, a human getting unnecessarily close to a pup could easily stress it out and may even stop its parent from coming back to feed it.*

---

* If you *ever* find any lone seal pup that you really do believe has a problem, then the official guidance is to maintain a safe distance and call an appropriate wildlife rescue charity for further advice. Not least because, no matter how cute they *might* look, all seals are armed with sharp reflexes, even sharper teeth and very dangerous bacteria in their mouths. In the mid- to late 1800s, when seal-hunting was in its heyday, teams of seal clubbers would frequently report a condition that they called 'seal finger'. It presented after a seal bite and would see this radiating swelling, accompanied by a horrible discharge, around the bite wound site. It was actually quite a serious infection caused by the seal's mouth bacteria and, in lieu of a course of antibiotics, the infection often became so severe that amputation was seen as the only course of action. Under no circumstances should you ever try and touch a solo seal pup – even if you think you are doing a good thing – and please don't attempt to put it back in the water and *especially* (and I can't quite believe I'm admitting to this here) do not try and put it on a dog lead and take it home with you.

That 'seal pup discovery' happened not too long after I'd received a small black-and-white telly for my bedroom. Those were the days when programmes featuring Skippy the Bush Kangaroo, Flipper the dolphin, Tarzan and his ape sidekick Cheeta, and Gentle Ben the bear were at the absolute peak of their popularity. As far as we were all aware, kids *really could* be friends with wild animals and there was absolutely nothing wrong with that. In fact, if the fuzzy images presented by my all-new telly were to be believed (and why on earth wouldn't you believe *everything* the television told you?), then these animals would be only *too glad* to enter into a friendship with humans, with enormous benefits ranging from solving crimes to daring rescues.

Given our predilection for climbing sea cliffs and entering storm-force seas, why wouldn't we make friends with a seal? It made perfect sense to have this smooth-skinned, crime-busting partner that could also get us out of our inevitable seaside scrapes. Boat capsized? *Get a lift back to shore from the seal!* Plummet from a huge sea cliff and into the open sea? *High five the seal and straight back to land we go!*

Frankly, Norrie and I couldn't believe our luck. As far as we were concerned, *this* was a sign from the heavens, and, to our tiny minds at least, this seal pup was bang in luck too! *Obviously*, it had been abandoned. It was now on us to save its life and thus set in motion a reciprocal relationship where the seal would join our gang and help us from that day henceforth.

'This is going to be so cool!' I said to Norrie breathlessly. In no time at all, we not only had what we honestly believed to be a rock-solid plan for rescuing the seal pup, we had also projected an entirely imagined future with us and our new seal friend working together forever. We left our latest and coolest gang member back on the beach, and we were headed to Norrie's uncle Iain's to get a dog lead and collar to slip around its neck. As soon as that was done, we imagined the seal would gratefully flip-flop away with us, all the way to Tobermory, where we would house it in a giant tank owned by another of Norrie's uncles. He was a fisherman, and owned a huge concrete saltwater housing for storing live shellfish for the market. It was all so perfect!

Inevitably, on return to the beach, things did not go to plan. With Uncle Iain's dog collar and lead in hand, we attempted to cajole the seal pup into coming with us. Naturally, it glanced up at us a little warily, then hopped its way back down the beach and slipped away to the sea. Forever.

Neither Norrie nor I could quite come to terms with the fact that it hadn't worked out in the way we'd imagined. 'That's not what happens on TV,' we lamented, in what was clearly the only sensible thought to have come from either of us during that entire escapade.

Later in my life, clearly, my approach to wild animals did change dramatically. During my first job in wildlife filmmaking, in Sierra Leone, there was actually a period where I really was looking after animals that we had legitimately rescued. If I had been able to tell the young Norrie and Gordon about all that back then, well, I imagine they both would've been utterly amazed. However, I would've also let them know that whatever they had seen on telly was wildly off the mark. In reality, it wasn't just that wild rescued animals wouldn't form anything like a close bond with us, they would invariably completely disappear into the jungle from the very second they were ready to be released. Regardless of anything else, I soon grew to feel very uncomfortable with the idea of any wild-born animal being kept in an enclosure.

Keeping that seal, in what would have been, essentially, a big tank intended for shellfish, might've seemed pretty cool for a day, but I'm fairly sure we'd have gone off the idea once we had realised how unhappy it would've made the animal.

The Animal Families & Me series are the closest I've come to actually being part of a wild animal's world. To a degree, I would 'hang out' with the bears, wolves and elephants we featured – but any relationship, however transient and small, was always on that animal's terms.

Animal Families & Me was about both the wild animal and the wild environment in which it lived. For me, the two went hand in glove. They are completely inseparable from each other. Remove one from the other and the wild is no longer a wholly 'wild' place, and that wild animal loses all of its essential context and character too.

As Norrie and I reluctantly returned the seal-free dog collar and lead that afternoon, all of that was a very long way from either of our minds – but in our graduation from shells to rockpool fish, slow worms to newts, fledgling birds to rabbits, Norrie's dog and then to the seal, one thing was clear: the animals were getting bigger and our desire to be with them was growing too.

Luckily for us, and for the rest of Mull's wildlife, we did eventually find what we were looking for.

• • •

Norrie and I were 11 years old when we first started paying more attention to the horses on the island. I think we must've been cycling up from Tobermory to one of our dens in the woods, but I can clearly remember us seeing them all gathered in their field, chewing away at the grasses and trotting around with that real majesty horses possess. There was something magnetic about those animals. I'd spent time with other big grazing creatures like cows and sheep, but I knew horses were different. To be frank, the most obvious difference was that you could hop on their backs without complaint; sheep and cows had always objected to that notion! Those horses were part of a local trekking centre run and owned by the MacDougalls, and we knew we needed to have a go.

Norrie assured me that pony trekking wasn't just for tourist folk from the mainland – anyone with the cash could go. However, it was £2.50 to ride for half an hour, and an astronomic £5 for an hour. It was a lot of money for anyone to fork out, let alone a pair of local lads without proper jobs. I saved up all my birthday money and Norrie probably just pestered his parents to the point they'd caved, but both clutching our hard-won fivers in hand, we had our hour.

Seeing horses out in a field and being stood right next to one were two very different perspectives for a boy who was still very much growing. I felt dwarfed by their size and strength, but I wasn't nervous, intimidated or fearful. It was more a feeling of being in total awe. I soon recognised that here was an animal that would willingly allow you to interact with it – stroking, patting, feeding – for as long as you showed the right respect and behaved in the right way. I couldn't quite believe you could actually get on top of these enormous animals though. *Who first thought of that?* I pondered as my saddle was placed and I climbed up for the first time. I took a deep breath, clutched the reins and listened to the instructions intently. From that moment forward, I was completely hooked.

I felt an immediate sense of deep calm on horseback and took to it naturally. So much so that Robbie MacDougall, the son of the owners and the lad who was leading our trek that day, let Norrie and me ride without being led by his rope.

Looking back, I think with all that was going on back home, just the idea that I could follow a few simple rules and develop a meaningful connection with such a powerful animal meant an awful lot to me. I felt empowered by this horse's faith in me and the control I felt I had over it as a result. For a quiet lad who was lacking confidence and in real need of an escape from the things that weighed on my mind at home and at school, just trotting about with my horse was everything I needed – but then it got even better.

'Do you boys want to go for a bit of gallop?' It seems scarcely believable that Robbie said that on our first outing but we both felt completely safe, and not for one moment did we consider that going *much* faster was anything to worry about.

'There's an open gate up there.' Robbie motioned. 'Follow me through and the horses will know what to do.' Through we went and this great locomotive heave of energy surged up from beneath me. My horse powered forward and sent the air whistling across my face. I gripped onto my reins and just let this extraordinary sense of utter unadulterated freedom wash all over me.

This is it. This is really living.

I could've screamed it out loud. I knew I'd just found everything I had been searching for. *This* was the meeting of worlds that joined up all our thrill-seeking adventures and the wild spirit that existed on this island; it was here in this animal, and deep within me. I have never felt quite so liberated before or since and it was no over-statement to say that the horse I rode that day changed my life.

We went back the next day. Obviously, we had no more money, but Robbie, who was probably only about 16 himself, didn't mind that we had rocked up again. Luckily for us, he was an exceptionally nice person and a real good laugh to be around. I think he understood how we felt and allowed us to get involved. He showed us how to saddle up the horses and prepare them for a trek, and when we came back the next day again, he even got us to lead the horses down from the top field. That was it. I was 'in', and horse riding, horse trekking and all their care would come to dominate the rest of my childhood.

There was no need for an interview. I started working at the MacDougalls' trekking centre purely through persistence and enthusiasm. Norrie's parents soon bought him a horse, so he stopped coming, but even if I *could* have afforded my own horse, I wouldn't have ever wanted just *one*. I loved the variety of horses the MacDougalls owned, from the smallest Shetland pony to the biggest Clydesdale crossbreed; gathering in, grooming, feeding, saddling and all the rest of the duties were never a chore for me. It was all part of deepening my connection with these incredible animals. Riding at a flat-out gallop or charging at a fence, secure in the knowledge that the horse would fly me over, were the cherries on what was already a very sweet and delicious cake.

From that point forward, every day after school, every weekend, every holiday, if anyone was to ask 'Where's Gordy?', the answer would always be the same: 'He's over at the horses.'

• • •

Willie MacDougall and his wife, Netta, owned the centre. I worked alongside their son Robbie until he went to the mainland to train to be a riding instructor, before his equally great sister, Janet, took over in his stead. We worked together until the point she left to further her own education too.

The summer after my first ride out, it was agreed that I'd initially be paid a fiver a week. Given how much time I would then spend with their horses, that fiver a week in the holidays probably only worked out at 5p an hour. Not exactly a lucrative summer job then, but I saw my 'payment' more through the opportunities it gave me to develop my own riding. That steep learning curve saw me graduate to more challenging horses and riding competitions, and the thrill and sense of achievement that came with that was something that no amount of money could buy.

The 'trekkers' were mainly plodding Highland types of all shapes and sizes, but the MacDougalls also possessed some cracking horses that you would never have put your average tourist on. Graceful and athletic horses that would be shown and jumped competitively by Robbie and Janet. The Pegasuses among the ponies.

With Robbie gone and Janet outgrowing some of the competition horses, Willie instructed me to give them a run-out. That really helped elevate my riding to the next level and I even joined a local branch of the Pony Club. Soon I was entering showjumping competitions on the mainland too, and, for the first time in my life, I even started to win.

It wasn't all sunshine and rainbows. The lack of regular pay aside, Willie was an incredibly hard taskmaster and working outside through the winter's dark, cold and rain was brutal, but I'd pull on my mud-spattered clothes and fake Barbour jacket and head out every single time. I knew the horses always needed to be fed, regardless of how hard the wind or Willie's tongue would whip, but fundamentally, and more importantly, I also knew that I'd found something that I was really good at. It was something that could make me feel amazing too, and I wanted to stick at it no matter what.

Handling horses, riding them, knowing how to behave around them, how to work them, how to get the best out of them, and finally, how to compete, saw my own confidence and sense of self-worth begin to bloom. It was also the first real indication that humans could form meaningful relationships, and a bond, with the right sort of animal. Developing a sensitivity to each horse's needs, and seeing them as intelligent, independent individuals in their own right, would help me enormously when it came to working with animals later on in my career – but things were going so well at the trekking centre that there was a period where I couldn't imagine anything other than working with horses for the rest of my life.

Surely, I thought, there is nothing out there that is more adventurous, more exhilarating, or more worthwhile, than this? At one point, a wealthy man with an interest in competition and racing even offered to fund my riding. He recognised how hard I worked and told me that there was always a job in his stables, should I ever want it. After that, I thought very seriously about just skipping my exams and leaving school as soon as I turned 16. Ultimately, though, when I did turn 16, I had come to think that there probably were different paths out there.

Working with horses, and riding them, had given me the confidence and control that I needed at that stage in life. When I was competing on those horses, I didn't feel the need to hide or become invisible. I was wholly comfortable with being *seen*, and, my growing self-belief and personal sense of pride aside, that whole period also underlined that I didn't need to settle for the conventional life mapped out for me by other people either. That it really wasn't silly, or childish, or beyond me, to dream of something bigger and better out there. Among those special animals,

I had found credible evidence that genuine opportunities could come out of left field. I just needed to find ways to remain open to the next one that came along.

The next break really would change my life for good, but it was the horses that started everything. There is, though, something far more important to add about that whole period. My time on Mull was largely beautiful, and completely carefree, but back home, things were getting a lot more complicated. A new man had entered our lives. A wolfish outsider, who I had very good reasons not to trust.

In those stables, though, Willie, Netta, Robbie and Janet had provided me with a sanctuary. I think that the MacDougall family had somehow known that there were times when I just needed somewhere else to go, and for that I will always be grateful.

Wolves and Us

Wolves have been absent from our island for at least the last 200 years, and yet the wolf has pressed its prints deep into the consciousness of the British people. The complexity of our relationship with this animal is one that I don't think is quite matched by any other predator on earth.

The wolf encapsulates the spirit of our once ancient and untamed wilderness. It is a throwback to a primitive bygone age, when our island was shrouded in forest and dominated by beasts far wilder than us. It's a paradoxical animal: widely viewed as a formidable and ruthless killer, yet also considered to be highly intelligent and pragmatic. Like us, it collaborates effectively in a pack and will display an emotional range that encompasses anger and fear, curiosity and playfulness, caring, sharing, loving and even grief.

Observing their co-operation within the pack, and in the time I spent with them as individuals too, I could sense a range of common talents and emotions. Traits found in both human and wolf society, that both species would've once identified as good reasons to attempt to cross the divide between our two different worlds.

It is widely believed that it was sometime during the Palaeolithic era that the nudge towards the very first 'domestication' of the wolf occurred. I hesitate to use the word 'tamed' as, having walked with those wild wolves, the idea that *we* instantly brought this intelligent animal to heel, curtailing its naturally strident independence for our own ends, feels almost offensive. I just can't see the wolf ever being up for working with us straight away, especially if it wasn't getting anything in return.

Recently, behavioural ecologists, who have studied both ancient indigenous wisdom and the wolf, have drawn the logical conclusion that it was likely the wolves who approached humans first. Perhaps what once began as the wolves' natural curiosity graduated towards a tolerance of our presence, which later evolved towards the recognition of a mutually beneficial opportunity to get food or protection. An initially passive and agreeable relationship, which eventually set the wheels in motion for the development of the domestic dog, an animal that so many of us have warmly welcomed into our homes and families, thousands of years later.

It is quite odd to look back now and think about quite where, and when, it went so badly wrong between the wolves and us. The mark of the dog is everywhere in Britain – we are a nation of 'dog lovers' – but the wolf would become a pariah.

Certainly, back in the Palaeolithic era, if humans had only ever seen the wolves as our sworn enemies, then they would never have allowed the wild wolf to get close in the first place, regardless of how nonthreatening their initial approach might've appeared. The later demonisation of the wolf must surely have its roots in the period where farming and livestock rearing became much more widespread and established in Britain – but that swing, from having respect for this one-time icon of our wild, to seeing it almost universally as the enemy of our flocks, still feels extreme.

Officially, the last wolf in Scotland died at the hands of the Clan Cameron chief, Sir Ewen Cameron of Lochiel, while he was out hunting in 1680, but folkloric tales claim their presence clung on up here into the eighteenth century, before their inevitable, and total, eradication. The slaughter of a wolf was seen as a heroic deed. Wolf skins were given as a tribute among kings and the nobility, generous wolf bounties were raised and criminals were even spared death sentences if they agreed to spend their days out hunting wolves, presenting their tongues as evidence of their industry. In the parts of Scotland where wolves were numerous, compulsory wolf hunting became enshrined in law, with hunts deliberately planned to coincide with the wolf's cubbing season. That sustained hunting and trapping effort, combined with extensive habitat removal through forest clearance (for yet more farming and industry), all but sealed the fate of the British wolf.

But why? Long before the wolf's extinction was confirmed on our island, the theories that drove its extermination had evolved well beyond any credible threat posed by the animal itself. There was no doubt that wolves did kill sheep sometimes, and very occasionally, a deeply unfortunate person, but that was nothing when held up against the severe penalty they paid for just behaving as wolves do.

The truth was, the human idea of the wolf had morphed into something entirely separate from the animal itself. Folklore and fairy tale taught generations that there were no depths that the 'sneaky' wolf wouldn't plumb to kill. In tales like *Little Red Riding Hood* and *The Three Little Pigs*, parables such as *The Boy Who Cried Wolf* and even sayings like 'a wolf in sheep's clothing', 'keeping the wolf from the door', 'wolfing down your food' or 'thrown to the wolves', the symbol of the wolf represented everything from lying to laziness, to speaking to strangers, to telling who can be trusted versus who can't, to being too greedy, or too poor.

The wolf was used to model *bad* human behaviour, or a terrible outcome for a human, against what was considered to be truly good, righteous or honest behaviour. As such, the image of this 'totally evil' wolf was shaping the way in which society was expected to behave. A pretty convenient tool if you were a landowner or a powerful person, someone who needed things to happen in a certain way to maintain control of their land and make money. It all sent out a very clear message: livestock, whether that be the sheep in the field, or the deer among the trees, were the sole preserve of the human owner and should anyone, wolf or not, threaten that, then they could expect to be dealt with extremely severely. By extension, it also said that if wolves, this seemingly untameable symbol of everything that the British wild once was, could be domesticated, or eradicated in totality, then just imagine what could be done to you too, if you were to step out of line and demonstrate apparently 'wolf-like' behaviour.

I'm sure the extent of wolf killings and threat was wildly exaggerated, but via hearsay, rumour, fairy tale and fable, the 'wolf' became something no one wanted to be. Darker still were the long-held rumours that wolves may have also taken the blame for some human-on-human murders, disappearances and the most brutal acts of domestic violence. Thanks to the wolf's reputation, the guilty perpetrators, it was said, walked away free of consequence. Humans, it transpires, were always the real 'wolves' in sheep's clothing.

The animal, and the environment it depended on, became something that humans no longer felt they required, and all the positive memories of our ancient working relationship with the wolf were lost – but I still maintain that there is good will towards wolves out there. That somehow, in spite of it all, wolves continue to find something of a positive place in many of our consciousnesses.

Certainly, they have in mine, and wolves will always stand among my favourite animals on earth.

Loner

'This is the closest I've ever been to a wild wolf …'

It was 2014 and I was breathing deep, steadying my nerve while somehow trying to both stay safe *and* do my job, which in that moment was presenting an opening piece to camera for *Snow Wolf Family & Me* while this simply enormous white wolf eyeballed me from just a few metres away.

Slowly but deliberately, I manoeuvred myself to the other side of a small mound of our equipment and tried to articulate what was happening. *No one* had anticipated we would be this close to a wolf, this soon into the expedition, and no one had planned for us to be this exposed either. I was fully aware that this wolf could comfortably leap over the gear, or round it in an instant. Our presence, though, was clearly a surprise to this wolf too.

It stared over at me, sniffing away at something hanging in the air between us.

I imagined it must've been wondering where on earth this odd-looking bipedal interloper had come from. He'd seemingly dropped out of the sky with all his smelly friends in tow, and landed smack bang into the middle of a space that was very much *their* world, and usually *their world alone*.

The wolves on Ellesmere Island were the top predator and could comfortably take down prey four times our size. The crew were all stood back, filming me on a wide angle as this great wolf stared on and on. It didn't present any signs of aggression whatsoever, but I knew we were all in very real danger should it have suddenly decided that we were, in fact, lunch.

There have been other times in my career where my gaze was held by a predator that could have seen me off this world in a heartbeat. A heartbeat that, in those moments, I could feel heaving away hard at the centre of my chest.

It is an almost indescribable feeling: a primal intensity mixed with an immeasurable, adrenalised sense of raw excitement. If you can get somewhere beyond your fear of a grim and grisly demise, you know that somewhere deep inside that hyper-aware, hyper-vigilant state, you are truly at your most alive.

I kept talking. The wolf kept watching.

· · ·

I was way north in the Canadian Arctic. It had taken us almost ten days to get into the field, culminating in a helicopter ride that took me and our small crew sweeping across a place that crested out somewhere close to the roof of the world.

On Ellesmere, immense tundra folded away to the horizon, fractured only by swollen rivers of snowmelt and the occasional patches of ice and snow that were clinging on from the previous winter. It was an immensely wild place that was so remote, with winters that were so savage, the wildlife here had virtually no experience with humans. Certainly, we would be the first people this wolf pack had ever encountered.

We were arriving for spring at the start of the wolf's pupping season, and hoping to follow the story of a wolf pack right through to the start of the following winter – but we had zero idea how the wolves would react to our very sudden ground presence in their territory. Our helicopter banked over vast rust-coloured grasslands and there they all were, way down below: a pack of six wolves, puncturing the brown earth with their brilliant white coats. It was truly a thrilling sight, even from afar.

A little further on, we were dropped down with a cargo net of supplies for the three weeks we'd planned to stay on our first visit. The plan was to carefully make camp and orientate ourselves for the days of wolf-searching that likely lay ahead, but no sooner had the chopper dipped over the horizon, a lone wolf from the pack had come circling right in on us.

For a while we gently danced round each other. The wolf one side of our gear mound, me on the other, the crew still at a sensible distance. 'Wolves,' I explained to the camera, 'are at their most dangerous when they lose their fear of people. And it seems that these wolves don't have any fear to begin with.'

Within a few intense minutes, the wolf had gathered whatever information it felt it needed and trotted off to the slopes on the horizon. It would become one of many such experiences, but that was among the most intense, in what really had been the most extraordinary start to the expedition.

It was beyond any of our wildest expectations – we had anticipated it might take most of our first trip to get anything like that close to a wolf (if we managed it at all). To be frank, we expected them to run even further than the mile they had been from us when we had first landed. I wasn't foolish enough to believe that just one good visit, from just one wolf, meant that all was now well and we were completely safe from the pack. These wolves may have never been hunted in their history, and they were bold for sure, curious too, but they were still potentially very dangerous.

I pitched my little yellow tent half a mile away from the crew and delivered a cheery piece to camera about a young man who had been out camping in Canada and was torn from his tent by a wolf pack. He only survived, I dourly recounted, by being with other people. Brilliant. If this were a Hollywood movie, it would be blindingly obvious who was getting it first. It would be the brave but, quite obviously, deeply stupid Scotsman. All tucked up in his sleeping bag on his own, like a canvas-wrapped sausage roll.

I knew I needed to be away from everyone else if I was going to increase my chances of getting closer to the pack. Very carefully, I strung a small battery-operated electric fence around the perimeter of my new territory for my protection, and then I tested it: twice.

On the morning of the second day, the wolf was back and this time he'd brought a friend. Slowly, they approached, playfully snapping at a flock of small birds while they closed in on me again.

'Hey, wolf!' I called out, turning the camera to show just how incredibly close they were to the perimeter of my camp. They were close enough for me to see how the wind ruffled the soft top of the hair on their backs. Close enough to see the point where their brilliant white fur melted into the shades of mustard found on their chests and undersides. Close enough to appreciate their enormity and the sheer size of their powerful teeth and claws.

'I'll tell you what,' I muttered to myself, 'this is quite unnerving.' I was being approached by wolves for the second time in 24 hours, and the shoelace of electric fencing standing between me and them felt incredibly insubstantial.

The new wolf snuffled a little closer, sniffing at the fence with its coal black nose. Its nose is thousands of times more sensitive than mine, and there it was: taking in its first scent of man. Close enough to poke. It lifted its head, now just an arm's length from my lens. 'Oh my god, look at those eyes. *All the better to see you with* …' I quoted from *Little Red Riding Hood*. She was a simply stunning animal with a piercingly bright stare. I was aware that we were both reading each other at precisely the same time. Taking in each other's unique bodies and movements. Trying to work each other out. To get a sense of what was really going on, and anticipate who might do what next.

Right there, written in her nose and auburn eyes, there was a wild intelligence hard at work. An intelligence we shared. I couldn't help but break out in a huge smile. She was one of the most beautiful animals I had ever seen and it was one of the most affecting wildlife encounters of my life. Steadily, I could feel the tension of some of my nerves easing into the background. Something more, I knew, was going on here.

. . .

We discovered the location of their den and I began to identify the differences between the wolves in the pack. The varying tones in their coats, their characters and behaviours, even the distinct 'howls' possessed by each individual animal. That once amorphous white pack of animals, first spotted from the heights of the helicopter, was separating out into a collection of unique individuals. It took me a couple of days to surmount my, I think, very reasonable fears about their deadly potential, but, by the middle of the first week, I felt like I knew what I was doing. Or, perhaps more accurately, I had learnt what I needed to do to avoid making myself any more vulnerable than I already was.

I was looking for opportunities to inch my way closer to their world (and further away from the sanctuary of an electric fence that was already being picked at by the pack's two yearlings) when, early one morning, while the rest of the pack were out hunting, I spotted that the top female had stayed behind to watch over the den. I had named her Luna, owing to the creamier moon-like colourations on her coat, and, very carefully, I made an approach.

Acting submissively, head down and making muted whining noises, I moved towards their home. This was the most precious place of all. The place where we all presumed their cubs were living.

I paused. Luna eyed me cautiously for a while, before leaving the mouth of the den and padding over a shallow bed of river-rolled rock towards me. I made myself smaller still; I crouched down deferentially, making sure she knew that she was the one in control. That I wasn't a threat to her, the cubs or the den.

I juggled some stones as she continued to watch over me, seemingly wrestling in herself between playing it safe and backing off, and the compelling curiosity that I must've presented. The conflict in her was writ large as she padded to and fro across the inch-deep stream of water that separated us. Eventually though, she'd seen enough, and turned back to the den. It was another small but significant moment. The wolves all wanted to know more about me, and I certainly wanted to continue edging my way ever closer to them.

The wolf in that series that probably left the deepest impression on both the viewers and me was one of the yearlings: the pair of wolves who were little more than a year old. Scruffy was the larger and bolder of the pair. He was the one who consistently moved and gnawed away at my camera traps, and the one who took the keenest interest in testing the electric fence around my camp. By the second week, it wasn't just me inching closer to their world: Scruffy had fully entered mine.

'Keep away from my stuff, Scruffy,' I nervously implored, while slowly walking back towards my campsite. There he was, seemingly without a care in the world, tossing my camping stool around *inside* the electric fence's perimeter. Soon, he was outside my camp again, but he was moving off with my stool gripped firmly in his jaws. It was important that I made my own boundaries very clear (at least, the ones that hadn't already been crossed). Should I not at least try to get my stool back from Scruffy, then he was likely to assume that my entire camp and all my possessions, food and camera gear were fair game. With almost two weeks still left on Ellesmere, I imagined it wouldn't be too long before the whole place was ripped apart by this very playful wolf. I needed to try and make a point.

I followed Scruffy across the tundra, making noises that were closer to howls, rather than the muted submissive whines I'd offered up to Luna days earlier. He dropped my stool in the grass and turned sharply. His eyes were firmly on me now. He didn't have the wise reticence of age and experience that Luna had – Scruffy was a teenager and the world was all his to discover. There was to be no tentative back and forth this time: *Scruffy was coming.*

I sat down and made a sound approaching a moan through my cupped hands – thinking it might just get him to think twice about his very direct approach, but instead, he came straight over towards me, pausing only when he was within a few feet of my boots.

This is too close. This is too close. My index finger was fixed to my deeply furrowed brow and Scruffy's eyes felt like they were boring right through me. There was absolutely nothing I could do. Either I was safe enough in that moment, and my instincts about these wolves' pure curiosity about me were accurate, or I was in the deepest imaginable trouble with no way of doing anything to make myself in any way safer. I had to just hold my nerve. We both did.

'Jesus wept, oh my god. That is unnerving,' I whispered into the radio mic fixed to my neckline. I rotated my body in the grass as Scruffy moved around me. I did not like him moving behind me. 'Hey, Scruff.' Up close, he was absolutely huge. In no way would you think he was just one year old. His actions might have seemed 'puppy-like', but his thick back heaved up from behind his head and formed a dome of pure muscle. With me sat down, he stood well above my shoulder line.

He circled behind me again, and, with our eyes temporarily unlocked, he suddenly shuffled closer. I turned and he paused his approach, flinching as he flicked his head about, trying to sense something from whatever was left in the now extremely short distance between us. I howled again. 'You like that, don't you?' I whispered, almost laughing as a beautiful inquisitiveness danced across his eyes.

I had come to Ellesmere to get close to these animals, and this was a monumental stride forward in that closeness. I sensed he was still nervous (we both were) but I could also tell that he really did want to know me. He'd already been in my camp, taken my stool, chewed at my camera traps, worked a way around the electric fence, and now here I was: the thing he'd been studying from afar for a week and a half, sat a mere metre away. Really, we both had exactly what we wanted.

Of course, there was no way of knowing what was really going on in his mind all of the time, but there were no signs of aggression or hostility there either – just that same sense of nervous discovery that we were both now experiencing together. I certainly didn't feel that I was in the presence of the 'ruthless killer' of the wolf's worldwide reputation. Were that in any way accurate as an image, Scruffy would've dispatched me in an instant.

Eventually, he had gathered whatever it was he felt he needed to know about me for that day, and off he went. Leaving behind both me and, happily, my stool.

• • •

When it comes to getting close to *any* animal, a degree of personal judgement must always be applied. There are always going to be those species that are potentially more dangerous than others – but it is also really important to distinguish between individuals within a group. As with us, different animals within the same species are liable to behave in different ways. Taking my pack on Ellesmere as an example, each wolf had a very different approach. Some were far bolder, like Scruffy, others more reticent, like Luna; certainly, you can expect to get a very different response from wolf packs that have had different experiences with people too. For the 2016 BBC production *Life in the Snow*, I filmed a sequence with a group of wolves in northern Norway who were entirely habituated to people. They licked at my face and nose without a care in the world, allowing me to stroke their bellies and even gently part the hair on their back to study the insulative properties of their coats.

Obviously, there was no way I'd be doing that with Scruffy or Luna, but it wasn't an impossibility should I have stayed on longer.

I would have never threatened their lives in any way, and they never seemed to see me as food or consider me to be dangerous. However, in the places where wolves have far more experience with us, and especially where they are persecuted by us – for example, the parts of North America where they are trapped, shot and killed by people – then naturally their wariness of humans could, and would, slip into a far more aggressive defensiveness. *People are killers too*, they'd think, and absolutely *not* to be trusted. In many wolf-on-human attack cases, the wolves had become habituated to closely associate human populations with food, whether that be from within their rubbish dumps, the pets they kept outside, or from the relatively docile livestock they kept on their farms. In those places, the wolves' behaviour has been modified by our own, and they have moved into far closer proximity with our populations as a result.

There is always the potential for outliers – those exceptionally rare cases where wolves have hunted and killed us for food – but you have to judge that against what circumstances you'd need for that to actually ever happen. Given I was having regular visits by Scruffy, who I believed was clearly no instinctive 'man eater', I thought it might be interesting to very gently probe the boundaries of what I might have to do to trigger his hunting response towards me. I know how mad that sounds – but I was a bit bored and very curious (probably both Scruffy and I were, at times) and by the time I thought about my experiment, I really was convinced that he would never have attacked me. So, one ordinary day, when he was hanging around with me and all was calm, I decided to make myself really small, hide from his view and make a deliberate high-pitched 'chirrup', which sounded like a small rodent.

Immediately, his behaviour flipped. Scruffy assumed a predatory prowling posture – head and nose down low, eyes alert, ears pricked – and made slow, deliberate movements towards the noise. Were I a lemming, the ending would've come all at once: with eyes, nose and ears triangulating Scruffy's body to the exact place where the little mammal lay in the grass, a short leap forward would have placed it well within his crushing jaws.

Oh fuck, I thought as he crept closer, *this is what it's really like to be stalked.* Scruffy was inching towards me and the nervous jumpy 'puppy' was all but gone. I didn't leave it too long before sitting up. The Scruffy I knew sprang up from his crouch. 'Where did that little mouse go?' was writ large across his very confused face, as he swivelled his eyes across the grass I was sitting in, scanning for his meal.

I didn't mess around too much after that, but I did try it just one more time, only to be sure it wasn't all a fluke. A little 'chirrup' and there he was again: predatory switch flicked, crouching, alert and ready – until the point I sat up, and that disarming confusion washed back over him.

It made me consider the one story I had followed of a fatal wolf attack on a person, and the host of variables needed to be in such a desperately unlucky position.

I was in Alaska and we'd flown out to a remote Inuit community to record the story. A young woman had been working there as a special education teacher. She was flying around various Inuit communities for a short period of teaching, and she'd decided to go for a run after work. Originally, she was from Pennsylvania, not a place where wolves still lived in the wild, and she was exceptionally small in stature: just 4 foot 10 inches tall and slight of build. She was actually training for a marathon at the time, and, having taught the local students on her first day of work, she changed into her Lycra running gear, put on some headphones and started to run down the only road in the community. That road ran west along the side of a hill – and the west wind had picked up her scent and floated it across to some hungry wolves.

Moose were the primary prey species for the wolves in the area, but they also hunted smaller prey, such as caribou, salmon, rabbits and small birds. They likely saw humans as a threat, but this woman probably didn't represent a human shape or behaviour they immediately recognised. To them, she was a tiny, vulnerable-looking creature, running away from a community of people who were typically much larger, wrapped up in thick winter clothes and, more often than not, travelling in trucks or on snowmobiles. Did she look like a baby animal? I was told that the wolf tracks had indicated they had followed her for some time before they attacked. Perhaps they had been weighing her up? Trying to figure out what she was, as they crept closer to the heels of this poor person running along with her headphones on, completely unaware of the very real danger she was in, right before the fatal attack.

Some people said that the wolf tracks had led back to the local rubbish dump too, and that wolves had been known to exploit gaps in the dump fence to eat from the community rubbish there. Potentially, a dangerous connection between people and food could have been established among some of those wolves then, but the official report flatly denies that any wolves had ever had any access to human 'food attractants' and asserts that the dump was entirely enclosed within a chain-link fence. It did concede that wolf tracks *were* observed around the perimeter of that fence, and a dog was also observed 'dragging a bag of garbage toward the perimeter of the community six days after the attack', which would suggest their rubbish wasn't entirely secure. The whole thing felt a bit odd. There followed a concerted effort to cull the area's wolf population, leading to the killing of eight animals – but it was always unclear exactly how many wolves were involved in the attack, and there were mixed reports about whether or not any of the culled wolves had been involved. The official report stated that one of the culled wolves had left its DNA evidence on the woman, but when we tried to follow up with interviews, I was given very short shrift by one of the people involved in the investigation.

There might've been a few discrepancies in the story, but whichever way you looked at it, there needed to be a lot of extenuating circumstances for a person to ever be vulnerable to a wolf attack and, even then, the chance of it actually happening was still extraordinarily small. Of the 70 years of records held between 1950 and 2019, there are only 25 verified cases of wolf attacks in North America, and of those, only two fatal attacks were caused by healthy wolves. You would then have to go back to 1920 to find the next fatality that wasn't due to a wolf being either rabid or captive.

The fact remains that you are far more likely to be killed by virtually anything else in your life than by a wild animal. In fact, if you were to combine all the average number of human deaths per year due to attack from sharks, bears, lions, hippos, elephants and crocodiles, you are still only looking at around 2,500 fatalities. You may still think that sounds like a lot, but set against the 400,000-plus human homicides a year, the 800,000 suicides or the 3,000 people who die every single *day* in accidents involving cars, it really is not. Twice as many people die from mishaps involving vending machines as they do sharks, but I guess that doesn't quite make the sexiest-sounding Hollywood blockbuster, does it?

My work with wildlife has placed me in potential 'harm's way' many times, but consider how often I've been in the rare and privileged position of being so close to so many of the animals that we consider to be the most dangerous, without anything remotely bad ever happening at all. Let's face it, in spite of my rigorous early combat training with my siblings, I represent pretty easy pickings for any large wild animal that would want to make me a meal, or, at least, give me a very robust instruction to leave their territory with immediate effect, and yet the only injury I've sustained was when that capercaillie bit my finger in Scotland.

Even the most powerful predators are pragmatic. If they have the option of fleeing the scene and leaving you behind, then they'll more than likely take that over the chance of having a crack at you. The vast majority of scary and dangerous animals we think about meeting in the wilderness never actually make our acquaintance because they will have fled the moment they heard us coming, with all our heavy steps and foreign noises. That is precisely why we, in the wildlife filmmaking world, have to go to such enormous lengths to find, and then hide from, so many of the so-called 'dangerous' predators we wish to film.

You *might* be weak but they don't know for sure that you *definitely* are – especially if you already deviate wildly from the type of animal that they would ordinarily expect to encounter within their territory. As with all potentially lethal creatures, a few small and sensible precautions will keep you almost completely safe, but, if you were ever in a situation where you were actually attacked, that natural instinctive fear they have of you is precisely why so much of the advice requires you to amplify that sense of doubt. In some cases, you might shout, scream, make yourself larger or charge in their direction. In others you might want to make yourself small, avoid eye contact or flee from the scene fast (or slow!) or you might even climb a tree. It is best you familiarise yourself with the exact strategy (no one wants to inadvertently charge at an animal that they really could've walked away from!) but, in sum, you are either building on their natural apprehension and fears of you, or you are providing them with the clear opportunity to leave you well alone by putting a safe distance between *you* and *them*. Shoot at it, hurt it or wrongfully attack it back, and you're much more likely to cause a panic response that ends badly all round.

Most importantly of all, the majority of potentially dangerous animals will give you a clear warning if your presence is making them feel in any way uncomfortable. A 'threat display' could range from a false charge to a growl, or a howl, or just them making themselves appear larger: puffing out their chest or arching their back. It is vital that you then *heed their warning* and back off, as opposed to getting closer in an effort to capture a better shot, or – worse still – misinterpreting the entire display as some sort of charming performance put on purely for your benefit. Among the most common 'wild animal attacks' are the huge numbers of tourists bitten by wild monkeys, simply because they misinterpreted a primate that was baring its teeth, or flapping its lips in caution, for them smiling or blowing a few kisses their way.

• • •

By my third week on that first trip to Ellesmere, I knew the wolves had begun to trust me. That initial nervous curiosity had shifted towards an acceptance which gently morphed towards something that felt far more integral. I learnt a vital lesson about behaving more naturally myself. Instead of simply staring over at them all day, I would carry on with my everyday activities without stopping to acknowledge their presence around me. I was behaving far more like a 'pack member' than an observer if I cleaned myself, cooked my food, and *especially* if I mimicked wolfish behaviours like drinking from the stream on all fours.

As long as I projected an atmosphere of total calm around them, then they would happily pad around me and my campsite, and allow me to freely work and move around their home too. A big moment came when I realised they had peed all over my binoculars. They might've smelt pretty pungent, but the scent marking was an instinctual move on their part. It spelt out that my things and I were being properly embraced into their group for the first time. Then, as if that point couldn't have been made any clearer, at the climax of the first trip I found myself lying right on top of their den.

I had spotted the first pup on the long lens, as it poked its head from the den and out into the sunlight. Later on, a remote-controlled car we'd fitted with cameras revealed that there were, in fact, three youngsters hidden down there. For most of that first trip, Luna had stood guard over the den. Feeding the pups her milk and being fed in turn by the pack when they returned successful from a hunting trip. I could feel the real strength of the pack's bond in those moments. How they worked together, howled and hunted together, shared their food, raised and protected those pups – and then right at the end of my stay, the entire adult wolf pack went to hunt, with Luna included.

Perhaps you could put it down to the cubs now being a certain age and somehow capable of being left alone regardless of their small size; perhaps you could rationalise that the pack wanted to be at full strength for that particular hunt, but after that moment, the cubs weren't being watched over by a member of the pack – they were being watched over *by me*.

There, on my tummy, out in the high Arctic sunshine, I observed the three adorable pups playing with each other, calling out with their little squeaks and 'yips', seemingly without a worry in the world. I was scarcely able to conceive of how incredibly lucky I was to have got so close to this most hallowed ground of all wolves, and it took some considerable effort to pull myself away from the den and return to my actual home.

By then, I had fallen for those wolves in quite a big way. At one point I said that it felt like 'I was becoming part of the pack'. It felt a bit hokey, but there really was that feeling. I'd started that series on the very edge, an observer on the pack's periphery, eyed with a suspicion that leant towards curiosity, but by the end, my psyche, my physical presence and my personal motivations had all shifted. I was in there, moving around the wolves as they moved, worked and socialised around me too.

In the Arctic autumn I returned once more, and the pack had moved some 20 miles away from the den, but everyone was alive. I can't pretend I was anything other than thrilled to see them all. The pups had grown, they looked strong and far more independent, and this time they were around me from the very moment our helicopter touched down. I didn't even think about protecting myself, or dancing around behind a mound of our gear.

That trip, the wolves were to spend their time fattening up in readiness for winter, feeding off a carcass and hunting for fresh food. I spent my time keeping up with the pack on a quad bike in a hunting territory that could potentially expand out to 7,000 square kilometres, far larger than that of the American wolf populations further south. Often, they'd head off over huge areas: down ravines where we couldn't keep up, crunching through territory without much effort that would then take us hours to negotiate. Time and again, though, we would assume they were gone, only to find them waiting for us just beyond the crest of the next hill, before they'd pick up the pace again. Had they wanted to leave at any point, they could've easily left us far behind – but they never did, and they returned to us at our base camp too.

There was no obvious incentive for the wolves to choose to be near us. They gained nothing from us in the way of shelter or food, and we would've offered little in the way of protection. There was no overt reason for them to wait for us to catch up either. Ellesmere was a savage and highly marginal habitat: vast and relatively short of wild food options for the pack. A place of stunted grasslands grazed by small creatures that could comfortably hide below ground, or the strong musk oxen that would spread out across massive areas. I got the impression that the wolves had to adapt to periods of starvation, literal feast and famine, between their musk oxen kills, and it became so clear to me then that they needed to work really hard to survive. If there was ever a time when they could've turned on me, then that would have been it.

It was hard seeing the younger pack members go hungry, but not at any stage would I have fed them. Forming a connection between humans and food has had historically bad outcomes for humans and wolves. We didn't carry food on us and we kept our own supplies behind the electric fence, tightly sealed in cool boxes that were semi-buried in the ground – but there was one very small 'benefit' that they did glean from us.

We were pretty much completely self-contained as a crew – all our kit was well organised in camp, with food and waste systems sensitively managed so nothing would ever really encroach on or alter their habitat. All apart from one thing: we had no toilet.

When it came to having a 'big jobbie', the 'number two', you'd take yourself away to wherever you could have a bit of privacy (not easy in a wide-open tundra), crouch down and do a wild one – which you then buried. What I discovered fairly early on, much to my surprise, was that on a subsequent return to *my spot*, it was obvious that my previous donation had been removed. Yes, I am afraid to say, the wolves were eating our shit.

It certainly wasn't enough to have kept the wolves around us in itself. I highly doubt they were *that* nutritious and the wolves needed huge protein loads to survive – but I did wonder if that 'token gesture', if you will, could have been something of an accidental olive branch once offered by our early ancestors, when our relationship with wolves was in its most infantile stages. A lot of the theories of how humans and wolves first forged their relationship seemed to revolve around the types of animals we both hunted, and possibly shared, without considering the fact that there were also dozens of human bum-holes dumping daily wolf snacks out into the environment. That mutually beneficial 'snack provision and waste collection service' isn't something I've ever read about in the history books, but I am yet to find a dog that doesn't take a real interest in the faeces of other creatures – so who knows?

There were so many other moments where I felt their closeness, but the one where I really felt everything had shifted between me and the wolves made up quite a short sequence in the series. The wolves had pretty much finished what was left of the carcass and were howling away into the sky, rallying the pack for another big move across the tundra. I had shuffled in among them as they picked off the tiny slivers of meat that still clung to the bone – but now it was time to leave, they got up and moved off as one.

Far away from the filmmaking process, and really, some steps removed from all the things we think and do, I felt deep in my gut that they wanted me to follow them. In the weeks before, such a thought would have seemed crazy, but the signals from the wolves were clear enough. I just had to accept them for what they truly were, and go.

I got to my feet and went with them. The wolves were behind me, in front of me, alongside me, as I walked within the heart of the pack and at my own pace. I felt this incredible sense of peacefulness, security and belonging. In that moment, I had crossed wholly over into their world.

For some time, we just walked together and I had a near overwhelming compulsion to keep going. To stay within my pack. To slip the collar and lead that was holding me back in my world and keep going onwards, up and over the horizon. It was quite dreamlike, and out of all the animal families I would live with over all the years of filming the Animal Families & Me series, it was only within the wolf pack of Ellesmere that I instinctively felt that connection.

• • •

Alastair, my mum's new partner who she met after moving to Mull, would call us the 'timber wolves'. It's actually just another name for the North American grey wolf, but many Americans view them as a smaller and weaker subspecies of the grey, which will sometimes be found in marginal habitats foraging through the bins for food.

Alastair had meant it in a derogatory way. He was saying that my brothers, sister and I roamed around together as a somewhat mangy and feral foursome. That we were a bit uncontrollable. A wee pack of 'outsiders' from a place far away from Mull, who were now all tucked up in the trees, on the fringes of Tobermory town.

I knew he had meant to demean us with the 'timber wolves' term, but I wore his slight like a badge of honour. Long before I'd had any interactions with real wolves, I had always liked the idea that he thought of us as being a bit like them and everything that they represented.

I was proud to be associated with the wolf. I certainly didn't see them as an inherently bad animal at all. I wonder if he was slightly wary, if not fearful, of the four of us – and I liked the idea of that too.

We might not have been completely wild or wolf-like, but Alastair was using the historically negative connotations of the 'wolf' as a vehicle for his own resentments about our presence – and especially the love and attention we took from our mum, the woman he was now with. The four of us got in his way, and I have no doubt he came to wish that we weren't around at all.

Ironically, if there was any traditionally lupine metaphor to be drawn, then by far the stronger version was the one where it was *Alastair* who represented the perfect central casting of that 'wolf-like' outsider. Here was a sly person who people would readily trust. He worked himself right into the heart of our flock.

He even became our stepfather.

Predator and Prey

It all began in early 1980.

Our mum went to the pub one evening and all of us were stuck, very reluctantly, in the caravan with a babysitter. I felt, right away, that something was up, but in reality, our poor mum had probably had a gutful of us through the week, and was only going out for a bit of a break. Nonetheless, it was down the pub where she first met Alastair, and it wasn't too long before they were properly dating.

He had this swarthy, Burt Reynolds look: dark curly hair, mutton-chop sideburns and a thick sculpted moustache, which was very fashionable at the time. He was also tanned, tattooed and powerful looking. He had the air of a pirate about him, this Jack-the-lad 21-year-old, and he was very well known around Tobermory.

Superficially, he came across as a great bloke. Someone who was charming, charismatic and always ready to laugh. He was one of those jack-of-all-trade islanders who did a bit of joinery, building work and fishing. He was quite capable of turning his hand to any manual task, even off-shore scallop diving for sale to the posh markets and restaurants.

I remember, as a kid, thinking about how incredibly intrepid the diving sounded. That there was a way, with a bit of scuba diving kit and training, that you could escape into a vast unseen and unknown world deep beneath the sea. That was all before you'd even considered the pay. Sure, there were risks involved, but if you got good at it, it looked like it was as simple as diving down and picking pound notes clean off the seabed. Another local diver had put it best when he'd simply said, 'The seabed is my bank, and whenever I need some money, I just dive down and get it.'

For those without university degrees, this was one of the very best paid local jobs you could get, and it seemed to us that these teak-tough diving men were absolutely rolling in it. Alastair thought my mum was quite a catch too, and it was actually she who paid for a fleet of prawn creels for him in 1982. So, he couldn't exactly have been rolling in it.

One day, Alastair proudly declared that he couldn't even swim. *How brave must this man be?* I thought to myself then, without really considering that was actually pretty stupid too. I just thought it was really cool. Initially, there was a bit of hero-worshipping, and I was really excited when he took me out on the boat to watch him dive. Whether this was performative or not, he explained to me that to acclimatise his hands to the cold temperatures on the seabed he would plunge them into a wooden whisky barrel filled with freezing cold water. Brave and very hard then, but there was something else about him too. He had a powerful magnetism: a pervasive aura that made him the kind of person that others were attracted to. At least in the very early days, I liked him, and I wanted him to like me back.

I never felt like he could ever be a replacement for my dad, but I recognised that we had that void in our lives on Mull and that, with him around, all those questions about who or where our dad was might have less of an edge. Initially, I hoped Alastair could be good for us all. Not a father, but possibly a father figure, or, at the very least a new male role model to look up to.

As hopes go, that one didn't last very long.

I'm pretty sure Alastair knew exactly what he was doing. His charm was working on me, probably on Stewart, and certainly on Maggie too. I remember him taking me out into the woods to make a bow and arrow: how he'd paid attention to what I was into and brought this very impressive Swiss Army knife to do the job. But none of it ever worked on Sandy. Not for one minute. Sandy was the oldest, the most mature and experienced, and he was also the one who'd spent the most time with our dad before the break-up. He wasn't going to have his head turned by anyone. Especially not Alastair.

It's a very strong emotion to place on someone so young, but I'd go so far as to say Sandy hated him from the get-go. Fairly soon, Alastair was meeting Sandy's ire with ire, and he certainly had a huge hand in ensuring that Sandy left home pretty much as soon as he'd turned 16.

• • •

Like most islanders, Alastair had a nickname. Almost everyone called him Wheachkie. I think it was because, when he was a wee boy, he had struggled to say the word 'whisky'. It wasn't an obvious nickname like Curly, nor nearly as obscure as Beeve, but that was how he was widely known, and, as my respect for him evaporated over the years, I reverted to calling him Wheachkie too. It was as if to say, 'You don't deserve for me to call you by your given name.' It was a small but significant act of disrespect and rebellion in my own mind, and it has only been in very recent years that I've been able to start referring to him as Alastair again.

Even before anything really bad had happened, I came to realise that a significant part of that unspecific aura of power was the shadow he cast through the rumours of rage, and rage-filled violence, that had followed him around. It wasn't just the violence that he might have been involved with himself as an adult, but that he also could've been subjected to some bullying during his childhood.

Many local men expressed themselves through their physicality on Mull. There wasn't much room for deep discussions about how you felt about something, or elongated attempts to try and understand someone else's point of view. People didn't tend to 'agree to disagree'; if someone had acted in a way that you didn't like, especially in the pub, then that could easily wind up with a 'do in'.

'Intelligence' was knowing where the best spot to find scallops was and 'emotional intelligence' was pretty much non-existent among the vast majority of the local blokes. This was not an enlightened time. Mull, for better or worse, had always felt at least a decade behind most of the mainland.

To some of the men, anyone who openly expressed any strong feelings of happiness, sadness, interest or ambition was 'gay'. If you used words like 'excellent' or 'fascinating' then you were 'probably gay', if you said 'I love this' then you were '*definitely* gay'. Expressions of pleasure were best limited to a mumbled 'that's fucken' good' and fascination should only be conveyed with a muted 'quite good, aye'. Norrie and I were in the pub one evening when a drunken man rolled up and slurred something into Norrie's ear. 'Pardon?' said Norrie innocently. 'Pardon?' repeated the man incredulously. 'It's fucking "what?"!'

Both men and women were guarded with their feelings. It just wasn't the 'done thing' to air your dirty laundry in public, or to be seen spilling your guts to everyone about something that was considered private, and there was definitely a culture of favouring the stick over the carrot. The idea that someone might be a bit of a brawler wouldn't really have raised any red flags. However, even in this deeply old-school, rough-and-tumble community, there were unwritten rules and social conventions. A very obvious line was drawn between the use of fists to settle a score between two equally matched men, or a clip to a cheeky kid's ear from a parent or teacher, and someone who bullied the weak, or worse, was a wife beater. The rumours around Alastair suggested that he was a man who might've crossed that line in the past. And that he would very likely do so again.

I wasn't aware of any of that as an eight-year-old. I don't think any of us were. But a cruel side to his character started to seep into his everyday behaviour. At first, it started fairly small. He'd regale me with stories of his physical conquests. Street fights, where he'd come out on top against other blokes. It might not have been that unconventional that he was a fighter, but it was definitely inappropriate that he was going into unnecessary levels of detail about precisely how he'd beaten someone to an absolute pulp.

Then his early comments about us kids being 'timber wolves' escalated into more direct slights. 'Look at the fucken' arms on ya,' he'd say to me, in front of everyone. 'I've seen bigger arms on a Sindy doll!' or 'I've seen broader shoulders on a Pepsi bottle'. It was always delivered in a jocular way, so I couldn't really say anything back without being accused of being oversensitive, but it was a very deliberate and pointed humiliation.

If ever I was clearly upset and crying, he would put his face right up to mine and mimic my tears: 'Boo hoo hoo,' he'd say, before ending with a fucking annoying flick right onto my nose. He was a man with zero empathy who let me know, persistently, that I was physically inferior to him. Me, this little kid, who was less than half his age and size, with my spaghetti arms and obvious relative weaknesses when compared to him: the living incarnation of Popeye the sailor. A burly, hard-working, hard-drinking, fully-grown fighting man of Mull. He was so *obviously* stronger than me that it was perverse to point it out – but Alastair, despite projecting this air of being a hard bastard, carried deep insecurities. Insecurities that he sated by proving himself to be 'the alpha' in whatever arena he could.

I recently asked my sister Maggie if she had any photos of Alastair from that period and she messaged back with: 'How about this one of him wringing the bird's neck at the lighthouse?' It is grimly ridiculous, yet so typical as an illustration of what he was like. We'd all gone off on this nice family walk on a Sunday afternoon. We were dressed up for the occasion, the boys in smart trousers and shoes, nothing more than a stroll out, but then there was this shag, the long-necked and dark-plumed fish-eating bird, looking a bit too dopey and docile.

'Look!' we'd shouted gleefully. 'There's a bird over there that's not flying off!' Slowly, we kids had crept up on it – anticipating that it might fly off any second – but it didn't. Clearly there was something very wrong with it, and obviously, as a normal(ish) parent, my response in that scenario would've been to quietly shepherd my kids along and leave it for nature to take its course. Not Alastair though. He just grabbed its long neck and snapped it right in front of us. Killing it instantly. In the picture, the lighthouse looms large behind him and his smart flared trousers. The recently scragged bird is gripped firmly in his left fist and a taut muscle is rippling away down his forearm, as thick as a ship's rope.

It probably was a sick and dying bird – you could say that it was a mercy killing to spare it a grisly death from starvation or worse – but there was something pretty pointed about how he'd wanted to execute it in front of us all.

Come mid-October 1980, we were renting a small prefab-type chalet on the other side of town. No one could face another winter in the caravan, so our mum found us this flat-roofed three-bed place, just to get us through the coldest months. That became a theme of the next couple of winters. We would spend the summers back in the caravan, and then head to a rental chalet, until the spring of 1982 when our mum managed to get us into Abeona, a house on Victoria Street. It was a white-washed mid-terrace house with two floors – no less! We'd gone up in the world, literally! It was on one of the highest streets in the town with a magnificent view over the bay towards Calve.

In the rental chalets, I continued to share a room with Stewart, but the place still felt like an immense palace compared with where we'd been staying up until that point. It probably would've been a palace, too, had Alastair not been present.

By now, my mum had told me that they were getting married and my immediate thought was that this was definitely not a good idea. Not for one second did I think, *Ah well, you're an adult, you know what you're doing*. I *knew* it was a big mistake from the off, not least because, just a few months earlier, he had hit her for the first time.*

I don't know what had triggered that first violent incident. More than likely, he'd come home pissed from the pub and my mum had said something to him. She might've been small, but

---

* My mum and I have spoken about this period at length. A lot of this is my recollection of a gradual escalation of violence, but it is from the viewpoint of a child. She points out that the actual acts of violence were limited to just a handful of moments over the years they were together. That is not down-playing it at all, rather, it is to make the point that for her, it was his use of a far subtler emotional abuse – his continual criticism and gaslighting – that really eroded her confidence and self-esteem.

our mum wasn't a pushover. Probably, she'd gently put him in his place, and he, feeling inadequate, or just frustrated at being ticked off, had lashed out in the only way he knew how.

I was in another room when I heard my mum's head being slammed up against the wall. I can remember feeling shock at hearing this terrible new sound, while still knowing *exactly* what was going on. It was as if I had always somehow expected that something bad was going to happen one day, without ever really knowing exactly what that meant, or what, precisely, it was going to be.

That first time, it all stopped pretty quickly. I remember thinking it was because he knew we could all hear it, as opposed to him coming to his senses and realising he had just done something inherently wrong. A massive line had been crossed and that sense of threat never left from that point forward. I knew that if it had happened once, it would happen again.

There was quite a big gap till I became aware of the next incident. I was with my mum, just walking down the street together, and she was wearing a headscarf around her neck. She never wore that type of stuff, but I didn't think anything of it. Then we bumped into one of her friends. 'Ooh!' she exclaimed in admiration. 'It's not like you to wear a scarf!' She tugged at it to get a closer look, and there, on my mum's throat, were his hands. The bruised indentations of terrible thumbs and fingers. My mum went red and quickly covered herself up. Nothing was said.

The third time was during a New Year's Eve party, and Alastair's brother and sister-in-law were over. We had all gone to bed after the midnight bells, when I heard muffled noises and violence breaking out in the other room. Clattering and shouting, and there, right in the middle of it all, I could hear my mum choking.

'Calm down, Ali! Calm down!' his brother was shouting and breaking it all up, and I remember lying there, and just feeling so incredibly grateful that he was there to handle it. I was a child. We were all children. Alastair had long since proven that we were physically inferior to him, and I just felt this utter sense of impotence in the face of his superior power.

His brother broke it up, but who was going to stop him when it happened next? Me? I stood no chance. And with that, the dreadful realisation dawned that this man could kill our mum and there was absolutely nothing I could do about it.

• • •

Alastair and our mum were married in an Oban registry office in October 1982. We were each bought a new set of clothes: smart white shirts and sweaters for us brothers and a new dress for Maggie. I stood there then, fully believing that our escape from Alastair was all but impossible.

At one point, her wrist had to be bandaged up after a fight, and then one Christmas Eve, Stewart and I were watching TV and it all kicked off in the hall. Him back from the pub and her screaming again. Her being slammed up against the wall by him, again.

By this time, Stewart and I were a little bit older, a little bit bigger and a lot bolder. I might've only been 11, him just 12, but with no one else around we knew we had to do something. We jumped up, threw open the living room door and saw he had a hold of our mum. 'What's going on!' screamed Stewart. 'What the fuck do you mean what's going on?' Alastair shouted back, letting go of her and rounding on us both.

That seemed to be enough. The shame and embarrassment that these two boys had whipped back the curtain and witnessed his behaviour seemed to stop him. Perhaps he was taken aback that the two youngest boys in the family had confronted him for the first time: the 'timber wolves', pulling together within their tiny pack.

That incident was enough for my mum, too. Unbeknown to me, she had already begun to make plans to get Alastair out of our home and into a place of his own – before the incident in the early summer of 1986 firmly hammered the final nail into the coffin of their relationship.

I don't know if he had been to the pub or not, but my mum was fast asleep in her bed and in he'd walked. He scooped up the hefty plug-in alarm clock on the bedside table and smashed it down on her head as she slept.

I was 14 years old and had been out that evening, knocking about as usual, but when I walked into this utterly broken home of broken things and a carpet coated with blood, I panicked. I remember racing up the stairs, following this horrible crimson trail into the bedroom where her blood was everywhere. There was so much blood, I assumed he'd dragged her down the stairs and taken her out of the house himself.

'He's done it. He's fucking done it,' I said. The very worst of my absolute bleakest fears flooded into my brain as I searched for my mum. But she wasn't there. *This is it*, I thought, *he's killed her.* Then, a neighbour, one of her friends, came into the house. 'Gordon', they said, 'she's with the nurse getting patched up.' Alastair was nowhere to be seen, but at least my mum wasn't dead.

I asked my mum what had actually happened. Apparently, she had fled to a friend's house who had then called for the nurse. Alastair had left, turning over her pillow before he went, in a ham-fisted attempt to cover up the blood. But she came home later that night, with all her wounds bandaged up. The next day I did what was probably the first truly mature thing I had ever done. 'Mum,' I said to her, 'he's gonna kill you. You have to get rid of him. We've got to go to the police and do something.'

From all the brawls with my siblings I knew that arguments could become heated. That there could be a misunderstanding, perceived slight or provocation that could lead to blows. But we were just kids.

A man, a grown-up, a husband, just walking in and battering his wife while she slept? That was really fucked up and totally warped. If that could happen, then I felt that the absolute worst would eventually happen too.

'I'll come to the police station with you,' I calmly continued. 'We'll just tell them all about what's happening. About what's been going on.'

It might have been taboo to talk to people about the problems you were having behind closed doors, but there was always another side to that: no matter how private you were as an individual, in a small community, everyone knows everyone else's business anyway.

It was obvious. I'm even going to go out on a limb and say that the police must've known too. Perhaps they'd even had words with him at some point? But my mum didn't go to the police. In fairness, why would she if they'd most likely do nothing much anyway? Our mum had made up her own mind though. She told him it was all over now, and that he had to go.

I wouldn't speak to Alastair, or even look at him other than from the corner of my eye, ever again. He was an invisible man in our life. Drifting around without any acknowledgement from me, and by the end of that summer he was gone.

Except, of course, he wasn't really. Gone from our home, yes, but he resided as a dark presence in my mind for some years to come.

The Black Bear and the Hermit

Our seaplane floated above an endless early morning mist, hugging tight to the tips of a vast forest of pine in Minnesota. The northern states of the Midwest hold so much of the iconic backwoods of American folklore. Great lakes and long rivers carving space between dense swathes of forest. It's one of the last true wilderness expanses of the United States and most definitely 'bear country'.

It was late summer in 2010 when we started to film *The Bear Family & Me*. The series featured, in effect, two families: Juliet and her three cubs, and, to a greater extent, Lily and her cub, Hope.

Unlike the experience with the snow wolves of Ellesmere Island a couple of years later, I always felt that my bear family were simply tolerating my presence. In fact, there were times when I think they would've far preferred it if I wasn't there at all and, on occasion, they would exhibit a real turn of speed and disappear off to the bush without a trace.

I didn't slip into that same comfortable rhythm of life that I would experience on Ellesmere, that sense of being accepted and somehow part of something bigger. It was always at the back of my mind that I was on the margin of that family, especially on the one occasion when I opted to sleep out in the forest, just metres away from Juliet and her three cubs. We'd interviewed a hunter who had been attacked by bears – he had been hunting them, so there was provocation, but it wasn't unheard of for them to kill people who just happened to be in the wrong place at the wrong time. For a lot of wild campers in the American backwoods, a night-time bear encounter was something you'd take steps to avoid, yet there I was, choosing to sleep on a patch of ground right next to a family. Or not sleep, as was more accurately the case. Dark thoughts swam through my mind. What if Juliet woke, startled, in the middle of the night, and forgot that I was there? What if she, in that same half-dozing state, mistook me for some threat to the cubs?

The bear habitat itself felt quite hostile at night too. This oppressively dense, dark, swampy forest with my fairly ambivalent family of bears and other potentially deadly predators too. There were packs of wolves around, none of whom I was remotely acquainted with. How would they react if they'd been on the hunt and came across this person curled up on the forest floor? I really didn't sleep too well that night, and I did not opt to repeat the experience either.

The next morning, though, when I did wake with Juliet, she actually seemed fine, and had indeed remembered I was there. She looked towards me, perhaps not as friend, but certainly not as foe. She then let me follow her all morning as she foraged in the forest, before she stopped and suckled her cubs. After that, she dozed off, and through sheer exhaustion, I did too, waking again an hour later, again with Juliet, without her showing any sign that I was in any way unwelcome. I felt then that we had a good thing going, which was pretty remarkable given what she was.

• • •

It is extremely rare for an animal to make me truly fearful for my safety. Almost always, actual threats to my life have originated from the behaviour of other humans; especially if they were armed, angry, drunk or just terrible drivers out on terrible roads. Overwhelmingly, that sense of a human 'threat' has come from the behaviours of other men – and, for me, a natural wariness had probably originated from those childhood experiences with Alastair.

For years, I wasn't able to see a single positive thing about that period – but it took a chance, and very random, encounter with another man during the filming of *The Bear Family & Me* to help alter my perspective.

When it comes to anyone's work, there's the job itself and then there's all the other things that happen around it. Those tangential and incidental moments that often feel like they don't mean all that much at the time, but every so often they really can change the course of your day or week. On very rare occasions, they may even shape the rest of your life.

Away from the filming of *The Bear Family & Me* in the Minnesota back-country, I had an encounter with a hermit. Not all hermits, backwoods men and women, are the same. As with any group in society, there will always be those that may behave in ways, or hold opinions, that are deeply unpleasant, but there is likely something worthwhile in listening to the voices of those rare people who take themselves away from society and live in nature full-time. Perhaps living in a place where your own survival imperative is pulled into an acute focus helps the hermit cut through all of mainstream society's smoke and mirrors, affording them a keen nose for what really matters, and an even keener ear for all of our bullshit.

For hundreds of years, hermits were valued for their apolitical and incorruptible views. Because they didn't need, or want, the trappings of an orthodox society, they were sought out to pass their judgement from a position that was several degrees removed from everyone else. Many writers, artists and musicians have long since headed to the wilds in the hope of tapping into some 'purity of thought' that might also be found in a place that feels lost to everyone else.

I can't remember that dear old fella's name, so let's just call him 'Joe'. We were well into filming the series and his was a name that kept cropping up among the local Minnesotans. 'Interested in the bears, are ya? Ah, well you'll have to go speak with Joe. He lives well out in the woods and sees them there all the time.'

Joe wasn't exactly a man you could call in advance. That's sort of the deal with being a hermit – no email, no phone, no postbox – and he's not exactly going to trot to town and give you a piece of wisdom down the local Starbucks. No, if we wanted to meet Joe, we would have to seek him out on his terms, and head deep into the woods to find his home.

We were given some very rough directions and ditched the car close to a small track that was slowly being consumed by the bush. On we went by foot, winding through the trees and following a loose path cut clear by just one set of boots, until, eventually, we could see Joe's cabin emerging from between the pines.

If Hollywood needed a set for an American hermit living out in the woods, then Joe's place might fit the bill. He had the wood cabin, the Confederate flag, and then there was the hermit himself, sat alone on his porch chair, staring down at us with an inscrutable expression. The only things Joe failed to have that morning were a banjo in his arms and a rifle laid across his lap.

'Here come the Red Coats!' he called out in a thick Midwestern accent. I knew then that he had been forewarned of our visit. That was definitely a good thing, as I'm sure there were several guns lying around in that cabin, but the use of 'Red Coats' as slang for us? Perhaps that was less good. He was very likely referencing the British Red Coats' defeat at the hands of the American Patriots during the American War of Independence, and I needed to get, at least, a little bit closer to Joe, just to figure out quite how seriously he took events that had happened two and a half centuries ago.

It turned out that he took them very seriously indeed, and he had clearly been waiting some time to deliver a long monologue titled: 'Why the British are fundamentally responsible for everything that's gone wrong in the United States today'.

But it was all a bit tongue-in-cheek really. He seemed to enjoy us gently bantering back and forth with him, a good-natured ribbing until, and I can't remember precisely what it was that I'd said, but Joe snapped, 'You wouldn't say that in front of your father!'

I took a step back, momentarily breaking the flow of our banter.

I immediately thought of my stepfather, Alastair. In the end, I had spent much more time under the same roof with him than I did my actual dad – certainly as a child, going through my most formative years.

'Ah, well Joe,' I answered honestly, 'that doesn't really apply to me.'

We had come to Joe for his opinion on bears and so far received his opinion on the British. Perhaps that was a fairly predictable outcome as foreigners to a man who was the true 'outsider's outsider', but I hadn't anticipated I'd be hearing his opinion on a personal life that I had always kept well guarded.

I sensed that Joe had the measure of me pretty well. His eyes sparkled with a different kind of knowing.

'You, young sir,' he began, quite pointedly, 'you have to be thankful for *everything* that "father" has done for you.'

He saw my face, likely expressing a wordless, but quite obvious, absolute disagreement with that statement. 'Because,' he continued, much more earnestly this time, 'he showed you the man that you never wanted to be.'

Those words caught me completely off guard. It was quite something to hear all that from a hermit way out in the woods, but

I knew he had a point. When Alastair and our mum had married there should also have been a commitment to love, honour and cherish her children, his stepchildren. Joe was right: in Alastair, I had been shown the exact type of man, father and husband that I didn't want to become.

Joe had probably seen something that I'd scarcely been able to admit to myself either. Alastair's actions had left some wounds that had sunk deeper than I'd probably realised. As an adult, I might've tried to airbrush out a lot of the bad things that happened, to downplay them, or just make it all into a bit of a joke. I certainly haven't ever discussed any of this publicly, but no matter what I did to extinguish those memories, the feelings of insecurity still clung to my skin like a sweaty shirt.

It would take me a very long time before I accepted that those events had affected me in any way whatsoever. Maybe I'd just wanted to forget about it all, or maybe I was in denial, but it wasn't some-thing I would spend too much time thinking about as I grew older.

Whenever I thought back to those times, I would focus on the great many things that were really good. Soften the bad times with the thought that there were plenty of people who were much worse off than me, and always outwardly present the image of the boy who'd only ever had this incredibly privileged immersion in the wilds of Mull – while quietly manoeuvring around some of the bleaker reasons why he probably felt he needed to be outside quite as much as he did.

I still feel really lucky to have had all of those great things in my early life, but I did continue to mistrust adults, especially men, for a very long time after. Alastair was still in there then. Undeniably etched into the deeper parts of who I was as a person.

As a child, it added to a general feeling of 'vulnerability' I already had. This feeling of 'weakness', an omnipresent feeling of 'threat', which, as I grew, morphed into a sense that, no matter how many good things I had going on in my personal or professional life, everything could quite easily, and quite dramatically, go catastrophically wrong. That there was always this unforeseen and unpredictable crisis waiting around the corner. That I needed to be on my guard and always prepared – even if the 'crisis' never actually arrived.

For many years of my working life, I tried to use those private emotions as my secret superpower. I thought that this inner sense of disquiet could give me an edge over others who didn't have it. That it would stop me from settling and push me on to produce work that was better and bigger than before, never resting on my laurels when things were going quite well.

The problem with doing that in the long term, though, is that it means you never appreciate any experience for what it is. You are forever 'on to the next thing', and you are always listening to your inner critic too: telling you that you are no good, or at least not quite good enough.

Ultimately, using any negative feeling as a fuel can only work for so long anyway. Eventually, it'll catch up with you. It certainly did with me.

• • •

You might wonder why my mum put up with such a character when he could be so abusive and she had her own kids to think of, but it's always easy to be judgemental from outside of the reality of a situation. Don't ever think she didn't, or doesn't, feel very upset about him being inflicted on us.

She is not to blame for *his* actions. Our dad was gone and our mum was a lone young woman with four young children in a new place. She worked incredibly hard to provide for us, often balancing several jobs – cleaning, restaurant jobs, a bar job, shop work – all around our care, to make sure we never went without – and things could have been easier if she was in a loving partnership with the right person.

My mum is a remarkable woman in so many ways. She has an inner strength and a complete lack of spitefulness and hate. I think she pitied Alastair, realised that he was broken and maybe thought that she could *fix* him. Believing someone can be a better person is hardly a flaw. He wasn't always all bad, either, but predatory men have an instinct for vulnerability. Once they have got their hooks in, they'll dominate and manipulate their partner in a way that will isolate them exponentially.

Domestic abuse isn't just physical violence. It is about the progressive establishment of one person's dominance and power over their partner. Abusers often make their victims feel responsible for all their abusive behaviours. They gaslight them incessantly. Bringing them down, belittling and humiliating them, creating an atmosphere of total fear while gaining complete emotional, and often financial, control.

Once any pattern is established it can be incredibly hard for someone to leave. These people are masters at crushing independence and self-confidence. They make their partners feel powerless to go – and often bloody scared. The domestic abuse charity Refuge estimates that the police receive a domestic abuse-related call every 30 seconds, yet less than 24 per cent of all domestic abuse crime is reported to the police. Shockingly, in England and Wales, two women are killed every week by their abusive partners, and it takes, on average, seven attempts at leaving before they finally leave for good. It takes even more bravery to build yourself back up again, emotionally and likely financially too, having spent potentially decades being told you're worthless.

I can look at Alastair in a completely different light today. He was only just an adult (scarcely older than my eldest child now, in fact) taking on a whole family when he was woefully ill-equipped to handle such a responsibility. There were those insecurities he had too. The bullying he might've been subjected to in his own past, added to the idea that it was all quite possibly far too much for him, far too soon. None of that is an excuse for what he did, and maybe my lack of bitterness is inherited from my mum, but I do actually feel sorry for Alastair. I couldn't when I was a kid, when it was all happening, but I look back now and all I can see is a damaged young man.

I know he continued to abuse women after my mum though, and for many years I hated him. Back then, the only way I could see to stop his violence was with an equally violent force. I fantasised about the day I would be strong enough to look him in the eye and make him feel just a fraction of how scared he must've made our mum feel. I promised myself that I'd make sure that I got that done as soon as I was strong enough. That I would get revenge on behalf of our mum, and for some time it was the sole ambition in my life. I gave no thought to jobs, or travel, or education: my need for violent retribution consumed me completely and I carried it around with me like a poison-tipped arrow clutched tightly within my fists.

That day inevitably came, when I was 17. There was some sort of community bash going on. A marquee was erected in a field and I was asked to go along and help out. There he was. Alastair. Seemingly without a care in the world, projecting that very same public façade of the charming, cheery, cheeky chappie that had once sucked in my mum, and doubtless several other women too.

I stood, watching him. *He probably hasn't given me a second thought*, I realised. He saw me and tried to interact with me. I can't remember what he said, but it would've been something pretty glib and only served to further underline to me that he had absolutely zero feeling for all the upset he'd caused.

I knew, right then, that I could've smashed his face in and it wouldn't have made a blind bit of difference to the way he was, and nothing would've fundamentally changed in terms of what had happened to my mum. He wouldn't have been punished, not really, and nor was he likely to have had some extraordinary revelation about the consequences of his own behaviour. I didn't know what depth of feeling he was truly capable of at all; really – I didn't know *him* at all – but I did have a choice in the way that I felt about him.

I had to let go of all the hatred and move on with my life. Hate is a poison that will suffocate you completely if you let it spread inside, and this man was definitely not worth that. Actually, I realised, he wasn't worth anything to me at all, and from that day I resolved that he wouldn't get any more emotions out of me. Dropping those intense feelings – my childhood promise, my primary life's mission, my primal need to exact my revenge on this person – was incredibly empowering.

Alastair died in his fifties from a cardiac arrest, following his third and final marriage. I have very good reason to believe that his last wife didn't realise we existed and I'm quite sure that Alastair easily erased us all from his memory too.

And that, as they say, is *that*.

I guess I'm a 'glass half empty' optimist – if it is possible to be such a thing. As far as I can say from my experience, dark events in our lives may bruise us within, but there's often little point in looking for deep meaning in the toughest cards that life can deal. Especially as a child, when your life is largely controlled by others anyway. You can only accept and hope that you can reverse the polarity in later life. Turn the negative into positive. Let all the *good* you experience shape you, and hope that it will eclipse the bad.

As the hermit said, Alastair did show me the man I never wanted to be, but his behaviour showed me my mum at her strongest too. The way she managed that whole period, as well as the other tough cards she has been dealt over the course of her life, only makes me admire and respect her more.

She has given me uncompromising love, taught me resilience and shown me what a truly good person looks like.

Sliding Restaurant Doors

I can still sometimes feel a bit backward about coming forward. Even if I'm asking for something completely reasonable, or something that has been promised to me already, or something that really is not that much of a big deal *at all*, I'd far rather not say anything about it, and then just feign surprise if something *entirely expected* does come my way.

My first paid job had come when I was only nine. A house was being built opposite our chalet and the bricklayer showed me and Norrie how to lay a couple of bricks. I probably only laid two, but from that point on I'd proudly tell people, 'See that there? I helped build that house.' I went over again the next day and the builder got me to clear up a bunch of empty cement bags and some wood off-cuts. Then he gave me a *fiver*! *Woah, this is alright!* I thought to myself, so I went back again, but I just didn't have the confidence to actually ask for another paid job. Backward about coming forward, I hung about waiting to be noticed, until all the workers went home.

I didn't have an ongoing job until I started working with the horses, and I stayed there until I was 16. By that time, most of my friends had jobs that were paying them decent regular wages. They could afford the occasional day trip to Oban or even Glasgow and were able to buy the highly coveted Hi-Tec trainers and stone-washed drainpipe jeans from the only clothes shop in Tobermory. Goodness only knows why we ever thought we looked good in those skin-tight jeans. I remember one of Sandy's friends, Wiggy, once bought a pair that were so tight that, legend goes, the only way for him to get into them was if they were held open at the bottom of the stairs, and he leapt in from four steps up.

Our drinking had recently graduated from the occasional prize can of cider from the town's coffee-evening bottle stall, to frequenting the shadows of the local pubs where a blind eye was turned to our actual ages. I needed much more disposable income than I was ever going to get at the trekking centre, plus I'd had a growth spurt and was physically outgrowing a lot of Willie's competition horses. With the start of the tourist season approaching in the spring of 1988, it was a very good time for a hardworking teenager to find himself a new job in hospitality.

The Captain's Table was originally a Spar corner shop, but it had been converted into Mull's newest restaurant and, to my mind, it was the one that represented the very *finest* of fine dining. In the 1980s, restaurants in rural Scotland left a lot to be desired and I thought that the Captain's Table was properly posh, offering well-presented local produce with fancy French names; what I took as 'scallops in a cream sauce' was labelled there as 'Coquilles

St Jacques' and 'prawns in tomato sauce' was 'Prawns Provençal'. *Ooh la-la.* Even some of the desserts had a fancy name: 'Captain Bligh's Chocolate Fudge Cake'. *Double posh!*

It probably wasn't just that the Captain's Table seemed to be on some elevated gastronomic plane, it was as likely that the very idea of eating out *anywhere at all* would have felt really unfamiliar to kids in our town. You might have the occasional pub lunch or fish supper instead of dinner at home, but eating in a restaurant at night? That was for the tourists!

The owners of the Captain's Table, Ann Gordon and her husband Nick, were really curious too. They had moved to Mull from England, created a beautiful home in a renovated cottage, built the restaurant from the ground up and just seemed very different from everyone else I knew around our island. I wanted to get to know them both better, and, given my mum and sister were already working in one of the other three restaurants in Tobermory, there was another really good reason to apply for a job at their place instead. (Another major contributing factor was that Ann was incredibly good looking. I deduced that if I was going to be spending my evenings and weekends sweating it out in any kitchen, then I'd far rather be doing it in hers than anyone else's. Funnily enough, while her husband and I grew incredibly close in the years that followed, I never brought this up in conversation.)

To apply for a job, I knew I'd first have to surmount my anxiety about putting myself 'out there' and asking for something. Nervously, I knocked on the door of their house, only for Ann to tell me to come back to the restaurant in a few weeks and ask again. That was fair enough – we were still some time away from Easter and the first big wave of holiday-makers on Mull, so I waited, and then went direct to the Captain's Table.

To my absolute horror, I entered the restaurant as Ann was in the middle of breastfeeding her newborn baby girl. She hurriedly covered herself up and I, quite frankly, could've thrown myself clean out of a window. I could not have left the Captain's Table fast enough, and I think Ann probably only gave me a job in her own haste to get rid of me.

That first role saw me washing the dishes. I think I was a pretty good scrubber, but of far greater importance to me was the restaurant's landline. It happened to be located right above my dishwashing station. Naturally, it would mostly ring with customers wanting to book a table, but once in a blue moon that phone would go off and I'd hear Nick's voice breaking through on a crackling and very distant-seeming line.

It felt like he was always on the other side of the planet – over in China, the Middle East or somewhere in South America – and even though my call-handling role was limited to saying 'hello' and 'I'll get Ann', I wore our transcontinental communications as a badge of honour. *I have just spoken to a man who is not in this country. He's not even in Europe!* I'd think, mind blown, while standing there gripping my dishcloth and brush, with soap-suds running up my forearms.

It transpired that Nick was a wildlife cameraman. Unbeknown to me at the time, he was only just beginning his career, but back then he was simply the most extraordinarily adventurous and exciting person I had ever heard of. As soon as he was off the phone to Ann, I'd grill her for all the details of exactly what he was off doing, and, as my confidence grew, I'd probe Nick for more information on these calls too. 'How are you?' 'Where are you?' 'What are you filming?' 'How long are you there for?' Poor Nick. Obviously, he hadn't called to speak to the lad who was meant to be washing the dishes, but *my god*, I would think to myself every time he called through to our kitchen, *what a job!*

Although I had spent almost my entire childhood surrounded by nature, it was the allure of Nick's travelling that initially attracted me to the idea of his job. I'd always loved watching wildlife documentaries, but I hadn't ever considered that there were people out there who were being paid to go and film them. TV just sort of happened, didn't it? You just turned on the telly and there it all magically was. Those phone calls with Nick had blown my whole world wide open and, from that point on, like a six-year-old telling an adult that he wants to be an astronaut when he grows up, I would always answer, 'I want to do what Nick does,' whenever anyone asked me about my future.

Nick returned from a filming trip in Guyana, all tanned with sun-bleached sandy-blond hair and a faraway look. (I later learnt that he'd been putting a product in his hair to enhance its colour in the sun, but, as far as I was concerned, just seeing the way he looked after these trips served to double my resolution to somehow get into his line of work.) I asked Ann if she thought Nick might be able to give me some advice, and she told me to go around to their house and find him in his study.

Nick's office appeared to me as an eccentric collection dedicated purely to his artistry. There were flight cases scattered on the floor, some open, some not, plus camera equipment, lenses and rolls of film stock lying around piles of his books, photographs and a cornucopia of items collected from his travels: tribal bows and arrows, dried piranha bodies and jaws, wood carvings, fossils and tropical-looking feathers. It had its own unique smell – a slightly tart, acidic scent, like a fusty vinegar, that was probably emanating from all the film stock and mixing with the lingering jungle damp. It was an aroma that I'd forever associate with Nick and I resolved, in that moment, that however long it took, I would one day have a room just like his.

I tried to play it cool, but Nick must've seen that my eyes were popping out on stalks. He could not have been more welcoming, though, or more mindful of putting me at ease. We sat down together and he told me all about his life. How he hadn't done too well at school either, that he hadn't gone to university, and about the various jobs he'd navigated before he'd got his big break in filmmaking. He was from a wealthy family and was public-school educated, but he hadn't just waltzed into his wildlife career – not at all. It had taken him 12 years, during which time he'd studied to become a chartered surveyor, found work during a particularly colourful period with the Blackpool-based tycoon, estate agent (and now convicted criminal) Owen Oyston, before he eventually bought and ran a very successful fish and chip shop in Blackpool with Ann.

It was scuba diving that had first introduced Nick to amateur wildlife filmmaking, and it was during a club diving trip to Mull that he decided to sell the fish and chip shop and come to our island full-time, by which point he had also been picking up work as a news cameraman through BBC Manchester. He was in his early thirties when he received his maiden UK commission from Survival Anglia to make a wildlife documentary in South America, and had probably only been doing that sort of work full-time for around five years by the time I'd entered his study. That room alone gave me the singular impression that he was a man who was born to do that job, and, as he regaled me with more extraordinary stories from the jungle and deserts he'd visited, I could no longer hide how awe-struck I was by everything. *Especially him.*

He did everything he possibly could to help me out from that meeting onwards. When I made to leave his study, he lent me a couple of books: one on the practicalities of filmmaking, the other the 1984 edition of Sir David Attenborough's *The Living Planet*. I devoured them both within a couple of days. I had never felt so motivated to read anything in my life, or so engaged by the subject matter, and I was soon back knocking on his door.

'Didn't get along with them, did you, Gordon?' said Nick presumptively. I told him I'd read them both and received a look of very happy surprise in return, and, crucially, an invitation back into his incredible study. He loaned me more of his books and even invited my school biology teacher over to discuss what I might consider taking for my Highers (the Scottish equivalents of A-levels) to help me on the academic side of things. It was a truly incredible display of faith in itself, given I was lucky to scrape some passes in my O-grades.

Nick would often give me a shout to do little errands for him. 'Can you run these letters to the post office?' he'd say, which I would literally do, sprinting up and back. He had me erecting his canvas hides in the back garden – watching me carefully to see if I could figure it all out, which I duly did, revelling in the smell of the wild as I unfurled the material and pushed poles and pegs into the structure.

The more time I spent with Nick, the more I came to see how incredibly hard he worked, but also the real passion he possessed for what he did for a living. On Mull, people often worked hard, but their success was measured by the size of their boats, homes or cars; nobody ever expressed a love for their jobs, which were seen more as a functional and practical necessity. Nick might've been partial to a flashy statement in the things he bought for himself, but he was also the first person I had ever met who clearly loved what he did for a living. If your regular Mull bloke had said the words 'follow your dreams' or 'shoot for the stars', as Nick regularly did, then they'd probably have been run out of town, but here was a man who would proudly wear his joy for work and express his most romantic ambitions without feeling a single shred of embarrassment. For Nick, wildlife filmmaking was more than a way to make ends meet; it was the embodiment of who he was as a person, and he would stop at absolutely nothing to be the very best at his trade.

I don't know when he first seriously thought about taking me on as his assistant, but in all of those little tasks he'd set, I had proven myself to be enthusiastic, competent and a very quick learner: someone who Nick recognised he could completely trust to do any task he set without complaint. He'd already had two camera assistants walk out of the job because they hadn't been able to adjust to the working conditions and had felt too home-sick to continue. I might still struggle with homesickness or find the work gruelling, but he would've known there was absolutely no way I could've afforded to abandon him given my obvious lack of any back-up plan. I had spent some considerable time working with Ann in the restaurant by this point too, right in the heart of that very stressful environment, and I know the fact that we had always maintained a great relationship must have helped me enormously. I'm sure she would've put a good word in for me, and so Nick decided to roll the dice on me.

I knew he had a commission for a wildlife film in Sierra Leone coming up, and I also knew he was interviewing candidates to be his assistant, but it would never have crossed my mind to ask him for a job. Then, one evening, he just came out with it. 'Gordon, what would you think to coming to Sierra Leone with me?'

I was 17, and a year into studying for my Highers in Oban, but I didn't even pause for thought. 'Yes,' I replied instantly, 'of course.' Nick then explained that it wasn't exactly a done deal. Survival Anglia, the company that had commissioned him to make the film and the Norwich-based equivalent of BBC Bristol's Natural History Unit, would have to approve my employment too. That meant cancelling my first ever foreign holiday, a lads' trip to Corfu with my great childhood friend and Oban coursemate Alan Malloy, to attend a 'Wildlife Symposium' in Bath. That was tough. That holiday had occupied all of our thoughts for the last couple of months, plus it had cost me all of my savings and was completely non-refundable.

I gave it a couple of days' careful thought. What if I cancelled the holiday, lost all my money, went to Bath (wherever that was, to attend whatever a 'symposium' was) and then got turned down for being some daft teuchter teenager with zero experience or qualifications? It seemed so unlikely, but how could I really live with the decision of not having given it a shot? I might not have realised quite how big an opportunity it was, but I wasn't daft enough to turn it down without first giving it my all. I told Nick I was coming. I think he might've then mumbled something like, 'Well, you've got the job then kid,' and off we went to the symposium together.

A few days later, Nick called me to his study. 'Well, Gordon. They've advised me against it because of your age, but they were really impressed with you too, and have said that if I think you're the right person then …'

My whole life hung on his next words.

'… *we are going.*'

• • •

When I got the job with Nick (and in spite of what the careers officer had said at school) there was, in fact, a very well-established and well-trodden pathway towards a career in wildlife filmmaking, and it definitely did not run anything like: 'Go and knock on the door of the person you most want to work for'.

Firstly, you needed to succeed at school and head off to a good university. Ideally, you would be studying for a relevant degree in wildlife sciences – zoology or something similar – at one of the top red-brick universities or, best of all, Oxford or Cambridge. With that all in your back pocket on graduation, you'd look for an entry-level job in wildlife filmmaking.

If you were more interested in *producing* wildlife films, then the BBC's esteemed Natural History Unit would occasionally offer positions on their 'trainee scheme', or they might offer up jobs for runners – the first rung in television, where you work in an assistant role doing things like carrying kit, looking after tapes, making cups of tea, driving people around and logging shots for the edit. You might find similar jobs advertised by independent production companies too, but if working as a camera operator was your goal, your best shot was to try and get a position working as an assistant to an established wildlife cameraperson, like Nick. Again, you'll be carrying their gear and looking after their rushes (then the tapes, now memory cards and hard drives with the shot material stored on them) and you might also go out in the field with them, building their hides or wildlife viewing platforms and sorting out any number of issues with logistics, local staff, lost bags, broken camera kit, missed transport, missing food and seemingly endless red tape – while your boss gets to frame the shot, hit record and take all the glory. (I'm joking! Well, sort of …)

In any of those cases, just a handful of those opportunities might come up in an average year – so, to demonstrate you have the higher levels of competence and commitment required to elevate yourself ahead of the hundreds of other applicants you'll likely need to go above and beyond. Besides the academic qualifications, it would certainly help if you had already filmed some wildlife and made a showreel of your shots, for which you'd need access to your own camera kit and something to edit with. Work experience within the industry was hugely useful too, especially if you'd rubbed shoulders with a few good contacts – but that would more than likely be unpaid as well. Finally, any experience of travelling overseas, especially to some of the places you might wind up working, would be of real benefit.

All of those things took a serious investment of your time, and you would likely need some money behind you too – and that's without taking into consideration the fact that you needed to be ready to drop *everything* if that golden ticket did come your way and you finally got your foot in the door. If you had a background like mine – scant qualifications, let alone a degree; no foreign travel experience whatsoever; and certainly no spare money or 'parental safety net' to buy you some time – then the odds of breaking into the industry were very much stacked against you.

That meant that wildlife filmmaking was often populated by people who shared a very similar set of backgrounds and experiences. Of course, many of the people who came into the industry on that more traditional pathway are hugely talented and responsible for producing countless ground-breaking wildlife films. But, looking back now, it wasn't right that there were so few opportunities for people from different upbringings and social circumstances. It took a long time before any formal routes really started to open up for those from diverse or working-class backgrounds, and I'd say we are still a long way from having true equal opportunities in wildlife filmmaking (or even careers in television generally), but things are better than they were.

When Nick agreed to take me on, I knew that this wasn't just a big chance to get started in a career in wildlife, it was also *the* opportunity to change how I saw myself. But big pressure came along with that. If it all went wrong with Nick, for whatever reason, then there would be no second chances and no way back into the world of wildlife filmmaking. It was 'all or nothing' right from the start.

Back in 1989, when Nick confirmed that I had *definitely* got the gig and that we were leaving at the start of 1990, I knew it was a big deal – but I probably wasn't that aware of how monumentally massive it really was going to be. I was a 17-year-old boy stood on the precipice of the adventure of his lifetime and the next step was going to be a total paradigm shift. I wasn't simply leaving your average Tobermory street for the sensory overwhelm of Nick's study, I was entering *his world* entirely, and leaving my own far behind.

There was nothing about this opportunity that made me think I was remotely better than anyone else. It was more that I had been gifted the chance to be *something* else, or, at the very least, to *experience* something else. The best piece of advice I've ever had was from my mum, given to me close to the eve of that trip: 'Remember who you are.' I didn't ask her to elaborate. I took it to mean: don't ever pretend to be someone you're not. Being you is good enough. Remember where you come from. Remember that you are my son.

In the end, I certainly didn't forget about Mull or my mum. In fact, for a large portion of the 18 months that followed, *all* I could think about was coming home.

The Box in the Basement

Sierra Leone has been buried in my basement for a very long time.

In part, I mean that metaphorically. The manner in which we were forced to leave, and all the aftermath, was so deeply upsetting that I felt compelled to squirrel it into the very darkest recesses of my mind. Rarely, if ever, to be explored again. But my actual diary of that time is, quite literally, sat in a box in my basement too.

I closed the lid on that box some 30 years ago. You might imagine a leather trunk with wooden strapping or a big rusting tin case with a squeaky hinged lid, but this box is cheap plastic, dirty and cracked with busted corners. Unremarkable, but for the fact that it has remained unopened for three decades. Not sealed with a strap, a chain and padlock, or even cheap brown parcel tape, just by my own reluctance to look back.

The problem with any long-term denial is that, however hard you try to forget about something, it always finds a way to cling on. It sucks away at you like a leech, gradually draining you while swelling itself exponentially. Out of sight, perhaps, but never really out of mind. Given enough time it'll grow arms and legs and a life all of its own, evolving into something entirely separate from the experience itself, and, more often than not, something far worse.

Before I was required to revisit both that box and my memories for this book, that entire period had long since been defined by how we'd fled the nation at the outbreak of the Sierra Leonean Civil War, and the unimaginable horrors that had followed in its wake. However, when I did finally muster the courage to head down the stairs and open up the box, I didn't find piles of diaries filled with traumatic reminders of that moment; I found just one plain black hardback Collins diary. Scribbled inside were mostly very straightforward accounts of a dull daily life in a jungle camp, rubbing up against a truly wild existence surrounded by monkeys, chimpanzees, exotic birds and many more creatures, the likes of which had been utterly alien to me.

I began to read, and all the memories of actually being out there, working away in that incredible patch of forest, came flooding right back …

Saturday 24 February 1990

'Into Africa'

Just before the door shut tight on the Tri-Star aircraft, I took a last breath of real British air and within hours of take-off we were over the snow-crowned peaks of the Pyrenees. Two hours later we were over the vast Sahara Desert. At last, I was on my way to Sierra Leone in West Africa. The months *of waiting were over. It was exactly a year on from when I was told by the careers officer to 'think of a more realistic alternative than being a wildlife cameraman'.*

As we landed in Lungi airport, I could see the heat haze drift up from the tarmac. Walking off the plane, a pleasantly warm air filled my lungs. It did not last long. Going through customs with thirty-five large shiny cases of camera equipment was a bit like walking through a pack of sausage-eating Dobermans with thirty-five sausages. We finally got out of the airport. From then on, all I'll say is that the culture shock was totally unexplainable.

The doors of our aeroplane had swung open at Freetown's Lungi airport and it felt like the whole continent just swept right in: a great tidal wave of African equatorial heat, foreign noise and riotous colour. Immediately, the wheels melted away from the base of my Argos suitcase and, 15 minutes after that, the handle snapped clean off too.

You absolute fucking twat, I thought to myself as I struggled to carry Argos's biggest cuboid across the sweltering airport forecourt. *You have just made the biggest mistake of your life.*

It turned out that Freetown's airport was actually located on Lungi peninsula, some ten miles from the capital across the saltwater river estuary of Tagrin Bay. We had to haul all our gear onto a ferry for the crossing, and it was there that I noted that there was a large fire engine accompanying us. Later, I was told it was cheaper to employ the fire service to bail out all the water, which was continuously pouring into the boat due to a leak, than it was to stop the ferry service and actually repair the hole.

The 'culture shock' I was feeling was not 'unexplainable' at all. To put it very bluntly, I had never spoken to a Black person before in my life. There was just one Korean lady living on Mull and that was the entire extent of my experience of ethnic diversity up until that point. Nick was the most 'foreign'-seeming person I really knew, but now I was in this place where absolutely everybody looked very different from me. They spoke in a different way, ate different foods and lived in a completely different climate and environment. All of that would be surmountable in time, but there was no avoiding the fact that this complex and exhausting documentary project was taking place in one of the poorest and most corrupt countries on the planet too. That fundamental fact wasn't going away, no matter how hard I tried to adjust. I was always going to feel like a fish who was (as long as the Sierra Leonean fire service kept pumping) out of water – but my goodness, I knew that I had been desperately naïve too.

In his book *Tarantulas, Marmosets and Other Stories*, Nick focused mostly on the next project we would work on together (his film *Tarantula!*, about the Goliath bird-eating tarantulas of the Amazon basin) but he was moved to write:

With the benefit of hindsight, I was far from convinced that leaving school was the best thing for Gordon. I told him to imagine his worst nightmare and then double it ... Forty-eight hours after leaving Scotland the 17-year-old had caught dysentery, was vomiting every hour and had seen his first dead body. Shocked doesn't do justice to what he must have felt. There were only two of us, and from the moment we arrived it was a seven-day-a-week job – no time off in the normal sense. I was well used to this kind of dedication, but Sierra Leone unsettled me too.

Nick was a man who wasn't averse to putting a little bit of topspin on his anecdotes, but all of that was true. The poverty in Freetown was extreme. Many people were living on the street with next to no money or possessions and virtually nothing to eat; we met people who had horrific diseases that we had all but eradicated back home. There was the occasional dead body lying on the pot-holed pavement too.

I'd flown out with wildly misguided preconceptions about what Sierra Leone was going to be like. This was well before a quick Google search could give you an idea of what lay ahead. Of course, Nick had tried to warn me, but I'd turned the volume right down on all the potential horrors he'd described. My focus was solely on this fantastical and glamorous jungle adventure that I felt sure I was going to have from the very moment we arrived. The poverty in Freetown brought me crashing back down to earth with a bump, but escaping the city was not something that was going to be possible for us anytime soon.

To execute Nick's ambitious film, alongside all the camera equipment we had just arrived with, we'd also put seven tons of steel scaffold, an inflatable boat, an engine and a generator on a cargo ship from the UK. Unfortunately, a storm in the Bay of Biscay had meant it took a whole month before the rest of our gear made it out to us on the West African coast. Nick, though, was not a man for hanging around. We got to work straight away, filming a huge fruit bat colony in a park in Freetown and shooting with a man who was keeping chimps in cages, which, despite his protestations to the contrary, we were fairly sure were being sold for scientific testing. None of this was what I'd had in mind when I'd been dreaming of the job on Mull.

We soon got in with the expatriate community in the city and were invited to meet the British high commissioner. That was another huge culture shock: they may have been mostly white and British, but it was my first experience of anything that approached 'high society'. I couldn't quite get over how large and ostentatious all their grand-looking homes were – particularly in light of the dire situation for the people on the street. The high commissioner's residence felt near palatial; he even had servants who drifted around in immaculate white uniforms with gold epaulettes on their shoulders. I wrote in my diary that one night I had 'been served some cheese and port', as if I was describing some utterly novel indigenous ritual, which, at that point in my life, it essentially was.

The dwellings and lifestyles of the expatriates were some significant distance removed from our own. We were staying in the 'Conservation Society Rest House', which, despite the homely-sounding name, was actually a dingy, neglected, mosquito-infested bungalow with neither running water nor electricity. It was a dump, but reading back through the early diary entries, I noticed how I had been very careful not to write anything too negative. I was petrified that Nick might read it, and then realise the extent to which I was struggling with everything. After all the trouble he'd undergone to get me out here, I didn't want to let him down in the first week.

In that first week though, my most urgent challenge was simply not to puke or shit myself in public. At one point, I actually wrote that I thought I might die, and all I could keep down was hot water. However, with Nick preoccupied with the work, I had to just try and get on with it. I put on a brave face, but in reality I was already desperately homesick, as well as actually sick. It even got to the point where I would think about the sorts of non-life-threatening injuries I might be able to self-inflict to get myself sent home for good.

• • •

Nick's film, *Tiwai: Island of the Apes*, eventually took us away to a remote uninhabited jungle island. It was swept on all sides by the mighty river Moa, a great watercourse that rises in Liberia and splits Sierra Leone's eastern districts from the rest of the country to the west. The island itself may only have been 12 square kilometres of mostly secondary rainforest, but to the local Mende tribespeople it was a truly scared place. Many of the Mende believed that the spirit of their dead lived on in the animals there, so hunting, logging and slash-and-burn farming were all strictly prohibited, and its position on the river had made it near impassable during the wet season, when rainfall would swell the Moa's flow into a torrent for almost half the year.

In more recent times, the money brought into the community by wildlife researchers and eco-tourism ventures has helped Tiwai Island enormously, but it was already something of a safe haven for wildlife before we'd arrived, and just a couple of years previously it had been formally recognised as a wildlife sanctuary by the government. It was incredibly important that the island was protected. Although it was relatively small, it represented one of the better examples of the Upper Guinean forest belt left in the area. The belt was once a vast swathe of unbroken jungle that stretched more than 1,000 miles from Ghana to Guinea, but in recent times, logging, agricultural encroachment and mining had seen almost three-quarters of its total coverage disappear. Of the remaining chunks, mere islands in themselves, many were rapidly degrading and highly fragmented.

The Upper Guinean forest belt remains one of the world's 25 hotspots for biodiversity though, with some of the most endangered wildlife on the planet resident there. In fact, of the 1,100 mammal species found on the African continent, more than a quarter are found in the Belt alone, more than 60 of which are endemic. Forest elephants, clawless and spot-necked otters, red river hogs and leopards share their tracks with other extraordinary creatures such as the highly secretive pygmy hippo, the giant ground pangolin and the zebra duiker. But *Island of the Apes* intended to focus right in on Tiwai Island's primates, ranging from the 'vulnerable' sooty mangabey to the 'endangered' Diana monkey and red colobus, and sat right at the very top of our tree of targets were the 'critically endangered' western chimpanzees.

Once we had cleared all of our remaining gear from customs, it was, at long last, time to leave the city behind and head off to Tiwai. The 200-mile journey to Kambama, a Mende village sat on the banks of the Moa, and the launchpad to Tiwai, took nine bone-shaking hours in a bashed-up Land Rover. In my diary I wrote that it was like 'being rattled about in a sticky jam jar with a twelve-week-old piece of stilton', but once we were there, it was just a short downstream hop in a dugout canoe to finally set foot on Tiwai Island itself.

I'd love to say that I immediately recognised Tiwai's astonishingly singular richness, but given I had absolutely nothing to measure it against, I just assumed that this was what all jungle was like. Monkeys were scurrying everywhere, with me comfortably able to tick off three of the resident species within the first hour of our arrival. This was *exactly* as I expected it was going to be: just like all the wildlife documentaries I'd watched and not a million miles away from *Tarzan* either. We pitched our tents in a clearing and settled in for our first night, and that was when I really did experience something that I was entirely unprepared for: the nocturnal noise. Croaking frogs, chirruping insects and piercing screeches. Swoops and booms from countless species of bird and bat. Scurrying sounds in the leaf litter. Rustles, thuds, growls, groans, hoops and whoops. A cacophonous wall of sound reverberating relentlessly from the forest floor to the very top of the canopy, from right outside my tent, and off into the very depths of the island's forested interior. I had never known anything like it, and that first night I just lay in my tent and listened to all that life thrumming away from dusk till dawn.

My broken night's sleep met a very early dawn rise, and then the real work began. I was responsible for ferrying the seven tons of scaffold across the river and onto the island. Using a hand-paddled dugout canoe and the small inflatable dinghy we had brought from home, it took two full days of back-breaking labour just to get everything over, and then Nick announced that he wanted the scaffold towers erected immediately, so he could start shooting right away.

It was physically punishing work but I found it strangely satisfying. Like a supersized and dangerous Meccano set, it was pretty much 'build them high and don't die'. Of course, it had been a doddle to erect the scaffold towers during the single morning of training I'd received in the weeks before leaving. I'd even written 'pimps' (*simple*) in my diary. But Tiwai was a very different proposition altogether. That morning in the supply company's yard, we'd only thrown up a single section of scaffold on a flat concrete base, but in Tiwai I slogged it out in sweltering conditions, carrying scaffold through the jungle with a local crew before we threw up three 100-foot-plus towers of steel on the forest floor. It was only then that I came to realise the full, terrifying extent of my own fear of heights.

What should've been a single day's labour stretched across a four-day jungle ordeal for just the first tower, and then it became immediately apparent that the monkeys were absolutely uninterested in going anywhere near our scaffolds anyway.

That was a surprise. From the moment we had arrived on the island it had felt like there were monkeys everywhere. They scurried along the riverbanks and forest floor, chattered away in the canopy and chased each other from tree to tree. So what was keeping them away from the scaffold? Initially, Nick's assumption was that they were simply scared of the reflections from the steel poles and the aluminium ladders. Later, I wrote:

When we realised that they may not have come close enough due to the aluminium ladders, which were still unpainted, we straight away set our expert painter Hasan onto the job of painting them. When he returned to camp that evening we saw that, unfortunately, he had started from the bottom upwards …

So, that was poor old Hasan, now painted almost completely green, with the rest of the laborious paint job left to do. Painting seven tons of scaffolding was a major chore in itself, but Nick was a massive perfectionist and he absolutely insisted that every single square centimetre of that galvanised steel had to be coated in our green camouflaging. We did it exactly as he'd asked, but it didn't work.

Next, we tried moving the towers to points where Nick hoped the monkeys might be, and, when that also failed, he got desperate. For two weeks straight, he had us chasing monkeys around the island. Flushing them up from the forest floor and attempting to *somehow* shepherd them across the canopy in the direction of an increasingly flustered Nick, concealed in his tree-top hide with the camera.

In those early weeks, I was completely knackered an awful lot of the time. As any parent of teenagers will tell you, 17-year-old boys need to sleep *a lot*. I was fundamentally a stretched-out version of my 13-year-old self: still growing and acquiring a lot of my 'man strength', but nowhere near the finished article. Building scaffolds all day, walking through the jungle with heavy loads, frequently getting lost, doing the painting and then getting up long before dawn to record monkey calls, before these fruitless chases all over the island, was exhausting in the extreme. If there is one running theme to pluck out of the diary from that first six months on Tiwai, it was the sheer number of mornings that began with Nick screaming at me to 'get the fuck up!'

Looking back, it must've been really frustrating for him, but he knew how dedicated I was, and, given I was a total blank canvas, he admitted he could mould me into exactly the sort of camera assistant he needed. That wasn't going to come overnight though. I was desperately 'green', after all (and not just from the scaffold paint), and on a very steep learning curve. But it turned out this was new to Nick too.

On Mull, I'd had this vision of Nick as a highly experienced, well-travelled and highly decorated man of wildlife filmmaking. He always came across as someone who knew exactly what he was doing. Self-assured and hugely confident, here was a man who, according to the dust jacket of his own book, was 'Biggles but better. Indiana Jones but true.' In reality, *Tiwai: Island of the Apes* was among his very first films for Survival Anglia. The pressure bearing down on his shoulders would have been immense, and we had not got off to a very good start at all.

This project was unlike any other. No other filmmakers had ever attempted what we were doing, so, in many ways, Nick was learning on the job too. We had made some pretty big mistakes (even I knew that herding monkeys was never going to work) and he was hard on me at times, but that was more than likely because he was absolutely shitting himself. A month into the project, Nick had almost nothing whatsoever on film.

By now, it was painfully obvious that we couldn't just throw up a scaffold tower willy-nilly in the forest and expect Tiwai's wildlife to do the rest. Cracking it here was going to take careful study, sound decision making, real patience and a fair bit of luck – like playing a grand game of chess in which the board is a densely forested island and the animals already hold most of the pieces – but we pulled together as a team and figured out a way to make the very most of what we had until, very slowly, things began to turn in our favour.

Life on Monkey Island

Nick had actually been given a little guidance from a research scientist prior to our arrival. The scientist had been studying the island's primates and pointed out a few important trees in the monkeys' world, but what he'd seemingly neglected to say was that those trees wouldn't have any monkeys in them for 11 months of the year. We needed to figure out precisely when that critical month was in the monkey calendar.

The breakthrough came when we realised that the scaffold tower needed to be placed next to the right tree a couple of weeks before it came into fruit. We mapped out the entire island through those pre-emergent trees and the various possible timings of their fruits, then we got the scaffolding dropped and rebuilt right before they gave up their bounty to Tiwai's hungry primates. Each fruiting tree would only be at its very best for about a week, so the timing was absolutely critical, but Nick finally started to get some really beautiful shots.

It was far from plain sailing from that point on, but at least Nick was having a few days where he was feeling a little more upbeat and confident. I could judge the success of his entire day in the hide simply by the way that he'd say 'hello'. This was a time long before the digital revolution in cameras, when tiny cards could store hours of footage and mini-cameras could shoot in HD from virtually anywhere. We were lugging just one hefty camera and tripod up and down the tower with a pulley rope, as well as three large magazines of film for an entire day's filming – one of which could only shoot ten minutes of film.

It sounds pretty threadbare by today's standards (although it didn't feel it when I was carrying it all in!) but I never saw the lack of spare film as a limiting factor. If Nick came back with just a few minutes of material from an entire day in the hide, then that was really good; as the weeks ticked by, I started to collect a few more of his cheerier 'hellos'.

Nick and I lived together in a forest clearing near the western shore of the island. We had a basic tent each, with a thatched roof over the top for extra shade and shelter. Inside we both had a camp bed and a small desk with candlelight for the night. Later on, we replaced the candles with oil Tilley lamps, but it was always pretty gloomy after dark.

Food-wise, I'm afraid to say we didn't exactly make smart nutritional decisions at the start. Before we left Freetown, Nick sent me out to buy a six-month supply of Fray Bentos pies. At the very best of times, they are a pretty awful foodstuff to choose as your staple, but the first cooker we bought barely functioned either, so for the entire first month we were pretty much forced to cook everything over an open fire, which meant we were eating unrisen meat pies in a tropical climate.

Almost anything else would've made a lot more sense. It wasn't like the film budget was *that* tight, but I think Nick actually enjoyed having it all a bit feral and hard, especially in the very early weeks. I think he thought it would break us both into the jungle mould and mindset, but looking back, I can't quite see how a poorly cooked Fray Bentos was ever going to achieve that. The work itself was throwing up enough problems that were often completely out of our control; it didn't make much sense to make everything else hard as well. Nick could've easily afforded another gas stove on the film's budget, and he did get us one eventually, but until then all of the administration that came along with the fire-making and cooking fell onto my shoulders.

After a day hauling scaffold, I'd have to find dry timber and get the fire lit before I could cook anything, and then repeat the exercise for a cup of tea in the morning, and again every night for Nick's Horlicks. No offence to devotees out there, but I still have big issues with Horlicks, not for its taste, but for all the associated trauma. This was a drink just for Nick, who I think associated it with some sort of comforting memory from his school days. Every night, just as I'd be settling down into bed for some much-needed sleep, he'd call out, 'Is that you getting the Horlicks on, kid?' Honestly, it took every inch of restraint not to tell him where to pour his malty bedtime beverage!

It took us a few weeks before we realised that the locals we had employed were eating food that was far better than our own. After that, we paid one of our team to cook for us too, and we switched our diets to eat almost exclusively as they did. From that point forward, we'd sit around together, eating with our hands and spoons from a single shared washing up bowl filled with a delicious local lunch or dinner. It was probably only a rotation of four dishes, mostly based around beans and rice mixed with cassava or potato leaves, onions and a few hot spices, but it always had these beautiful red-orange sauces made from locally grown palm oil that was cooked up into a thick calorific gloop. Not only did it steer us away from Nick's pies, but it also meant I got out of many of my cooking duties!

Kambama village was a little upstream on the opposite bank, so the Mende who worked with us would paddle downstream in dugout canoes in the morning. Come the evening, everyone piled into the motorboat, and I'd give them all a lift back upstream whilst holding on to their dugout and towing it alongside.

In the early weeks of the project, I didn't hugely enjoy having to go to Kambama; I avoided it as best I could and would write about how tough I'd find it all in my diary. Usually, that was because I would be constantly asked for things on my visits: food, money or the clothes and shoes that I was wearing. The plain truth was that, despite the fact we were hugely under-resourced for your average wildlife film crew, for the impoverished people of Kambama, most of whom had literally nothing, we might as well have been multi-millionaires. The disparity between us and them made me feel really uncomfortable and I just didn't have anything like the depth of maturity to properly handle it. It was, of course, entirely unsurprising that they wanted some of what we had, and, since we were working adjacent to their land, we did give them as much as we could afford. We helped when people were sick, provided money for buildings and ferried people to medical services whenever we were asked.

Soon enough, we found our rhythm with each other and I began to really look forward to visiting Kambama. The people there were very friendly and welcoming, and they were something of a salve to my homesickness too. They were fascinated to hear all about what my own 'home island' was really like, so I'd spend long nights talking to them about our towns, villages and cities, and many things that I'd just taken for granted, like how amazing snow and ice-cream were, and then they'd share all their knowledge of their forest and its wildlife, in turn.

I became particularly close with the men we had employed as our crew. Minah, Momo, Mohamed and Hasan were with me nearly every day. They had a great sense of humour and were always quick to laugh and crack a smile, no matter how tough the work became. Together, we carried the loads, built the hides, erected the towers and looked out for wildlife for Nick to film.

Minah was the main man. He had been sent off to missionary school and was one of the very few people from the village who could read and write. He spoke excellent English and was a really bright guy. Very usefully, he had also been employed as the research assistant to the scientist who had been studying the primates before our arrival. He became the de facto head guide and would spend a lot of time working very closely with Nick, giving him advice and steering him towards the best of the fruiting trees. The rest of the team were nearly always off with me, doing all the grunt work. I made it a point of principle that I always did just as much of the heavy labour and lifting as everyone else. They never once complained, so nor did I, and I think, through all that shared hard work, grit and graft, a genuine sense of respect grew among us all. We would share an awful lot about our lives and we had a lot of fun together.

Pay for the team was pretty basic and pre-set by the regional chiefs. (We actually tried to up the amount of money a bit, but that wound up causing them big problems back in the village.) Some had felt that the work should be shared around evenly, with everyone taking turns at helping us out, but that was really problematic as the team we had employed were all learning how to become wildlife guides and had been carefully instructed on the specifics of tower building and wildlife filmmaking. We didn't have the time to start that from scratch every time a new crew joined from Kambama, so we had to figure out a fairer way around giving them something extra. In the end, we paid them the going rate in cash plus a supplementary income with rice.

The only issue we ever had was when the team had to explain to me that the Sierra Leonean standard 'cup' of rice was always heaped and *never* levelled off, but once that was sorted, we got on really well and they helped us out hugely. Especially useful was that they would always have our backs when any problems or misunderstandings came our way from the local villages. Most issues were easily resolved, but there was one time we came very close to landing ourselves in really hot water. The whole thing was a terrible mix of bad timing and pure accident on our part, and luckily the only real damage was to our pocket. Still, it was a really close call and wasn't exactly brilliant for our local reputation.

We were returning to a village located some distance from Kambama to chase up a possible monkey story. We had first visited about a month before, and had made friends with an elderly blind man who lived there. He was a really lovely old boy, full of stories and genuinely pleased to hear about what we were up to on Tiwai. On our return, he had immediately recognised the sound from our approaching engine and crunching wheels. Ours was the only vehicle in the area, so he knew it could only be us, and up he'd sprung from his hammock.

I can still see him stood there now, waving enthusiastically from beneath the shade provided by the large thatched roof of a community hut. We swung our Land Cruiser into the village, waving back happily, when, seemingly without reason or warning, the entire roof collapsed in on the man in a devastating plume of dust, snapped thatch and pole.

'Fucking hell!' Nick and I shouted in unison, leaping from the car and sprinting over to the scene of total destruction. That roof must've been six square metres of thatching supported by only a few wooden posts, and it had completely consumed our friend. 'Is he dead?!' I asked out loud, as the rest of the village gathered around in panic.

Incredibly, our blind friend not only survived, but he emerged from beneath that roof with barely a scratch on him. What was clear, though, was the washing line, *which we had not seen*, stretching tight from what was once the corner post of the community hut, all the way back to the roof rack of our car. We had swung into the village, snagged the line, destroyed the hut and almost killed our friend. It was definitely going to cost us.

Not long after that, we received a handwritten 'court summons' informing us that the paramount chief wanted to 'discuss' the incident. Nick steered himself well clear of that one and I was swiftly dispatched to agree appropriate reparations. The problem was, the chief wanted a significant personal cash sum for his back pocket, and not the actual repairs themselves. Ultimately, the whole accident was resolved with me having to return once more to the village (this time with all eyes on any errant washing lines) to employ a builder directly and pay for all the building materials in person – but at least it all got sorted, and our blind friend still gave me a warm and very welcoming wave.

• • •

You could never predict what strange new animal neighbour you might bump into in the forest, but generally the island routine was monotonous. Carrying in scaffolds and camera gear and keeping up with everything that needed to happen for the camp to properly function. Rinse and repeat every day, seven days a week, without breaks. At times, it was a total grind from dawn till dusk and the summer, when Nick and I would get to go back to Mull for a holiday, felt incomprehensibly far away in my teenage mind.

Things really came to a crescendo in the build-up to my 18th birthday. 'Just think!' Nick would harp on enthusiastically. 'In years to come you'll be able to tell all your friends that you spent it in the rainforest!' *My friends, Nick?* I'd think every time he brought this up. They didn't have the first idea where this rainforest was, let alone Tiwai Island, and even if they did, I imagined that they were far too preoccupied with the apparently unmissable cultural revolution that was happening right across Britain.

Once a week, I'd try and tune my wireless radio to the BBC World Service and catch up on a very crackly top 20 run-down of the music charts – and it always made me feel utterly dismal. There had been a huge explosion of exciting new music while I'd been away. All-new rave and electronic dance acts were erupting from a vibrant underground warehouse scene, and the precursor to Brit Pop too, landing with a big wave of Mancunian indie bands dominating the charts with all their guitars and swagger. It wasn't just the new music – it was all the new faces, the new ways of dressing, the new politics, almost an entirely new language that was being cultivated and curated by my very own generation. For us kids, throughout the 1980s, it had all been about America, but all of a sudden and against all the odds Britain was becoming the coolest place on planet Earth to be. Yet there I was, in a forest thousands of miles from home, with ringworm and jock itch and making a grown man mugs of fucking Horlicks to settle him in for the night.

In reality, of course, I wasn't missing out on much. It wasn't like your average Mull teenager was going to be tearing it up nightly in the Hacienda, but I'd still far rather have been down the local pub with my pals than spending my 18th stuck in the jungle with the nearest pint of cider and blackcurrant a continent away. The big day ticked round and I marked it drolly with the following diary entry: 'Opened cards. No celebration. I did manage to locate the source of the smell in my tent though. As I suspected, it was indeed an animal shit.'

Once a month, Nick would go back to Freetown to secure the film footage in a fridge he was borrowing to keep it safe from the heat and humidity. While he was there, he would pick up more supplies and crucially (at least for me) collect our post. I've kept so many of the letters I was sent from back home. Pages and pages of details about the comings and goings among my friends back on Mull. They are a reminder of just how dull life was for your average Mull teenager, but they also showed quite how much time we had for each other. My friends would sit down and write pages to me, and then I'd do the same back to them. Those handwritten letters really meant something.

There was another big reason to get excited about Nick's Freetown trips: the food. Whenever he went away, Nick made sure he brought back something of a treat for us all. One Christmas, he headed to the city to pick up his wife and daughter for a visit, and pulled off a real masterstroke. I'll never forget Minah's wide-eyed expression as he burst into the camp shouting: 'Nick's back from Freetown with not just Ann and Emma, he's brought a vulture with him!'

I sprang up and rushed to the riverside, only to find that this 'vulture' was, in fact, one enormous turkey. Minah had never seen a turkey before; this was the largest bird he had encountered in his entire life. Our little team was incredibly excited, and, in the week before Christmas, we did everything we possibly could to get that bird as fat as possible before the inevitable Christmas Eve chop. The turkey was a massive luxury for us all to share around, and it made that Christmas feel really special. I don't want to give the impression that having a live animal for the pot was the norm for us. It was an extremely rare thing, and obviously, if you are going to eat fresh meat in places where it can't easily be kept, more often than not you'll have to get accustomed to experiencing the death of a living creature.

Many would argue that if you are going to eat any meat at all, then you really should, at the very least, have that respectful association between the living animal and what eventually winds up on your fork. I might have always had that respect, but the actual killing bit was something that I never felt wholly comfortable with doing myself. Early on in our Tiwai stay, a chicken was brought into our camp for Nick and me to eat. 'Deal with that please, Gordon,' said Nick airily, in a way that suggested this was not a big deal at all.

Well, it was a big deal to me. However, I didn't want to turn around and say that I didn't want to do it.

'Sure, yeah,' I replied coolly, trying to imitate the tone of a man who kills chickens all the time. I rounded on the bird and

Tum-Tum the otter cooling off on road trip.

Nick and I at the sunrise spot on Tiwai Island, 1990.

Wendy and I at Tobermory Bay, circa 1998.

Wendy, Harris, Lola and I with a black bear in Minnesota, 2010.

Filming in Tsavo National Park, Kenya, 2016.

Setting up to film urban leopards in Mumbai.

With Scruffy the Wolf, on Ellesmere Island in 2014.

Scruffy the Wolf and I on Ellesmere Island in 2014

Selfie with Scruffy the Wolf on Ellesmere Island, 2014.

Filming polar bears from inside the 'Ice Cube' hide, Svalbard, 2012.

Inside the 'Ice Cube' in Svalbard, 2012.

Polar giant from a new angle.

Wendy, Harris, Lola
and I on the Isle Of
Skye in 2017.

Wendy, Harris, Lola and I
at Balmoral Estate, 2022.

grabbed it. I didn't have the first idea what I was doing, but I wrung its neck as best as I could before placing it back on the ground with a huge sense of relief. It lay there, still as a stone. The grim job was, at least, over.

Or so I thought.

'Bleargh!' To my utter horror, this chicken was spluttering back to life before my very eyes. 'What the f …' Before I could process what on earth was going on, this definitely now undead chicken had risen to its little reptilian feet and was lurching towards me maniacally with, quite clearly, a partially broken neck flopping around all over the place.

Naturally, I completely freaked out, grabbed an axe and started swinging wildly at the zombie chicken in a pure blind panic. Somehow, despite the state it was in, it managed to evade my best axe-wielding efforts and I wound up chasing it around the camp in circles.

'Gordon!' Nick's booming voice cut through all the chaos. 'What the FUCK are you doing?!'

My axe head mercifully met chicken. Heart pounding, and with sweat and blood streaking down my arms, I turned and screamed back in a mix of horror, anger and raw truth: *'Well, clearly, I don't know what the FUCK I'm doing, do I, Nick?!'*

Years later, I was working as a camera assistant for a man called Phillip. We were on a long night drive in between shoots when the car in front of us suddenly hit a pheasant and drove off. The poor pheasant was very badly mangled but somehow still alive, lurching around on the tarmac.

Phillip stopped the car. 'Gordon,' he said, in that airy tone I knew only too well from Nick, 'go and put that pheasant out of its misery.'

The anxious memory of the Tiwai Island chicken debacle was instantly resurrected from the deep grave of my subconscious, but I could hardly tell Phillip about that.

'Fine', I said resolutely, as I stepped out of the car and approached this all-new zombie-pheasant flapping around on the road. It looked awful, with all sorts of broken bits hanging off its body. I took a deep breath. At least this time I knew what *not* to do.

Confidence, Gordon, simply grab the bird by its neck, pull up and twist, I thought to myself, making my approach.

This time, in my determination to make a better fist of the job, I accidentally pulled so hard that the pheasant's head came clean off its body and out into the palm of my hand with a horrible 'pop'.

It was a spectacularly awful outcome, far worse than what had happened on Tiwai, and, in totally reflexive repulsion, I hurled the entire decapitated pheasant right down a steep bank and tossed its head out onto the verge.

Heart pounding, I returned to the car.

'What!' said Phillip incredulously, now the newest member of the extremely niche and always backseat non-bird-neck-wringing-cameraman-advisory club. 'Why did you just throw it away?'

Luckily, it was a really dark night, so he hadn't seen what had just happened to the poor pheasant. 'Well, I was only putting it out of its misery …' I proffered hopefully, as a reminder of what he'd originally instructed me to do. 'Anyway,' I continued, 'it's dead now, so …' I gestured to drive on.

'No,' interrupted this now *very much involved* townie vegetarian cameraman. 'We could have given it to Tilly for her ferrets.' Tilly was someone we had just been filming with, and this was probably quite a reasonable idea, were it not for the awful fact that I'd have to tell Phillip that I'd also ripped its head off.

'Ah well, something else will eat it,' I said, motioning that we really should get back to the drive.

'No,' replied Phillip with a real firmness this time. 'Go and get it.'

Now I was panicking. 'I lobbed it way down the bank, don't worry about it, Phillip,' I answered pleadingly, while thinking, *Fucking hell, he's going to think he's working with a complete psychopath here.*

'Fine. I'll go and get it then,' he said with finality, disappearing down the verge in a frustration that soon switched to awful surprise, punctuated with a sentence I never want to hear in any context again, ever:

'Gordon! Where's its fucking head?!'

It was a *very* quiet journey from there on.

Tum Tum

The weeks slipped by and Nick hoovered up more shots of Tiwai's wildlife. Monkeys were joined by Tiwai Island's birds, raptors, insects and reptiles. We even shot some sequences with the local people, about hunting and logging away from the island, artisanal diamond mining, the illegal wildlife trade and Mende rituals and traditional beliefs. We had come a long way from that clueless first month, but there was always pressure from Nick to get more. To get closer. To do it *better*.

One day, we heard that both a baby spotted-necked otter and a genet – a small, cat-like species of carnivorous mammal – had been brought into the local village. The otter had been dug out of its holt, presumably while the villagers were out on a hunt, and I imagine the genet had been trapped somehow too, most likely during some tree-felling for slash-and-burn agriculture. Apart from those on Tiwai Island, most animal species were seen as fair game for the pot, and the villagers were always on the lookout for any opportunity to catch themselves some valuable protein.

I wrote in my diary: 'The only thing on four legs that they wouldn't eat is a table.' But, of course, I had the distinct privilege of being able to see wild animals as more than just meat. In a place where food and money were both scarce, any opportunities to provide for your family had to be taken, even if that meant pulling 'cute' baby animals directly from their homes, growing them on in the village and killing or selling them for food.

Both the otter and the genet were scarcely more than two tiny balls of fur. With the otter in particular, I can remember having to very carefully unfurl it with my fingers, just to figure out what this minuscule creature actually was. It seemed so small and fragile and, without its mother, it had very little chance of survival; neither of them stood any chance whatsoever in the village, so we swapped the otter and the genet for six cups of rice each, and took them back with us to Tiwai.

This wasn't purely an altruistic move on Nick's part. We hadn't ever discussed using captive animals in the film prior to the acquisition of the otter and the genet, but, if we could somehow keep them alive, then they did also present a clear opportunity to get a few very intimate shots of animals that, back then, would have been impossible to capture in the wild. We went on to take in a pangolin, a couple of monkey species, an African civet, a porcupine and a water chevrotain – a nocturnal species that resembles a tiny deer – but Nick's trips to Kambama were not always successful. One day I wrote in my diary: 'Nick travelled to a village on the promise of saving a captive eagle today, but it turned out it was a duck.' That was one we did let drift off down the Moa, without it taking a turn in front of Nick's camera lens.

By now, in spite of my friends in our team and the village, and some of the campsite improvements, I was getting homesick to the point that my life on Tiwai had begun to feel like a prison sentence. But the sudden arrival of that otter and the genet brought new life to the camp and a big injection of energy for me. Suddenly, I had this all-new sense of purpose and something to do that wasn't just carrying scaffold or Nick's camera kit. Those animals needed my care and, more than anything, I wanted to keep them alive.

We managed to hand-feed the baby otter a little bit of milk, fully anticipating that if it wasn't dead by the morning, it probably would be by the end of the week. Nick's wife, Ann, and his daughter, Emma, were there at the time, and it was Emma who bestowed the baby otter with a name. It might've been a tiny fur ball, but it had a big round belly too, so Emma decided he had to be Tum Tum; not only did Tum Tum make it to the end of the week, but pretty quickly he grew and grew. After a few months we needed to feed him some solid food, which meant catching fresh fish.

I would go fishing around the island, spending many hours catching Tum Tum his solids on a bamboo pole, but Nick soon realised that this was seriously eating into my scaffold-carrying duties, and certainly wasn't going to be sustainable when Tum Tum's fish demands grew ever greater. The solution was found in Kambama village. A local teacher hadn't been paid his salary for many months, but it turned out he was a very handy angler. The teacher gratefully took up our side-hustle, catching Tum Tum all his fish for a bit of a wage from us, and, better still, Nick realised we would have to find a way to keep the fish fresh. That forced him to purchase a gas-powered portable fridge on his very next trip to Freetown, and, given there was plenty of room in that fridge for more than just Tum Tum's fish, he started buying in crates of beer for us too. In one fell swoop, Tum Tum had completely turned my life around and I could've kissed his whiskery little face. To be fair, I probably did.

Every day, I'd grind up a portion of fish for Tum Tum to greedily devour, but soon enough, we started to think about how we could teach him to catch his own. He was utterly clueless about what he was supposed to do in his natural environment. By the point young wild otters are eating fish, they would also be taught how to swim and catch fish by their mothers; so, in lieu of his mum, we took it upon ourselves to begin Tum Tum's apprenticeship in water.

First, we filled up a washing-up bowl for him to swim around in. Once that was mastered, we placed a small live fish inside, in the hope that this enclosed environment would make it easy for Tum Tum to learn exactly what he needed to do. Initially, it looked like all was well. His swimming went really well, and when Tum Tum dived into the bowl he immediately chased that little fish around in circles. All he needed to do was grab the fish with his claws or jaws, but, after a few attempts, it was obvious that there was something fundamental missing. He seemed to really enjoy swirling around in pursuit of the fish, but he didn't seem to make a connection between the living, breathing, scaly creature in his bowl and the mushed-up fish that I'd been serving him.

Perhaps the bowl is the issue, I thought to myself. With Tum Tum now fully capable of swimming strongly, we decided to take him down to the river Moa for the first time. His big brown eyes almost popped out of his head. 'No way,' he seemed to say with every hair on his slender body. 'I'm not going in *there*.' I got in and tried to cajole him in with me, but it took a few more visits before he eventually submitted to trying a wild swim. Once he was in, though, he flatly refused to put his head under. It was almost like he was too buoyant to dive down, or more likely, just extremely reluctant. Whenever he did stick his head under, he'd spring it straight back up again, almost in disbelief at this huge, terrifying water world that existed away from the confines of his washing-up bowl. It took many more visits before he would put his head under with any confidence, and more still before he could control his buoyancy and actually start to swim with any control, but then he really did crack it, and would look forward to our daily river swims as much as I did.

However, he still wasn't able to catch his fish.

Just like in the bowl, Tum Tum would eagerly chase the Moa's fish, and as he grew bigger and stronger, he could even get to the point that he would keep a perfect pace with them, but that final killer reflex was always beyond him. It became a real worry. The plan was always to raise the baby animals to the point that they could fend for themselves in the wild, and return to the forest for good, but nothing ever seemed to work with Tum Tum. We even stopped hand-feeding him at one point, just to force some sort of predatory reaction through pure self-preservation. He disappeared for a while, and we assumed that he must've figured it all out for himself, but two days later he wandered back to our camp looking very sorry for himself. He had obviously been off to the river to try to fish, and, having failed, he'd trotted back through half a kilometre of jungle pathways in total desperation. We fed him again after that, and, although we never quite gave up on the hope that he might catch something from the river one day, it never happened. Tum Tum's predatory instinct was missing and, for him, fish chasing was always one big game.

Tum Tum and the genet were free to come and go whenever they pleased, but they chose to be around us almost all of the time. That pleased me no end, as they were both an enormous amount of fun to have around. The genet would often just sit on my shoulder as I prepared things around camp, and going down to the river with my mask and snorkel on, watching Tum Tum as he swam around, felt like an enormous privilege. Down there I'd watch him transform into this lithe subaquatic mustelid: his fur slicked back in the wet, his webbed feet pumping at the clear river waters, working his body around the rocks, boulders and twisted roots beneath the surface. I'd dive down with him too, sending twin streams of our air bubbles pulsing up towards the Moa's surface.

Tum Tum always stayed in Nick's tent and the genet was in with me. That was fine for Nick, as Tum Tum mostly slept through the night, and he even used to get into bed for a little cuddle, but the genet was nocturnal and a very poor bedfellow indeed. It was a beautiful animal though, with a long ringed tail, a slender spotted body and a cat-like appearance; it was also armed with extreme agility and sharp reflexes. Even when it was very young, it would leap from my clothes stand to my bed, and back again, without any trouble at all. No hunting training was required here either. As soon as it was big enough, our genet took to hunting for itself with real enthusiasm. Better yet, it had a diet that largely consisted of insects that it could catch around the camp, which meant my tent was always well clear of beasties like forest cockroaches and giant spiders – but all those nocturnal antics definitely kept me up.

By now, my body had largely adjusted and I no longer needed as much sleep as I had at the start of the trip, but I still needed *some* sleep. Diary entry after diary entry reads: 'I didn't sleep well. The genet kept me up again. Rambling around my tent.' It also seemed to think my eyelashes were insects, and there were many nights when I'd wake up with the genet actually biting down on my eyelids!

We did get some useful shots of the animals we had rescued and looked after, and a really beautiful underwater sequence of Tum Tum swimming in the Moa, but the backbone of the film was always going to be the island's wild animals behaving in their wholly wild ways.

The Waiting

Over the course of my career, there were always going to be those moments where I haven't quite got the shot, for whatever reason. One that always stands out came during my first job as part of the team on the BBC's *Big Cat Diary*, working in Kenya's esteemed Masai Mara National Park.

It was 20 years ago now. We had a grand ambition within the crew to somehow capture a successful leopard hunt during the day. We didn't *have* to pull off that sequence for the whole series to work – we had plenty of other big cats to follow, chief among which were always the lions – but everyone knew that if we did somehow manage it, we really would have achieved something special.

Leopards mostly hunt at night, so exciting daytime activity involving the species is very rare. During daylight, they are far more likely to be resting or sleeping in the trees or bushes. Given we didn't have a permit to film in the Masai Mara at night, and no infrared cameras at our disposal even if we had, it was a bit of a pipe-dream, without quite being in the realms of total impossibility.

Bella the leopard cropped up in a few *Big Cat* stories over the various seasons. She was courted by males in one, and would have her cubs with her in a later one. On this particular day I'd headed to where she tended to hang out, over on the wide banks of the river Talek, and just waited. By this point, we'd been following her on and off for a couple of weeks, and had even had a few close calls where maybe, just maybe, the conditions might have been right for a daytime hunt – but it hadn't materialised.

That day, I had one eye trained on the spot where she was hunkered down, likely dozing, when I became aware of a huge herd of wildebeest approaching from the horizon. This was one of the mega herds for which the Masai Mara was most famous. A simply enormous mass of animals numbering comfortably in the thousands. The herd was so large it was turning the plains black, and so noisy I could hear them rumbling and grunting their way forward, their musky scent filling the air long before it was possible to pick out any individual beast with the naked eye.

Suddenly, Bella was alert and up on her paws. She padded her way out from the river's edge and onto the open plain. Clearly, she was surveying the coming scene, sensing, I was so sure, that rarest of leopard opportunities: fresh vulnerable meat flowing in her direction in the very middle of the day. As an ambush predator, there was simply no way she would attempt to take one down on foot, not in broad daylight with all that short grass, but, ever so carefully, she walked over to the one bush that stood between the wildebeest herd and her.

The bush was small, probably only four metres wide, but in she went – camouflaging herself completely. This had to be it. She surely could only be in there to make a kill. A daylight kill of a passing wildebeest. The thing we'd dreamt about achieving. I locked my camera in place and got ready.

For the next two hours, that huge wildebeest herd moved closer and closer. *God, she's so clever*, I thought to myself, training my focus on the little bush, *she* knew *that they were going to come to the river, and she* knew *that they were going to have to come past this bush.*

The whole thing felt inevitable. An hour later and they were 50 metres from the bush. Soon they were 20 metres away and I thought, *Right, as soon as they are within striking distance she's going to make an attempt,* so I punched record and started filming.

Things had advanced in camera technology in the years since I'd worked with Nick. Where he'd had cans of film that only lasted for ten minutes at a time on Tiwai, I was now blessed with film cassettes that could shoot a whopping 40. I ran the camera, maintaining all my focus and attention on Bella's ambush spot as the wildebeest drifted past the bush and settled down to graze. I couldn't believe my luck: they were so close now. But as the minutes ticked by, absolutely nothing happened.

She's just biding her time, waiting for the right wildebeest before she strikes, I thought to myself, painfully aware that the first 40-minute tape was coming to an end. By this point, there were hundreds of wildebeest circling the bush; some were even nibbling the grasses right by the bush's edge. They couldn't have been any more than a couple of metres from Bella; I knew she could be on them in the blink of an eye, but still, she waited.

I, however, couldn't wait a second longer. As quickly as humanly possible, I changed tapes, ditching the full tape with one hand and pushing a fresh one into the camera with the other. I was certain that the tape change would be the moment Bella chose to spring out from the bush but, luckily, she didn't. Huge relief – that was until another 40 minutes had passed and I had to do it all over again.

She was still in the bush, the wildebeest were still everywhere, and still I focused intently, sitting in that peak state of total concentration, ready to react should I see even the slightest movement from her hiding place.

Next the camera battery went, so I had to change that in rapid time too. Then I needed to change the tape again, yet still it didn't happen. As the hours ticked by, the amount of energy it was pulling from me, as I focused every inch of my being on that bush, was something else. She could've leapt out at any time from any side, so I knew I couldn't drop my guard for a microsecond. For four hours straight, I kept going, so sure that it was going to happen. *It's so easy*, I thought as the strain started to take a grip of my body, *they are* right there. *All she has to do is pounce and she's got one …*

Eventually, I had a small pile of utterly uneventful tapes and several drained batteries. The wildebeest had grazed their way past Bella's bush, crossed the river and even gone past me. I couldn't believe it. To compound the whole thing, Bella then strolled nonchalantly out from beneath the bush. She trotted back to the river's edge, took a sip of water and, with a flick of her tail, disappeared. I sank back in a deep state of total exhaustion, and some degree of exasperation too.

I can happily stick it out in a hide, even when nothing is happening, as long as I know I'm in the right place. That leopard was an example of something really special potentially about to happen, with me being in absolutely the right place at exactly the right time – but still somehow coming away with nothing.

There have been other times where I've just missed out, but usually the action, or the opportunity, was gone in seconds – not four straight hours of being on tenterhooks. But you have to be able to find a way of rationalising and processing those moments. This is *wildlife* filmmaking after all. Much of what happens in the natural world can feel foreseeable to a degree, but there are so many chaotic and completely unpredictable elements. You can only ever make your very best guess and prepare yourself in the best possible way; you'll always need an element of luck to pull it off. The animals are going to do what they are going to do, and all you can do is try to be there when it happens.

All of that, though, only comes with time spent in the field and experience. Back on Tiwai with Nick, I knew how hard we'd worked to get a few shots of the wild monkeys, but it was nothing compared with what came next. We still needed footage of the island's most iconic animal, and there was definitely a period where we began to wonder if that was possible at all.

Chimp Limbo Land

Tiwai Island's chimpanzees represented the backbone of the entire *Tiwai: Island of the Apes* film. They were the stand-out selling point for the whole project and, should we have returned without something of them, we may as well have never left Mull in the first place.

Going into the project, Nick had been advised by the locals that there was a site where the island's wild chimps would regularly go to crack their nuts. He was taken over and, sure enough, lying at the base of this large tree was the Tiwai chimps' 'stone and anvil'.

River-washed hammer stones had been carefully selected by the chimps for their perfect nut-cracking size and weight, before they were carried half a mile from the riverbank, and over to the buttress-root of the tree. The 'anvil' was actually the thick and hard exposed wood of that tree's root, and for decades, if not centuries, it had been used by the chimps for the task. The root had flattened areas on it where you could see the chimps had pounded away for many years – there was no telling quite how long it had been going on, who were the first chimps to have carried the stones in or who had figured it all out in the first place.

Periodically, we would hear the distinctive thumping sound of stone meeting nut, drumming out through the forest and signalling to us that the chimps were hard at work at their anvil. We hadn't seen a chimp, but it didn't seem, at least at first, like it was going to be too difficult to find them.

This was an incredible behaviour in itself. Presumably, all we needed to do was stick a hide next to that site and then get the shots when the chimps inevitably arrived to do their business. We also knew that this was going to be the very first time that this behaviour, among this particular group of West African chimps, had ever been captured on film. That was really important as, quite obviously, it would make for an immensely exciting and really significant part of our documentary.

At the time, it was widely believed that the chimps in that part of Africa did not know how to use any tools whatsoever. Among many primatologists, they were widely regarded as the 'dumbos' of the chimp world: a group that had evolved separately from the apparently 'intellectually superior' chimps found over in East Africa, as, until then, much of our early knowledge of chimps' tool-use had focused specifically on the Gombe chimps of northern Tanzania and the long-term studies conducted throughout the 1960s and 70s by the celebrated primatologist Dr Jane Goodall.

In Tanzania, Dr Goodall had observed various chimps stripping leaves from supple sticks and using them to probe mounds for termites. That, in itself, was a monumental leap forward in our understanding of chimps. Fundamentally, it challenged many of the long-held homocentric theories around animal intelligence and it directly contradicted those who believed that intelligent tool-use was something entirely exclusive to humans. Dr Goodall had, within those Gombe troops, found clear evidence that chimps were capable of complex problem solving and high levels of cognition. It was further proof that Great Apes were indeed our closest living relatives, but what of those poor 'thicko' chimps found over in the West African forest? It seemed to us that there was always a blind spot with our guys. They were perceived to represent something of an anomaly among chimps. But it was an anomaly that we now had a massive opportunity to disprove.

All we needed to do was to capture the nut cracking on film.

We erected a hide right next to the tree root and in Nick went. As ever, he was super-keen to get going. That first day brought nothing, but that was hardly a surprise: these were wild chimps after all, and highly wary of anything alien suddenly appearing in their world. The chimps needed to get used to our hide being around their stones and anvil, and no doubt the foreign smell of a human squatting somewhere nearby too.

The chimps themselves might've been widely regarded as 'sacred beings' by many of the Mende, among whom their killing was considered tantamount to a human murder, but that didn't mean that they faced no persecution from, or had no fear of, humans. Chimps, like all animals in the area, were frequently hunted for food by people from outside the Mende tribe, and a fair few within it too. There were plenty of differing opinions regarding the value of chimpanzees – especially those that entered farm-lands and ate crops – and Tiwai's chimps would frequently leave the island during the dry season, when the river was low enough to cross. Away from the island's spiritual protection they were seen as 'fair game', and most wild animals have a natural suspicion around humans anyway. These were nothing like Dr Goodall's Gombe chimps, who had become highly habituated to human presence through decades of careful study at close quarters. This was going to take time, and time was one thing we did still have.

Chimps might be big strong apes, clearing five-foot tall while standing, but that did not mean they were going to be easy to find. On Tiwai, they kept their distance from us and we couldn't even be precisely sure of how many there were. We thought it was one troop though, comprising, we guessed, maybe 20 individuals. What we did know was that they were definitely using the stone and anvil site, and that they were nearly always on the island somewhere.

As well as the occasional sounds of nut cracking, we would hear the chimps calling out to each other with regularity, espe-cially early in the morning, when they would vocalise right across Tiwai's dense forests with distinctive guttural howls or high-pitched shrieks. It was quite something and, whenever Nick heard them, he was like a dog with a bone. Clearly, the hide was posi-tioned in the right place (or so we thought) so whenever he heard them close, and especially if he heard the nut-cracking noises, off he would go, often well before sunrise. Each time, I'd drop him off in the morning and collect him again at the end of the day.

'Anything?' I'd say hopefully, peeling back the canvas hide cover and releasing a cloud of his body odour. 'Nothing,' would come the bleakest of replies.

Usually, after a week of failing hard, Nick would confidently announce that the chimps weren't coming back to the site anytime soon, and off we would go to film something else. Invariably, that was when we'd hear that singular 'thump, thump, thump' and an ashen look would descend over Nick's face. There wasn't anything we could do about it then. If Nick had attempted to walk back in while they were working at the site, they would scarper from the stones and anvil long before he could get anywhere close to his hide, but the sheer frustration of those occasions would always send him straight back in for another long and fruitless stint the very next morning.

Nick was locked in chimp limbo for months on end. The entire first six months of effort were an utter failure. We had our summer break on Mull, and Nick came back from it with a renewed vigour, but still the months slid by and he captured nothing.

It wasn't just that we weren't seeing the chimps cracking their nuts; we hadn't seen the chimps anywhere on the island at all. It seemed that their levels of confidence around us were so abysmally low that they would do absolutely anything to avoid being near us, even if that meant forsaking the entire nut-cracking enterprise for all the days that Nick was in the hide. They were like chimp-shaped poltergeists, moving around the stones and nut shells periodically, while sending out nothing but their noises in between the trees.

Then, one day, while I was alone and strolling along in broad daylight, I practically walked right into a chimp. I almost couldn't believe my eyes. This animal had so far done everything it possibly could to stay away, almost to the point that it was attaining a Yeti-like status, yet here it was: right on the path directly in front of me. It was an adult male, stopped side-on, and he was looking straight back at me.

He was simply enormous. A huge dark-haired ape with taut, lumpen muscles doming out of his body like he had just strapped several forest tortoises onto his arms and legs. I felt *tiny* and immediately sank down onto the ground, not, I should add, in a consciously submissive display of my 'non-threatening' status, but because I was genuinely terrified.

He stared me down for a bit and then sat down too. If that wasn't, frankly, unbelievable in itself, he then gave me a look that seemed to say: 'Watch this carefully now. I'm going to show you something *really* cool.'

He reached out for a supple stick from a tree, snapped it off and stripped it of all its leaves. Next, he punched a hole in a nearby termite mound – as easy for him as sticking your tongue through a piece of wet tissue – and inserted the whole stripped stick deep inside. He gave it a wiggle before pulling it out and licking off all the insects, as if it were one enormous termite-coated ice-pop stick. The extraordinary ape then rose up, with his point very much made, and disappeared back into the forest.

I was dumbfounded. It was clear proof that these chimps used tools – in fact, they were the very same tools that the Gombe chimps had been recorded using 3,000 miles away to the east – and I'd witnessed it all with my very own eyes. I should've been completely thrilled, but neither Nick, nor his camera, had seen a single thing. And now I had to tell him.

It is still one of my all-time favourite animal encounters – it felt like I'd just seen a unicorn grazing in a glade – but reporting that day's events back to Nick was almost as bad as if I'd forgotten to turn on the camera when Neil Armstrong took his first step on the moon. He sank into an abyssally deep pit of despair, before scurrying off to the hide for yet another week of desperate waiting.

• • •

In keeping with Nick's tough-minded mentality, his chimp hide was squatter than the squattest of squat toilets, and equipped with little more than a folding fishing stool for him to sit on for hours on end. He could've easily taken one of the chairs from the camp and sat on that instead, but by that point, it was almost as if he was punishing himself.

Nick's moods were now anchored entirely to what he shot while hunched over in his hide, which, in terms of the chimps, was nothing. But to make things infinitely worse, I was encountering even more things away from his lenses and out on my own. It was sod's law: the harder he tried, the deeper he failed, and the more the wildlife just seemed to gravitate towards me. I saw so much in those forests while trying to support Nick with the work we were supposed to be doing – and the next two 'chimpcidents' could very well have tipped him over the edge.

It was the middle of the day and Nick was, of course, squirrelled away in the chimp hide. Usually, that meant I'd be off organising the camp, out collecting water from the river or tending to our animals, but given Nick was definitely not going to show up any time soon, and it was a particularly hot day, I opted to climb into my hammock and have a bit of a rest instead.

In one corner of the forest clearing where we had our camp, we had constructed a thatched hut to act as something of a kitchen, and, on the edge of its roof frame, we had hung a big bunch of bananas. It was only about 15 paces from where I was now lying back, readying myself for a cheeky bit of a kip, when a sudden movement caught the corner of my eye.

I turned to observe yet another huge male chimp stride into our camp as brazenly as if he was just another member of our team. This chimp was actually walking like a human too, up on his two feet in a switch away from their usual foot and knuckle posture. He wanted to have a good look around to make sure no one was there, and, as yet, he hadn't spotted me gawping at him from my hammock.

He tiptoed in an almost cartoon-like way, creeping across the camp to that bunch of bananas, before unhooking them from the kitchen roof, tucking them under one enormous arm and scarpering back to the forest.

What. The. Fuck. I lay there motionless in my hammock, almost unable to compute what had just taken place in front of me. And then I thought about Nick. Off in his hide, doing every single thing he could to film a single chimp, while his lowly sidekick had just encountered his second without lifting a finger.

That evening Minah picked up Nick from the hide. I could tell from his slumped shoulders that it had been yet another bad day. 'No joy?' I called out. He looked up, turned and snapped: 'Have you eaten all the fucking bananas?'

• • •

Despite the months of blanks, we did at least know with certainty that the chimps were well used to our hide. We had left it in place the entire time and would regularly hear them cracking their nuts right next to it. Nick wondered if the sudden introduction of his camera lens poking out of the hide was the foreign factor that was keeping them away on his filming days. Looking back, we had probably placed the hide far too close to the site in the first place, just five paces away from the anvil, and the chimps were far too canny to be comfortable with a big change like a camera lens suddenly appearing at such close proximity. So we added a false lens hood to the hide, in the exact place Nick's would be on his filming days, and then just waited.

Eventually, early one morning, we'd heard their nut cracking resuming and knew that the chimps were now happy with the change. 'Okay,' said Nick, 'let's go back in and give it another go.' Off he went and, of course, captured nothing, but this time he broke from his 'totally hardcore' form and requested that I bring him some lunch for the next day's filming effort. I dropped him off the very next morning, and, at lunchtime, I packed him up a bit of pasta and made my way out to the hide.

I can clearly remember stopping well short of the area and waiting for some time. I listened intently for any forest animal sounds, especially any nut-cracking noises – lest I spoil Nick's shot – but the coast was clear. The place was silent. So, in I strolled with his bowl of pasta.

'FOR FUCK'S SAKE, KID!' spluttered Nick, with a tomato-red face. He was so apoplectic with rage he could barely get the words out of his mouth. 'There was one right here! It walked in and picked up a fucking rock above its head … and … and … I knew the point you'd got to the junction towards the hide because, Gordon … it fucking stopped and … it looked back up the path before it slowly put the rock down and crept away into the FUCKING FOREST.'

I gripped his bowl of pasta and wondered if he was about to put my own head on the anvil and split it open with his camera.

'What could I have done, Nick? How could I have possibly known? I listened out and heard nothing!' My protestations fell on deaf ears so I slowly placed down the bowl of pasta and crept away into the fucking forest myself.

Of course, he captured nothing again that day and returned to camp with an empty bowl and one almighty bollocking for me. He wasn't wrong about the way it had played out. Nick even showed me the footage he'd shot, with the chimp picking up the rock, looking up the path in my direction and then walking away. It was excruciating, though I wrote in my diary that night: 'There's just no pleasing him. He asks me to do one thing and I do it and that's still not good enough.'

Moments like 'pasta-bowl-gate' made me realise that Nick's expectations were impossible for anyone to meet. Throughout that period, I felt that he would regularly move the goalposts or contradict a lot of what he had already said or asked – all of which made it really hard to keep up with exactly what I was supposed to be doing. Ultimately though, Nick was great company. We laughed every day and, like all successful partners, we never went to bed on an argument. He went to bed on a belly full of warm Horlicks and I went to mine with a malty mutter.

When you consider the 20-year age gap between us, the conditions in the forest and the immense pressure he was always under, it's really quite something that we didn't ever fall out in a bigger way. Even though his delivery could've been a lot better, it did help to sharpen me right up and I ultimately left that whole experience surer of my life's path. We would continue to work together for several incredible years afterwards, but looking back to Sierra Leone, we probably could have supported each other better if we had both been more honest about our personal difficulties during that challenging time.

Nick was a very dear friend and mentor, and I marvelled at his drive and passion. I respected his sacrifices and valued his opinions. In all the years we worked together, in all sorts of rough and tough places, and so many crazy situations, we just got on with it, but more importantly we just got on with each other too. It was as simple as that.

That incident with the chimp and the pasta bowl really could've broken us, but the day did come when Nick laughed about it. Admittedly that day was a decade later, but it still came!

• • •

The day after the pasta mishap, I left Nick and the entire anvil area well alone. The evening came and I walked to the site to help carry back his gear and, to my horror, I saw that his lens was still poking out of the hide. Ordinarily, Nick would lift the hide flap as soon as he heard me coming. Why was his lens still primed on the anvil then? Surely I hadn't just done it again? Had I? Had he really just been filming? Had I scared off another chimp?

A new, far worse, thought suddenly entered my mind. A snake had slithered into his hide a few days before and he'd been really paranoid that it would return. *Maybe* … I thought, with rising panic, *he's not opened the hide flap because he's dead!*

I braced myself to see Nick's snake-bitten corpse, frozen solid with rigor mortis, with his unblinking eyes permanently fixed on the stone and anvil site. Slowly, like a coroner peeling back the sheet shrouding a corpse on some god-awful day-time detective soap opera, I lifted the flap to his hide … and was met instead with a *far* greater surprise.

'We got it!' Nick was beaming back at me from ear to ear. I had never seen him so happy.

We walked back together and the whole remarkable story poured out of Nick. It began with an adult chimp walking into the clearing, stood upright on its feet. It picked up a large hammer stone and walked towards the tree-root anvil, carrying the stone in two hands with a hunched back. It then sat down, gripped the nut with one hand and hit it repeatedly with the stone, before peeling it open and eating it. A pair of young chimps begged for a nut and the adult chimp repeated the process, showing the youngsters how it worked before sharing the spoils and going at it again. The sequence of events in the footage flows as naturally as if Nick's presence had never been an issue in the first place. Adolescent chimps join the scene, and a particularly young one arrives and tries to playfully tease a sibling. One of the youngsters attempts to have a go with the hammer and ends up accidentally dropping the stone behind its back, another uses both hands and a foot to exert extra power down onto the nut.

The footage made it clear that this was so much more than just smacking a stone into a nut. The selection of the right stone for the right nut was clearly very important, and the chimps would carefully manoeuvre the nut in their fingers to find the optimum angle to crack the shell without crushing the nut inside. Getting it absolutely right can take up to six years of practice, and there was an extra level of precision too. Nick captured one of the chimps stripping a stick into a fine pick, which was then used dextrously to pick out the small crushed pieces of nut that its fatter fingers couldn't quite prise from the shell.

The entire two-and-a-half-minute sequence had been shot in just 20 minutes of activity. I can't tell you how rare that is in wildlife filmmaking. So much of what we shoot invariably requires us to shoot more and more, often over many days. Gathering action from different angles and sometimes with different characters, just to make sure we've adequately captured a completely coherent story. Often hours of footage, composed from several days of coverage, is distilled down into a few brief minutes on the screen. After over a year of gruelling effort and hundreds of hours spent in the hide, Nick had got it all done in one.

'*We* got it,' he had told me. Not 'I got it'. Those words meant so much, and it tells you all you need to know about Nick. In the crowning glory of his career to that point, the very moment that made the entire *Tiwai: Island of the Apes* film, he had been mindful enough to stress that this monumental achievement was shared with me, and the whole of our team. So many camera operators would take all the credit in a moment such as that, but not Nick. All the stress and any ill-feeling were washed away in an instant, and my goodness me, we really *had* got it too.

It was a true testament to his extraordinary capacity for endurance and his unerring resolve that we finally got that over the line. What he captured was beautifully shot too, so good, in fact, that we broke down the hide and never needed to bother that extraordinary troop of Tiwai chimps ever again. In terms of the purity of what we captured that day, when held against the monumental effort and commitment it took from us both, it's very hard to think of anything else in my 30-plus-year career that really compares.

The celebration, however, would be short-lived. Serious trouble was brewing over the border.

All Out War

In 1961, Sierra Leone gained its independence from the United Kingdom in the second wave of British decolonisation after the Second World War. After a relatively positive start to its autonomous governance, the political landscape found itself mired in allegations of corruption, mismanagement and gross misuse of public funds.

By the time we were there in the 1990s, it was often said that Sierra Leone was the 'poorest rich country in the world': ample natural resources, particularly minerals, and *especially* diamonds, but a government unable to pay many of its public workers, including the teachers. This caused a lot of educated professionals to leave the country for good, and left huge swathes of the youth with very few prospects and extremely limited opportunities for gaining paid work.

To compound the situation, just over the border in Liberia, the war criminal and warlord Charles Taylor had received funding and training from the Libyan dictator Muammar Gaddafi, and launched an armed uprising to overthrow the Liberian government. As a result, 80,000 Liberian refugees fled across the riverine border and into Sierra Leone, and Taylor's army brutally seized power in the Liberian capital in September 1990.

The resulting Liberian Civil War was happening as Nick and I were busying ourselves with the second chimp-chasing stint on Tiwai, just 20 miles from the Liberian border, yet for us, and all our Mende friends, it could just as easily have been happening on another planet entirely. The local people didn't seem worried at all. Liberia had always felt like a very different place from Sierra Leone, and most of the Sierra Leonean discontent was confined to the townships and the capital – not the deeply rural villages dotted around our patch of forest.

Around the time that Taylor was taking over, I can remember being back in Freetown at another one of the high commissioner's gatherings. A BBC World Service journalist was over from London and the Liberian Civil War was a major topic of conversation. The consensus among the expats, matched by that of the locals we worked alongside, was that a war like that could *never* happen here. The BBC journalist listened to all of this before saying, in quite a matter-of-fact way: 'Within a year and a half, this place is going to go up in flames.'

No one could quite believe what he was suggesting; in fact, one businessman was confident to the point that he bet the journalist £100 that he was wrong. But of course, he was absolutely right. In the end, it all took a hell of a lot less time too.

The Revolutionary United Front (RUF) was initially formed around a group of Sierra Leoneans who had helped lead Taylor's rebel army in Liberia. They marched under the slogan 'No More Slaves, No More Masters. Power and Wealth to the People', which gave the distinct early impression that their goal was to overthrow the Sierra Leonean government, give the power back to the ordinary Sierra Leoneans and redistribute the national wealth, particularly the diamonds.

Their rhetoric really chimed with a lot of disaffected young people, and especially those who were living close to the Liberian border. The RUF were greatly assisted by Taylor, and, leaning on their populist aims, they quickly found support among the Sierra Leonean youth and many of the Liberian refugees who had been displaced during the war and were now living in desperate conditions over on Sierra Leone's far eastern borders. However, it soon became apparent that the RUF had no clear ideology or plan for formal governance. Their initial aim was to gain control of the border's diamond fields for the purchase of their weapons, and they largely achieved that by attacking villages, murdering, mutilating and raping civilians, and recruiting soldiers to their numbers through the most extreme acts of violence. Infamously, the RUF army eventually included an estimated 11,000 children, some as young as five, many of whom were given drugs with their guns and instructed to murder their own parents or have the initials 'RUF' carved into their own chests in macabre tests of their loyalty to the cause. In a matter of weeks, the border provinces were under RUF control, and this whole thing had gone from unimaginable to a national nightmare.

On 4 April 1991, I met an American Peace Corps director in the forest who had just driven from Freetown to make contact with their projects out to the east. He explained to me that he was there to pull out all the Peace Corps workers 'and the girls', which I took to mean the local women in the villages they were working in. I wrote in my diary that I'd come back and told Nick the news and that he was now wondering what to do. I finished that entry ominously with the words: 'nothing or everything could happen'.

We had recently heard on the BBC World Service that the Sierra Leonean army had been dispatched to tackle the RUF in the east, and we were heartened by the thought that they'd likely get the whole thing under control pretty quickly. After all, these were professional soldiers fighting against what most people presumed was a small rag-tag army of untrained rebels. In reality, in their attempts to locate the RUF, the army were often as brutal as the RUF themselves were with their takeover. This alienated many Sierra Leoneans and forced them inevitably towards the RUF, and, with their own pay packets, rations, ammunition and morale at rock bottom, many of the national soldiers either switched sides to the RUF, or abandoned their positions altogether. The World Service news report that came through on that night of 4 April served to confirm the inconceivable. The Sierra Leonean forces had lost in the east and the rebel army were now spreading west like wildfire – and bringing their war crimes with them.

We decided we had no other option but to leave and began to pack everything up in readiness for a departure the very next morning. At daybreak on 5 April we loaded our Land Cruiser, said goodbye to our friends and left Tiwai behind.

It is incredibly hard to think back to it all now. The truth was, as we said our goodbyes to our team at dawn, we were still firm in the belief that nothing much was likely to happen in the area we were working in. At that point, nothing had changed. The jungle, the village, the island, everything was the same as it always was. There wasn't any doubt in anyone's minds that we would all be back together soon. 'Just a couple of weeks,' we said to each other, all sure that it was most likely just a case of the Sierra Leonean army regrouping, probably with international military support from the United Nations or Britain. As far as we were concerned, our departure was just a precaution. We certainly weren't planning on leaving the country any time soon; we were just going to head to Freetown for a spell, wait till we got the 'all clear' and then resume the work on Tiwai. We even took a list of the things the team wanted us to bring back from the city, and I selfishly thought about how it would actually be quite nice to have a short break.

Once we had left the forest and hit the open road, though, the devastating reality of what was really happening away from our little island bubble became clear. There were people everywhere. Entire families, men, women and children, stretching out in great long lines, all walking westwards towards the horizon. They carried their entire worldly possessions on their backs and their chatter was of real terror. This was no longer some amorphous news report crackling away on BBC World Service, nor was it a lone Peace Corps director out in the forest; these were *thousands* of refugees fleeing for their lives from a very real war.

The RUF were hot on our heels. At 11am we passed through Potoru, the first real town on our journey back towards Freetown. By that afternoon, the RUF had completely overrun the place and brought their mass slaughter and torture with them. We were later told that the locals confessed that two Brits were living on Tiwai Island. It wasn't just the diamonds the RUF were after; they were looting villages and skinning the entire area for anything of any value. We might have been living simply by Western standards, but we had a generator, diesel, the vehicle, the boat, the boat engine, food and cash with us. A huge amount of stuff that would've been of real use to any rebel army. Had we left any later, I'm absolutely sure that I wouldn't be here now to tell you about it.

We had friends in Freetown who had agreed to take Tum Tum in and look after him. They had a pond in a large back garden and it seemed like the most obvious place for him to go full-time. They'd taken him in when Nick and I had gone back to Mull the previous summer, and it had all worked out really well. The only issue then had been on the long car journey between Tiwai and Freetown. Getting Tum Tum adjusted to the heat away from the forest had proven difficult. We'd had to stop frequently to give him the chance to cool down in any water we could find, be that roadside rivers and ponds, or even pothole puddles, but on that retreat, with the car completely packed to the gunnels, the RUF coming and the roads filling with fleeing refugees, we just had to keep going.

I still managed to throw a few, very occasional, cups of water over Tum Tum, in a desperate effort to keep him going, but by the time we made it to Freetown, it was too late. Our beloved otter died from heatstroke in the boot of our car.

After 20 days in Freetown, we were placed on a special British Airways flight bound for home. Nick and I would never return to Tiwai. The Sierra Leonean Civil War would last for over a decade, killing 50,000 people and leaving many more victims of rape, mutilation and limb dismemberment. An estimated 2.5million people, over half the population of the entire nation, were displaced during an unremittingly brutal conflict.

Nick later wrote in his book that the RUF had swept into our area instantly, killing 300 people, and that we had 'missed this same fate by some half an hour'. It was impossible for either of us to drive through that immense heaving mass of humanity, all fleeing on the hoof, and not think that we had just abandoned all of our friends to their own fates too. We had left our boat behind with Minah, though, and we did hear that he had piled his family into it and fled downriver to hide in the forest – as so many of the Mende had done – but beyond that, I still don't know what actually happened to our team, and I haven't heard from any of them since.

A lot of time has passed, but the shame and guilt I feel is immense and still very raw. I knew on that drive that we had gravely underestimated the scale and seriousness of the conflict. We were far from alone in that mistake but the people we left that day were very dear friends of ours, as well as colleagues, and the thoughts of all the terrible things that could have happened to them haunt me greatly. Although we had no choice, it has always felt like we ran away.

The Ice Cube

If you listen very carefully, in the brief pauses between the violent pounding of Perspex and metal, the scrapings of immensely powerful claws and teeth, and the guttural grunts from the giant polar bear, you can actually hear my heart beating.

In that moment, it was beating so hard that my radio microphone was able to pick out each individual thump. There have been some seriously intense moments in my life working with wildlife, but that (now quite famous) incident trumps the lot.

'Hey bear.' It had begun quietly. She stood sniffing in my direction, just a few paces from me. Her nose, a fist-sized lump of coal, ahead of twin jet-black marble eyes, all fixed within her huge white head. Her sense of smell was many thousands of times more sensitive than my own. She was gathering information. Planning her approach. Just as she would if she were stalking a seal. But she wasn't stalking a seal. She was stalking me.

This had most definitely not been part of our plan. She was supposed to have stopped at the seal breathing hole some

50 metres away, but she had spotted me and come here to hunt instead.

It would've been over very quickly were it not for the 'Ice Cube'. I was sat within a human-sized reinforced box with my camera and tripod. In the footage, you can clearly see the markings of how it had all been slotted together. Guidelines, measurements and letters were written onto the metal struts with a permanent marker pen: roof frame, side frame, door, the places where A and A met and so on. It might've given it a feel not too dissimilar to a piece of flat-pack furniture brought home from Ikea, but this was no flimsily assembled piece of kit. Made from Perspex, aluminium and an awful lot of nuts and bolts, the Ice Cube had been carefully engineered to resist attack from even the largest and most powerful polar bear. We had built it specifically so I could get closer to a polar bear, but no one had ever wanted to see it actually put to the test. Least of all me.

She slowly sniffed around to a small gap in the door and suddenly crunched her two hefty paws directly onto it. The Ice Cube lurched and the attack began.

'Okay.' I tried to stay calm. 'I'll just check that's locked.' My hand worked away at the spring-loaded locking mechanism on the door as her breath steamed up the plastic sheet that was stood between life and death. The Ice Cube rocked back and forth with each of her heavy blows, but held firm.

Her nose swept away and then she got right up on her hind legs – seven-foot-high, possibly 500 kilograms in weight and towering above me. Testing the roof panel of the Ice Cube, inserting her claw tips into the gaps between the fittings – prying for any weakness that would allow her to peel the Cube right open, as if it were nothing more than a crude tin of Scottish kippers.

'Being this close, you get an appreciation for what this animal is. She's one of the most powerful animals on the planet …' I spoke steadily, alternating between delivering my words to the camera lens in front and glancing warily over my shoulder, as the bear ground away at the Perspex panel directly behind me. 'One of the most intimidating animals on the planet …' She paused in her violent industry and briefly peeped in from behind me, almost comedically, like we were engaged in polar bear peek-a-boo. '… and one of the few animals that actually see us as food.' And then she was back to shaking the Ice Cube again.

Soon, she found what she was looking for. A gap no more than a few inches wide, but still wide enough to almost insert her entire glistening nose. I could've wiped it for her, but then in came her claw tips. Still no give, so she reverted to pure brute force. Clubbing the front of the Ice Cube with both her paws, scratching the Perspex and flexing it with her teeth in a way that we hadn't even managed to produce when our strongest crew member had tested it with an almighty blow from a sledgehammer.

Minutes slid by like hours. 'Not sure if I like that. Not sure if that's good.' The polar bear was stooping right over me again and I began to wonder how much more of this any one of us could take. Me, the Cube or the bear. Which one was going to crack first?

There have been times in my career when I've been made to feel physically inferior to the animals I filmed. Most notably captured on film with the eyeballing and muscle-flexing of Chimanuka, the silverback gorilla in *Gorilla Family & Me*, or with Juliet, the protective black bear who false-charged me in *The Bear Family & Me*. Off camera, I've also been charged by tigers, twice chased by elephants, and there were even times when I felt wary of the wolf pack on Ellesmere Island during *Snow Wolf Family & Me*. Mostly, that was out of pure respect for the huge differences in our physical capabilities, rather than anything the wolf pack themselves ever actually did by way of a 'threat'. But the major difference between those experiences and what was playing out in *The Polar Bear Family & Me* was that they had all been cases of 'performative' violence to get me to back off.

That day, that polar bear had definitely wanted to eat me. And should she have managed to break her way into the Ice Cube, I have absolutely no doubt that is precisely what would have happened.

• • •

We were working in Svalbard, a grouping of very remote Norwegian islands deep within the Arctic Circle. 'Svalbard' roughly translates from the ancient Norse to 'cold shores'. That was some understatement. Here was a place where everything felt extreme. Extreme isolation, extreme winter cold and extreme darkness, giving way to an extreme summer beauty. Vast tundra, immense glacier coverage and a seemingly endless series of interlocking mountain ranges, hidden valleys and fjords – all forged through Svalbard's ancient experience of multiple recurrent Ice Ages. It's a paradise for an apex ambush predator and home to one of the densest concentrations of polar bears anywhere on earth.

Here, human footfall is minimal and the sense of solitude can feel absolute. Being fit enough to endure the conditions is a pre-requisite of residency. There are no formal medical services. Births must happen away on the Norwegian mainland, and the permafrost means that no one can be buried without special permission either, because the bodies can't safely rot away in the cold. Svalbard's largest town, Longyearbyen, has a small permanent population numbering barely a couple of thousand very hardy settlers (who can comfortably lay claim to being among Earth's northernmost residents) but the wider archipelago is mostly given over to the wild. Truly, Svalbard sits comfortably among the most wonderful locations I have ever had the privilege of working within.

When we arrived for that first shoot in the early spring, it felt like an eternal winter was clinging on to the land. Snow coated the hills in dense white drifts and a thick ice had encrusted the ice-breaking ship intending to carry us deeper into the archipelago. We took it in turns with a sledgehammer to clear the bow and ropes of ice, working away as a pinkish dawn crept out across the Svalbard skies. It may have been April, but light itself was seldom seen during the pits of the Arctic winter and, where we were headed, human visitors were very seldom seen either.

'Edge Island' is nestled in the southeast corner of Svalbard. It was named after Thomas Edge, an English merchant and whaler who had plied his trade in these ice-filled waters during the seventeenth century; the island was now part of a huge nature reserve where populations of sea birds, Arctic foxes, Svalbard reindeer, whales, dolphins, seals and walruses were all present in numbers. But the island's most iconic species was undoubtedly the polar bear. The plan was to arrive right at the point a mother bear emerged from her winter's den with her newborn cubs.

The cold I had felt that morning was only relative. When we were chipping away the boat's ice coating at dawn, it had felt close to the most severe cold I had ever experienced, but a climatic truth was writ bare in the crumbling ice floes that slid by the hull once we were on our way. At that time of year, we should have been travelling by snowmobiles across mile upon mile of solid sea ice. The latest research indicates that Svalbard could be warming at a rate six times faster than the global average. If that trend continues, in the next 70 years its glaciers are expected to lose their ice at twice their current rate. This was the earliest boat crossing to Edge Island that our captain had ever undertaken and, as he navigated our course through the splintering sea ice, over four very long days, it was clear that these were disastrously warm conditions for the bears.

Their hunting strategy was hugely reliant on vast swathes of intact sea ice. Most of their food, and a large portion of their fat reserves, came from eating seals. The polar bears would wait out on the sea ice in ambush, crouching right next to a seal's breathing hole, before snatching them as they came up for air, or to rest on the ice. Seals bred on the ice in the springtime too, giving polar bears relatively easy pickings from their vulnerable young pups, or they could locate their snow-covered lairs, crash through and eat all the residents they found.

The highly fragmented ice floes, and far more open sea, meant that the seals weren't coming into the area in the same numbers that they had before. And the ones that did now had far more options to evade and escape the hungry bears, right out into the wide-open sea.

Across much of the Arctic, the disappearing sea ice has forced polar bears to look for alternative food sources on land. That might include animal carcasses, berries, grasses or eggs, but none are an adequate replacement for a blubbery seal, and their hunger has pushed them towards people too.

For the most part, in the places where people live closest to polar bears, that has meant an increase in polar bears visiting community garbage pits, food stores, dog teams or bins to scavenge for scraps and edible waste – but in some places, it has also seen a rise in the chances of being attacked by a bear, or even killed.

In the voiceover opening to the series I intone how 'I had come to the Arctic to get closer to polar bears than anyone before'. By which, clearly, I meant *filming* them at the closest possible quarters to further our understanding of their lives, and most certainly *not* placing myself in a situation where a polar bear may look to me for its next meal. We weren't naïve to the potential threat they posed. I knew polar bears were among the very few predators that could see us as food. It was precisely why the 'Ice Cube' was so important. It was built as a safety precaution for us all. Allowing me to maintain a respectful and safe distance from the polar bears, without disturbing their natural behaviour, while still having a defence that was strong enough to withstand an attack. What we absolutely did not want was to arrive without any sort of meaningful precaution or protection, and then be placed in the terrible situation where a polar bear could be shot dead while we had been working away in what was, very much, *their* territory, and they had just been behaving in a way that polar bears sometimes do.

• • •

After a couple of days searching Edge Island, our polar bear expert, Jason Roberts, located a den and, as we trained our lenses and binoculars onto a scrape in the snow, the adorable snow-white head of a young cub popped out of the void and into the light. It was a massive moment (one that could've taken weeks of searching were it not for Jason's skills) but, having already spent months in their warm winter hollow beneath the snow, this mother bear and her two cubs were now in no rush to leave.

Busying ourselves as we waited, we decided to try and get some footage of the island's other polar bears – and that was when the Ice Cube was brought into action. I can remember how nervous I was, sat inside the Cube, when it was first towed out across the sea ice. My biggest fear then was that the Cube could topple sideways into one of the great holes opening up on the ice. If it had then landed on the door, I would be completely trapped inside and submerged in sub-zero saltwater. A truly grim and grisly death by Arctic drowning. Okay, I was a little nervous about the Perspex becoming brittle in the cold air too, and more vulnerable to fracturing in the highly unlikely event of a polar bear assault, but a few durability tests with the sledgehammer had soon put paid to that.

The plan we had was simple: place the Ice Cube near to a seal's breathing hole and record a hunt on a long lens once a polar bear had arrived. That game of 'cat and mouse' could take many hours, with the polar bear waiting patiently by the hole for the arrival of a seal (which might never come). However, as it turned out, the action was almost instant. The polar bear arrived. She was female. She was enormous. She was hungry. And she completely ignored the breathing hole and made a beeline for me in the Ice Cube.

As her assault rumbled on, I verbalised my biggest fear. 'Her best bet …' I take a sharp intake of breath, 'would be for her to get her full weight on top of it. Just like she would when she's breaking into seal lairs …'

And with that she was up.

'Okay, don't get onto the top.' This was it then. A few more almighty blows from her and I admitted out loud that I thought she was actually going to do it, but then she was down again. Breathing heavily from 45 minutes of full-on effort.

Something vital had just shifted in my favour. 'Every time she pushes and exerts force, she uses up calories,' I remarked, as she sat back down on the snow to rest. 'Is there anything worth eating here? Anything worth using up energy for? Inside there is, definitely … little old me …' Both my voice, and the polar bear, had begun to trail off. She was done. Despite the near overwhelming encouragement from my scent and apparent vulnerability, she had finally realised it was just too difficult to break into the Ice Cube. She gave me one more glance back, just double-checking she was absolutely sure of her conviction, before slowly wandering off.

That ordeal had seen my fear far outweigh my fascination. It had been too close for anyone to have felt in any way comfortable, and it was not something I would ever wish to repeat.

The Polar Bear Family & Me, and that sequence of events in particular, generated an extraordinary global reaction. The series won an award at the Royal Television Society Awards, but the incident in the Ice Cube garnered worldwide press and video clips that have since gone viral many times over.

One of the questions repeatedly asked in the comments below those videos and press articles is how I had managed to stay so calm. The truth was, inside I was completely crapping myself, but, through the fog of all that fear, I was also aware of how extraordinary it was as a moment. That, right in the teeth of all that drama, there was this opportunity for me to talk about polar bears in a way that no one ever had before, or was ever likely to do again.

I think I verbalised my fears in an authentic way, but I also managed to deliver some of the behavioural science behind what was happening. In just doing the job at hand, I had unearthed something of a survival strategy. The process of recording and talking allowed me to unbuckle from the symptoms of being completely overwhelmed by my fear: shouting, crying, screaming, unlocking the door and trying to make a futile run for it. Ultimately, I had found a sense of measured calm and maintained my grip on the few things that I could still control from within the Ice Cube.

What is most curious about all this now, though, is how I can manage my mind in the intensity of a situation like that, and yet maintaining a basic peace of mind at home – where, as far as I'm aware, there aren't any polar bears trying to eat me – has often remained so elusive.

Perhaps, though, it is just a different type of beast?

Black Dog

At the end of our time in Sierra Leone, I knew full well what could be achieved with dogged determination and total commitment to a wildlife shot. That if you are willing to do whatever it takes, you can walk away with footage that would have been otherwise impossible.

However, there is one almightily big 'but' coming. The level of single-mindedness that Nick was willing to draw upon came at a huge personal cost. When our time in Sierra Leone wound to its conclusion, Nick's wife, Ann, told him she was leaving. Without going into the deeply personal details, the bare truth was that their marriage broke down because Nick wasn't home enough. Working as a wildlife cameraperson will inevitably take you away for long periods of time, but Nick's dream was to line up next to the world's greatest natural history filmmakers, and that extra level of sacrifice had ultimately compromised everything he'd built with Ann.

Nick is far from alone in that respect. There is a tragically familiar theme of relationship breakdown for many who choose to work within the wildlife film industry. I knew that I was going to have to be very determined to get ahead in my field, but seeing the collapse of Nick and Ann's marriage affected me greatly – even as a teenager.

Back then, I thought that if I was ever lucky enough to find the right person, then I wanted to make a proper commitment to them and build a marriage that worked. I wanted to be a father who saw his kids grow up too, and if that meant paying something of a price because I didn't get the ultimate shot or the ultimate accolade, then so be it. It was a price I knew that I was willing to pay – but, in reality, finding that balance was never going to be easy. Even if I'd been content with just being average at my job, I was always going to be absent for chunks of time. It was the nature of the beast, but that justification doesn't exactly help the partner who is left alone at home, especially when you have children.

My principal drive in becoming a presenter wasn't about being seen onscreen. I've never coveted the limelight and I am a shy person at heart. I reckoned that if I were successful in front of the camera, I could earn a bit more, which would mean I needed to go away less. But that wasn't going to happen overnight.

It took me years to get to a point where the camerawork was coming in with regularity, and a few years more before I landed my first solo series as a presenter. Things were very gradual in that respect – going from saying a few lines to the camera while filming leopards, to working within a team of presenters in iconic shows like *Springwatch, Autumnwatch* and those hugely success-ful Lost Land expedition series. It took till 2010 before the first

Animal Families & Me opportunity came around with the black bears of Minnesota. Inevitably, there was a long period where I was picking up jobs for both my camerawork and my presenting at the same time, but I kept justifying all the time away as part of my grand strategic plan.

I didn't feel like I could afford to turn anything down. Even when the presenting started to go well, I still felt like I had to keep one foot in the camerawork door, and keep pushing everything else along too. I told myself that there wasn't ever going to be a Gordon Buchanan-shaped space in the BBC schedule. That if I wanted to stay relevant on the BBC, I'd have to keep proving my documentaries were really worth their slot, time and time again.

Approaching my forties, I was getting opportunities to work on the sort of wildlife series that I could only have dreamt about when I was younger: amazing projects with great teams in incredible places, that brought encounters with wildlife and people that will live with me forever. I never lost sight of the massive honour and privilege that my work has been, but for that spell I was pretty much saying 'yes' to anything that would get me even a fraction of the way to the next rung of the ladder.

I should caveat all this by saying that I wasn't away all of the time, but, by the spring of 2011, trying to find that impossible balance was taking a terrible toll. I could sense something really big was brewing up inside me – and it was not good news at all.

I was on a long car journey in the Cascade Mountains in Washington State with my co-presenter Jasmine Minbashian – someone who I really didn't know that well at the time. We were about to begin filming *Land of the Lost Wolves*. It had been dawning on me for quite some time and I probably just needed to say it out loud to fully admit it. So I turned to her and said it for the very first time: 'Jasmine. I think I'm depressed.'

Poor Jasmine. She was heavily pregnant and probably wished that she'd got in the other car for something easy like a game of I-spy. But she listened and it initially felt good, or, at least, it felt less bad. It was also liberating. Telling someone made it real and helped me recognise it for what it was. We got through the shoot and I went home – but that's when it hit me like a shovel to the head.

I wish I had written down how that breakdown felt. I probably should've known that the day would come when I'd have to try and articulate that period of my life in a book, but when you're locked in it, that deep pit of depression, you're scarcely capable of getting out of bed, let alone possessing the clarity of thought to put the experience into words.

At a bare minimum, I knew I had to drop absolutely everything I was doing right there and then. I had just committed to live presenting three weeks of *Springwatch*, but there was no way that was happening now. Luckily, the series producer was a really old friend, but I still couldn't summon the energy to call him up and tell him what had happened. I doubt whatever I'd have tried to stammer out would have made any sense anyway. Instead, I sent him a text saying words to the effect that things had really fallen apart in my life, and, to his immense credit, he texted me right back and told me not to give it a second thought. That was the first roadblock seen off, but I didn't feel any better.

If I had to describe just a fraction of what was going on, I'd start by saying that I had no control over my emotions whatsoever. I could be in floods of tears at any given moment and had zero mental peace, just constant turbulence in my mind. I couldn't see a single positive thing to cling on to in my life. It was as if all of the joy, hope, happiness and good feeling had been extracted from my body, like I'd just had a meeting with a dementor, one of the deeply evil soul-sucking wraiths that haunt the skies in the Harry Potter films.

It had been creeping up on me for some time, but because I'd maintained a state of near total distraction through all my work and travelling, I'd somehow managed to tightrope walk across the chasm of depression that had been steadily opening up right beneath me. That was until I reached the point where I wobbled off my rope and fell right in, headfirst. And once I was plummeting down, I just couldn't stop.

When you break in that way, you need help. You are lost, not even a shadow of yourself, just an entity, more like an injured animal near the bottom of the evolutionary scale than who or what you thought you were. I did go to the doctor, and somewhat inevitably, the idea of 'suicidal thoughts' was mooted. I told him that it wasn't like I didn't want to 'be here'; it was just that my mind was this huge expanse of nothingness. A gargantuan gloom that I couldn't see any way out of. Initially, he suggested that it was burnout, but when I said that I thought it was a bit bigger than that, I was given a questionnaire to fill out.

'Ah right.' I sat down and filled out his 'depression' questionnaire, quickly pencilling in my answers to a range of queries about my life and feelings. The doctor picked it up, glanced at the sheet, then looked directly back at me with some degree of serious concern dawning in his eyes. 'Yes, I agree. This is not burnout. We will be getting you some medication.'

I left clutching my paper bag of anti-depressants and the knowledge that they could apparently take up to three weeks before they kicked in. *Three weeks.* I can remember thinking that was a colossal period of time to exist in this mental quicksand.

I slept. It was the only time my mind would dull, and then I'd wake up stuck in my depressive pit and stumbling through another day of darkness. But slowly, incrementally, the drugs did help to bleed some of the light back into my life. Eventually, I could feel a release from the hole. I was thrown a line, pulled up and out, but still sat on the edge. My legs were dangling down into my abyss, but at least I could stare into its depths without actually being trapped down there. I had some distance then, perhaps a little perspective on it, but now I felt numb – I was flatlining emotionally. Neither completely depressed nor very happy. Aware of what had just happened, and able to make sense of a few of the key reasons why, but with none of the emotional range I used to have: no lows, no highs – but at least I was back in the room.

I wish I could say that having reached out and received help, I was reborn like a phoenix from the flames and never looked back, but annoyingly this was just the first of several serious bouts of depression that I've suffered over the years.

I might have convinced myself that I needed to say 'yes' to everything because it would get me the 'security' I craved, but in reality, the whole idea of 'security', literally, feeling secure and happy, or even just 'content', was artifice. They are the things that I have found most difficult throughout my life – and were never going to come through work alone. For as long as I can remember, I've lived the life of a depressive. Not that I knew that as a child, or realised it in my teens, or even really recognised it in my twenties and thirties. Unfortunately, we can only ever view the world through our own eyes and I guess that I just thought that everyone felt that way. Distracted, sad and anxious, an awful lot of the time.

I don't know why it had taken me almost into my forties to hit the nail on the head. The blindingly obvious was in fact not that obvious. You create a mask to compensate and convince. If you can fool yourself, you can fool anyone. But even the most highly crafted mask eventually starts to slip. And not long after opening up, my mask dropped to the ground and shattered.

To a degree, I probably was burnt out from all the work and travel, but that driving anxiety had always been there and was unlikely to vanish no matter what I'd chosen to do with my working life. None of that elemental vulnerability had ever gone away and, left unchecked, it had gathered with all my other dark clouds to form the perfect storm in my mind.

That cloud of depression could always creep up on me at any point. Sometimes it would come on without any warning and I'd be left wondering *Why is this happening now? I've got absolutely nothing to worry about.* But that's not how it works, is it? I know now that I have had to make peace with the fact that it's in there, a part of me and who I am, and therefore it's on me to find the ways of catching it when it's coming out – so that it doesn't keep spiralling out of my control.

Winston Churchill, frequently crippled by despair, called his depression 'my black dog'. We actually have a black dog. His name is Stewart and, conversely, he helps me when my own beast begins to appear from the shadows. That's not why we got a dog, it was just an unexpected benefit. I've learnt that the deal you strike with dogs is that you pick up their shite and they'll make you smile. As much as dogs are a comfort to me, something much more powerful is needed to stop my beast in its tracks, or at least slow it down if it's a particularly big beast.

After that breakdown in 2011, I actually did find it a lot easier to just say 'no' and set very clear boundaries. I also came to realise that there was no point carrying on at all if I wasn't going to enjoy any of it. My work wasn't 'life and death', nor did someone have a gun to my head, forcing me to do it. I was, to a very large degree, living my dream, and if I was going to be miserable both home and away, then what was I doing the job for? I could just leave it all behind and do something else instead. After that, I found it a lot easier to appreciate where I was, and the enormous privilege of what I was getting to do when I was away, alongside the other once-in-a-lifetime opportunity that came from building a family of my own.

I made changes on a very basic level too. Now, whenever I feel that darkness creeping in, I do everything I can to stop it tightening around my ankles. I'll eat as healthily as I can, I'll take cold showers, I'll cut right back on the booze, I'll make sure I've got a proper bed-time routine, exercise every day, and I'll spend more time speaking to my closest friends and family. I'll make a conscious effort to get out there and talk to people in my town too, even if it is at the most superficial level of just going to the shops or getting a coffee – anything to stop myself from indulging the temptation to shrink away from it all.

It sounds so easy to do when you write it all out on a page, but whenever I'm on that downslide, just making those simple changes can often take the most monumental act of self-discipline. I really do have to actively remind myself of what I should be doing, instead of just choosing some short-term crutch, slouched on the sofa with a couple of cans of Tennent's and half a pack of Tunnock's teacakes.

The truth is, as you get older, life often gets more complicated. With more responsibilities and pressures, real bills to pay and more experiences that are inevitably tragic and sad. These days though, I do count my many blessings a lot more. I am very lucky to have a few good stories to tell and I'm thankful to still be around to tell them, but more than anything else, I am exceptionally lucky to have met, at a fairly young age, the person who I wanted to spend the rest of my life with.

Wendy & Me

In 1994, I left Nick after a long last shoot together in the Brazilian Amazon. I came home, took out a business loan and invested every penny into buying a camera kit of my own. I was 22 years old and going solo, but I had no work lined up and was now saddled with an eye-watering debt to pay back to the Prince's Scottish Youth Business Trust and Clydesdale Bank.

It might've been better were it not also for the fact that I very quickly came to realise that I had almost no clue what I was doing. Sure, I could point a camera roughly in the right direction, but over all the years with Nick, the fundamental reality was that I had been there to assist him in *his* operation of *his* camera. I might've recorded a few shots for him, but in reality, he had framed them up, having already done most of the legwork in terms of figuring out how to get that shot in the first place, and how it would all work in a coherent narrative for his documentary. All I had really done was press the record button.

There's 'imposter syndrome' and then there's actually being an imposter. I was hardly a cameraman at all, not really; I just had the camera. Nick let me use some seriously creative license in the putting together of a showreel of 'my' work, but really, I was the living embodiment of the saying 'all the gear and no idea'. To be fair, I didn't even own my gear either, the Scottish Youth Business Trust and the bank did.

With the loan long gone, I couldn't afford any film stock to practise filming by myself, so I was just going to have to learn on the job. I don't mean that in a heroic way – I wish I did – as for a large portion of the next two years I basically conned people into employing me with the sole aim of gaining enough experience to not get fired. As the length of time between starting a job and getting booted off it for incompetence slowly began to extend, I knew I was finally getting somewhere. I just prayed I hadn't burnt so many bridges during my secret apprenticeship that I had rendered myself completely unemployable in the UK.

Fortunately for me, the mid-1990s had seen a real boom for wildlife filmmaking. Many of the more established camera people were busying themselves on long foreign projects with big budgets or had long-term deals with production companies. That meant there were opportunities for younger and less experienced people on the smaller things, and that I had just a little bit more grace than you'd likely get today. I certainly wasn't going to be precious about being offered a job on the basis that the first, second, likely third, and possibly even the fourth and the fifth choices were all unavailable – and steadily, my shooting grew to a level of competence where I could just about get by.

In the early spring of 1997, my big break came. I was asked to film three half-hours for a 14-part wildlife series called *Wild Islands* for STV, the Scottish free-to-air channel. By this point, I had run up a significant bar tab at the last chance saloon. This was the one job where I could not afford to make any more mistakes or have any distractions. I moved into a gamekeeper's cottage in the Cairngorms and set to work right away.

I might've been a freelancer navigating his way through to his first meaningful job, but I had managed to have a couple of relationships in between all the work struggle and setbacks. I wanted to settle down some day, but the truth of it was that I hadn't met a single person that I thought that was possible with. By the time *Wild Islands* came around, I had reached the conclusion that for me 'the one' did not exist. I was destined to be single for life.

I hadn't exactly got the greatest blueprint to follow. Not that that's much of an excuse; lots of people from backgrounds with divorce find the right person and have great marriages in the end, but I didn't really know anything about how long-term relationships worked, or how you navigated through problems as a couple.

I didn't feel any pressure to be in a relationship though. It wasn't like I felt I *needed* someone. If that 'right person' didn't ever come along, or, more likely to my mind, didn't exist at all, then so be it. I knew I wanted to be a dad, but I just thought that, when the time came, I could investigate the other ways people brought children into their lives, outside of being in a conventional relationship. Things were moving in a much more progressive direction as the 1990s ticked forward, but I had a lot more work to do before I could even think about kids or settling down. I had to keep meeting the repayment demands of my loans for a start, and I still had a very long way to go before I had anything like actual job security. So, I was solely focused on *Wild Islands* and doing the very best job I could, when I discovered that the world had very different plans.

It's funny how often you speak to couples who say that they got together completely out of the blue. That they were both quite happily getting on with their everyday lives when this all-new, extraordinary feeling rushed in and changed their entire life's path. That was how it was for Wendy and me.

'I've got this friend … and you'd be perfect for each other.'

We've all heard that one, haven't we? Alison, Norrie's wife, was the first person to mention Wendy in such a sentence. To which the natural follow-up from me was always going to be: 'Oh, is she single?'

Disappointingly though, her reply was: 'No, she is not.'

Gotcha, Alison. 'Perfect' but for her long-term boyfriend!

I was still intrigued to meet this 'Wendy' though, more out of curiosity about what Alison had said than any real thought that we could be together one day. The first time we properly spoke we were both off to T in the Park, the largest music festival in Scotland at the time, and among the biggest in the UK. T in the Park used to be a rite of passage for many young people in Scotland. We were a bunch of 20-somethings crammed onto a big bus, wheeling our way to the festival site, and I was sat behind Wendy.

She was quite obviously beautiful, bright and very funny. But, more than anything, the thing that marked her out as someone special was (as treacly as this sounds) her magnetism. I felt drawn to her in a 'once in a lifetime' kind of way. I was completely comfortable in her company from the first second we spoke. We chatted away to each other on that bus like we had been friends for life, me leaning forward in my seat, her leaning back across the armrest, looking right back at me.

We laughed, joked and swapped ridiculous stories. We hadn't even arrived at the festival and I was already having the best day out. I didn't allow my mind to wander beyond the moment; she did have that boyfriend, and they'd been together for three years. To me back then, three years was an *eternity*, probably meant they were about to get married. He was a very lucky guy.

We spoke to no one else for that entire journey though, and as we got off the bus and went our separate ways I thought, *My god, Alison was right. We were perfect together.*

A year later, Wendy moved to London for work. I was a couple of months into *Wild Islands* and very much still in the *there's no one out there for me, don't even think about it* frame of mind, but I needed to go to London for a day's work too, and I had just discovered that the friend I usually stayed with was away. On a whim, I rang Alison. 'Do you think it would be really weird if I got in touch with Wendy and asked if I could crash at hers?' 'Oh god no, not at all,' she said breezily. 'I'm sure she'd love to see someone from back home.' Alison gave me her number, I called her up and that was that: I had found my digs for the night.

I'd asked Alison for Wendy's number purely because she was a really cool person who I thought I'd love to hang out with again. If she was a best friend of one of my best friends, then it stood to reason that we would get along great, and that was how I'd long since reinterpreted Alison's *'you'd be perfect for each other'* comment. The fact that she was so cool about me coming to stay – someone who she only really knew from a bus ride and a handful of other brief encounters – only served to double down on that sentiment. She really was a friend in waiting.

However, it soon transpired that she was now *far cooler* than I'd remembered from the bus. She was working on Channel 4's *The Big Breakfast*, one of the highest-rating breakfast TV shows in British history, and had been spending her days lining up celebrity interviews with Hollywood superstars like Harrison Ford, Kim Basinger, Keanu Reeves, Sharon Stone, Samuel L. Jackson and all of the monumentally massive UK music acts of the time: Oasis, All Saints, Robbie Williams, the Spice Girls. She'd even met the England football team multiple times off the back of their iconic Euro 1996 tournament, and the 1998 World Cup was right around the corner.

As far as I was concerned (she'll either love or hate me saying this but it was true), Wendy *was* the nineties. In the summer of 1997, Britain was still gripped by that Cool Britannia wave that had rolled in while I'd been dialling in from my radio in Sierra Leone, and it seemed to me that Wendy had been riding along on the crest of it all. She wasn't star struck by any of the people she'd met either, which, to my mind, made her the coolest person of all. She wasn't out to impress anyone; it was just her job.

I had enough about me to realise that she was working away at the heart of 'proper' entertainment telly, the brand of which even your great-gran would know about, right in the thick of one of the most vibrant cities in Europe. Whereas I, by contrast, was a novice wildlife cameraman making three half-hours for Scottish television from a 150-year-old cottage in the middle of a desolate moor in the Highlands.

She sounded so much more mature and established in her career than I was. I also hugely admired the fact that she'd upped sticks and left all of her friends in Glasgow to go and grab this whole new life for herself in London – a huge megacity where she knew very few people. I heard how she'd gone in for the interview for *The Big Breakfast* and been given the job on the spot, despite the fact that there were more interviews running throughout the day. Wendy, clearly, was someone who made things happen. A go-getter then, and I thought (quite rightly, as it transpired) someone who was destined to be very successful in whatever she did.

All things considered, and in spite of the news that she'd broken up with her boyfriend, if she were looking for a new boyfriend, she was hardly going to choose me. Quite honestly, I drove my car to her address in St John's Wood with no romantic intentions in my head whatsoever.

Looking back now, I think all of that perfectly set the scene when I did come to knock on the door to her flat on that June evening. I was still the 'friend of a friend'. There was no agenda. It was just a place to crash for the night in the company of someone who I liked and admired.

She lived in a shared flat with a few other young professionals. *Cool*, I thought. She'd brought home a bottle of decent red wine. *Hmm, pretty fancy.* She offered to make 'pasta pesto' for dinner. *What the fuck is that?* I thought. *Sounds cool and pretty fancy.*

These days, with many bowls of pasta pesto under my belt and countless more red wines under the bridge, I am marginally more sophisticated, but at the time I thought that this was seriously high-end stuff: St John's Wood flat, red wine, pesto, professionals and an ambitious and already successful Wendy in the mix. Still, there was not a single moment of awkwardness from the second she'd opened her door. We flowed along together like we had never stepped off that bus. She was exactly the same truly lovely, truly warm and truly interesting person that I'd met the year before.

We ate, we drank, we blethered, we laughed and we had the most amazing (and yes, platonic) night. In fact, I'd even say it was, by a million miles, the most enjoyable evening that I have spent with anyone, ever. Not only did I have this deep sense that I was in the presence of an extremely special person, I loved every single second of her company too. Given that we hardly knew each other, it was remarkably comfortable from start to finish.

'Thanks so much for letting me stay!' I called out as I left her flat and walked to where my car was parked.

We definitely hadn't just been on a date. Food, wine and merriment, yes, but no romance at any point.

But … *had this been a date* (which as I have already said, it definitely *was not*), it would surely go down in the record books as the most successful ever. And even though it *absolutely was not a date*, I was absolutely hopeful that we would get a 'date' in to see each other again soon.

Now, at the very least, we are definitely proper friends, I concluded, walking away from her flat. And while I'm now thinking of 'dates' in the more general 'calendar' sense of the word, had this been the *other* type of 'date', then this is exactly how I'd have wanted it to go. Fine? Good. That's all sorted then.

I climbed into my car to begin the long journey back up to the Cairngorms. I pootled away from St John's Wood, Lord's Cricket Ground and London Zoo, and just thought about Wendy. *I'm so glad my mate wasn't in London last night*, I thought to myself, joining the start of the M1. *If he'd been home, we would've just gone to the pub and I'd never have thought to even call Wendy — and now she feels like not just a 'friend of a friend', but my friend.* I crossed over the M25 and went past Luton. *That really was a great night with Wendy.* Birmingham, Stoke, Manchester. *Okay, you can probably stop thinking about Wendy now.* M6. Preston. Lancaster. Kendal. Penrith for some fuel. *Ah, it's okay. This is fine. It's normal that I'm still thinking about Wendy. You've got to occupy your mind with* something *on a long car journey like this.* Fuel cap back on, nozzle replaced. Fuel paid for. Back to the road. Carlisle. *Wendy.* Edinburgh. *Wendy.* Perth. *Wendy.* Pitlochry. *Wendy.* And back to the Cairngorms National Park. Yep: *still thinking about Wendy.*

In fact, for nine hours and 490 miles straight, the only thing I *could* think about was Wendy. I wasn't re-running specific moments from the night, things she or I had said, it was more that I was just trying to hold on to this lovely warm glow that I felt whenever I thought about her. I turned off the engine outside my little cottage. A bright moon lit up the dark clouds scudding across the night sky, and the brightest of stars seemed to twinkle.

I had to admit it to myself: Wendy wasn't only on my mind, she was under my skin. Moving through my veins and into my heart. If the 490 miles I'd driven that day had taught me one thing, it was that – and this may come as somewhat of a surprise to you all – I *really* fancied her.

Those *Wild Islands* animals weren't going to film themselves though. It was time to focus solely on the work – and ordinarily, that was something that came easily. However, I woke up the next morning and was surprised to find that the warm 'Wendy glow' was still there. I clung on to her to the summit of Cairngorm, and out onto the moors in search of ptarmigan, but I fully expected it to have passed come the weekend. Usually, if a love interest lived somewhere far away, any romantic flames would dampen down after a few days and the starry eyes would eventually dim. But her glow remained.

I knew now that I was experiencing something very different. Something that was completely foreign to me as a feeling. Something unfamiliar. And at first, I wasn't entirely sure what I should do about it.

Into the Unknown

For some hours, my eyes had been transfixed by the landscape sweeping past the helicopter window. Great chocolate-coloured rivers twisted their way through a rugged jungle. On the horizon, a long spine of misty mountains erupted skywards like the serrated scales on a dragon's back.

I was about to enter an area that ranked among the last unknowns on earth. It was quite conceivable that more people had stood on the moon than entered the place where we were headed. The forest-covered frame of an immense and ancient volcano slid into view. That was it. Our home for the next few weeks.

I was much more used to filming in jungles that were, to put it very simply, a lot flatter. The terrain down there looked formidable, but I knew I was going to have to figure it all out very quickly. We really didn't have that much time on the ground. The animals were all new to me too.

I openly admitted to the camera that I was feeling nervous. It was a huge leap into the unknown.

It was 2008 and filming was starting for the BBC's *Lost Land of the Volcano*. It was the third series in an expedition format that had already sent me away with teams of scientists and filmmakers to the jungles of Guyana and Borneo. The plan was simple enough: establish a remote jungle camp under a tarpaulin and search day and night for animals. The teams would split up and scour the environment for anything we could find, making new discoveries and filming wildlife in this thrillingly reactive 'as live' way. There was genuine jeopardy, too. None of us really had a clue what we might find (if anything at all) or what was going to happen to us while we camped alone in these extraordinarily pristine wildernesses.

The previous series, *Lost Land of the Jaguar*, had been hugely popular. Our audience had absolutely bought into the whole 'flying by the seat of our pants' feel, but there was now a pressure to go further, deeper and bigger than we ever had before. And that had led us right here, to the great forest island of New Guinea.

New Guinea is massive. It's the second largest island in the world, after Greenland, with vast swathes of swampland and forest, bisected by the highest mountain range between the Himalayas and the Andes. In total, New Guinea represents a little less than half a percent of the world's total landmass, but some scientists believe it might contain up to ten per cent of our plant and animal species – with many new species still out there, yet to be discovered.

By that point in my career, I'd had plenty of experience filming within jungles (and plenty more working in extremely remote places) but this island represented something else entirely. Going in, I had no point of reference to anything that had felt even vaguely familiar. There were no cats, elephants, rhinos, bears or even monkeys or apes. New Guinea sits on the Australian side of the 'Wallace Line', meaning its extreme geography shelters a curious mix of strange and unique Australasian creatures, including tree kangaroos, the long-beaked echidna, birds of paradise, the cuscus, and hundreds of other birds, fish, amphibians and reptiles – none of which I had ever encountered before.

Our volcanic destination, Mount Bosavi, hid a truly 'lost world' within its heart. Bosavi was an extinct Ice Age volcano whose cone had long since collapsed, creating a heavily forested two-and-a-half-mile-wide crater at its centre, with vertical walls stretching up some half a mile in height. The creatures living inside that void were highly likely to have never seen humans before, and there was every chance that some might have evolved into separate species too.

The helicopter touched down on a rocky bank and, as I rushed forward to escape the downdraft, I was embraced within the great bearded bear hug of an old friend. 'Hey, Gordon!' It was Dr George McGavin, a world-class entomologist and the leader of a scientific team that had been assembled from across the globe. Alongside them, we had expert New Guinean guides and trackers from the local Kasua tribe and the BBC production crew. As well as George, the three-person presenting team included the adventurer and naturalist Steve Backshall, and me, the wildlife cameraman charged with recording the most secretive creatures of Bosavi's crater.

I needn't have been nervous about finding and filming Bosavi's wildlife at all. I had scarcely unpacked my bags before a Doria's tree kangaroo wandered straight past the camp. Quickly, we followed her down the slopes and up a small ravine. 'They are one of the strangest animals that live in the forest.' I tried to catch my breath as my Papuan guide pointed over to this curious teddy bear-like creature, sat in a tree with its thick kangaroo tail hanging down below. 'I think that's because they are recognisable. They are kangaroos. But these kangaroos live in the trees.' I wedged myself in the tree opposite and started to film, no more than seven metres away from this incredible creature. It looked back down towards my lens with a wariness that leant towards curiosity, but not panic.

Steadying myself, I picked out its various features. It had more of a koala bear face than a kangaroo, a strong, short and stocky build and huge claws for climbing. 'The nails must be about two to three inches long,' I observed. Then, as if to make a point, it reached out and began to eat the leaves of the tree. 'Ah, lovely!' I exclaimed. 'Now that's a really good sign because animals that feed are relaxed.' I knew now, beyond any doubt, that I was working among creatures that had not seen a human before.

From that point onwards, things just got better and better. I found the giant footprint of a cassowary in the mud: a huge flightless bird that stands up to five foot tall, with a long neck and blue head crowned with a bony, horn-like casque. I would've dearly loved to have filmed one of those in the flesh, but I was soon distracted by other extraordinary birds: the courtship dances of both the king and Raggiana birds of paradise; and the pygmy parrot, a truly minuscule parrot species, hardly bigger than my thumb, that we had found nesting within a termite mound.

Soon, we had filmed our first forest rodents and a stunning striped possum, and a carefully placed remote camera trap had given us our first look at a cuscus – a shy, bulbous-eyed and very sweet-looking nocturnal species that I later captured 'live' on my infrared camera as it worked away in the trees. It fed on fruits and leaves, using its strangely hairless prehensile tail as an extra limb, gripping the branches and steadying itself as it quietly went about its business.

It was a thrilling start, but the dream within our team was the crater's potential to throw up species that were new to science. George had even set the target of us finding and filming 30 – but if that had ever felt like a stretch, Bosavi was to wildly exceed everyone's expectations.

• • •

It was deep into the expedition and everyone was feeling it. Among the team we had fevers, infected bites, stings and topical rashes of an unknown origin, and we were battling a camp-wide bout of intestinal worms.

I sat on my hammock looking very grey. 'We've got to take these tablets.' I held out a grubby palm and showed the camera lens my personal pearly white pill. 'They'll pretty much kill every-thing in our gut, but they make you feel very run down.' I ruefully swallowed it back and instantly aged a decade.

Bosavi was rotting us from the inside out. Even our local New Guinean friends were flat out on their backs. It would soon be time for us to all go home, and truly, if that had been that, the job was more than done. But Bosavi had one more wonder up its sleeve.

Throughout the expedition, I had worked closely with Dr Kristofer Helgen. Kris was a brilliant research scientist and was blessed with the ability to spot the difference between the 'extremely rare' and the potentially 'new to science' with his eye alone. By that point, we'd already met and filmed a number of iconic Papuan creatures, but our biggest hope for something really special had always lain with whatever might trigger the infrared sensor of my camera traps.

Unquestionably, camera-trap technology has been one of the most revolutionary innovations of my lifetime. Having that ability to leave a camera in one likely-looking place for days, if not weeks, has turned up no end of wildlife discoveries that you could almost certainly never have made if you'd just sat there in person. Camera traps made a huge difference on this sort of expedition series and, even with such amiable wildlife in the crater, *Lost Land of the Volcano* was to prove no exception.

One evening, as the rain poured down, Kris and I sat side by side and scrolled through the latest camera trap cards. I scrolled down and whipped through hundreds of photos in seconds.

'Me, setting up the camera,' I commentated as we went. 'Still me.' Kris grinned over my shoulder. He was well used to all this. Small common rodents flicked past other Papuan species we had already documented. A wallaby, another tree kangaroo, a cuscus.

We didn't take any of them for granted, not at all, but we were looking for something else now.

A string of pictures of our Kasua guides flowed past. They'd been over to check the cameras and had unwittingly set them off. Always a good laugh, but not exactly primetime telly.

'Wow…'

I quickly pulled my finger off the key. Kris was staring at the screen, eyes widening. 'What is that?' I asked.

'Have a look at that!' He gestured excitedly towards a long tail protruding from the rear of an exceptionally hairy new creature.

'What do you think that is, Gordon?' He was sitting back in his chair now, a huge sparkling grin breaking out across his face.

I *thought* I knew what I was looking at, but never in my life had I ever seen one as big as that. Its size was incomprehensible.

Kris was near certain we were looking at an image of a species that was new to science, but he really needed to see it in the flesh and fur to be sure.

When I look back and think about all the wildlife shoots that I've been on in my life, chasing and waiting for animals and capturing nothing, or capturing next to nothing, versus what had materialised at the very end of this expedition, it is still scarcely believable.

A few days later, our Kasua trackers were shouting out in the pitch darkness and pouring rain, and Kris and I were plunging forward through the slopping mud and roots. 'Oh my word. Oh gosh …' I searched for the words as I stumbled, it just couldn't be, but suddenly, there it was: the animal from the camera trap, illuminated by the head torches of our little team of trackers.

I looked at Kris, then turned to the camera. 'That is the biggest rat I have *ever* seen!'

I crouched down next to the almighty mammal. It stretched out almost a metre from nose to tail and had absolutely no fear of us. One of the guides lightly gripped its tail as it quietly groomed itself, licking its paws and nibbling on a fern, blissfully unaware that it was the undisputed star of our series, and one of the biggest wildlife discoveries anywhere in the world that year.

Kris was laughing incredulously. 'This is the world's largest rat … It is a true rat, the same family as the rats you find in the city sewers … This is absolutely a new species!'

The animal's teeth suggested it had a largely vegetarian diet and probably built its nests in tree hollows or underground – but this was a species we fundamentally knew nothing about.

I had to admit, this rat was adorable. All wiry woolly fur, long whiskers and intelligent character. 'Jeepers creepers! I had a cat and it was about the same size as this rat!' I joked, holding on to this awesome Bosavi species that we now knew, for certain, was found nowhere else on the planet. 'That is such a huge deal!'

Scientists do find new species every year, even new species of mammal, but they are nearly always really small creatures: bats or mice, or even smaller rodents. Hardly ever do they discover mammals as large as that rat was – let alone with cameras and a whole television crew, all present at the exact same time. The freshly christened Bosavi woolly rat was the most miraculous find.

It really was time to go now. Incredibly though, George had underestimated our 'new species' target. Alongside the rat, we recorded a new sub-species of silky cuscus, new species of camou-flaged gecko, fanged frog and grunting fish, plus a further 15 new species of frog, two more fish, at least 20 insects, arachnids and possibly a new species of bat. In total, we returned home with 40 new species waiting to be ratified.

I had arrived in Papua New Guinea with all those nerves at the helicopter window. A powerful sense of overwhelm, joining onto a much smaller hope that we would somehow overcome this environment to find something really special. A quiet instinct that we were in the right place, at the right time, with all the right people, all working together. But to then bear witness to a large mammal species that was new to science? To actually be there in person. To hang on to it as it lives and breathes, right there in front of you. That was something utterly unimaginable.

Before it happened to me, I would surely have assumed that experience sat firmly in the bracket marked 'things that can only ever happen to other people'. It is still an almost indescribable feeling: so intense and exciting, yet so utterly singular and deeply personal too.

It was, in some ways, a bit like the first time I properly fell in love.

• • •

A full week after our night together in London, I was shocked to discover that I was still thinking about Wendy. Before you huff up at my misty-eyed romantic overindulgence on these pages,

I should admit that, by this point, I was beginning to worry that there might be something seriously wrong with me.

'This isn't right. I'd better get this checked out,' I was thinking to myself. Given my brain and body had ceased to function in the way they normally did, I assumed I had some sort of illness. This 'warm Wendy feeling' was beginning to feel like a burden. It was like having a brain worm, a song stuck in my head on loop that I just couldn't shift, no matter what I did or where I went. For almost two weeks straight I hadn't been able to do anything about it. I was in the Cairngorms, all by myself, just living with this unseen force – like I was possessed by a benevolent spirit. Come the next weekend it was either going to be a trip to the doctor's to get checked over, an invite to a priest for an exorcism or I'd have to attempt something that was potentially even more drastic: admit how I was really feeling to a friend.

And if I went for that, there was only one friend I could call.

'Hey Alison.' I rang her full in the hope that she was going to tell me something that would burst this mental bubble – that Wendy hadn't mentioned me at all, or even better, that she actually thought I was a bit of a twat.

'Right,' I began, with the tone of someone who was about to confess to a truly terrible crime, 'I've got to level with you here. Since I stayed at Wendy's two weeks ago, I've not stopped thinking about her, and I really *really* fancy her.'

'Well, that's a coincidence,' she said. 'I've just come off the phone to Wendy and she is saying exactly the same thing.'

From that moment forward, though hundreds of miles apart, we were together.

Our two independent cogs had been wheeling away separately, but when we brought them together, they just fell into place and worked right away. That spark, or 'click', or whatever you want to call it, was so powerful, it became the foundation for everything we were able to go on and do in our lives together.

• • •

There hadn't been any pressure on us when we had met in her flat that night and there was still no pressure on our relationship after we got together. We had long phone calls into the evenings when we were apart, and then, every couple of weeks, either Wendy would come up to Scotland or I'd go and stay with her in London.

There was no timeline or target we felt we had to meet. No arbitrary pressure and no doubts either. We just remained utterly comfortable in each other's company and let our relationship flow forward naturally. We soon fell in love, but I guess you could say that the love had always been there in some form anyway – I had loved being in her company from the bus to T in the Park and during that night with the wine and pesto pasta in her flat – it was just that now, I also knew that I had met my soulmate in her.

I might've felt a bit inferior to Wendy when I'd first walked into her flat, but the more I got to know her, the more I came to realise that we had a whole lot in common. She was an islander too. Her mum's family were all from the Isle of Arran, a beautiful west-coast Scottish island nestled in the Firth of Clyde. She might've grown up on the west coast of the mainland, but she saw herself as very much *from* Arran. That's the place where she felt most at home and where she would spend huge amounts of her childhood staying with her gran and grampa and, as an adult, with her sister Tracy, who settled and raised her family on the island.

She'd experienced some turbulence in her childhood too. Her parents had broken up when she was young. After that, she didn't really have a relationship with her dad until adulthood, and neither of us had grown up around money. She didn't do too well in her Highers (although at least she finished them!) but she did eventually go to the University of Glasgow and would shine during her internship at STV: her first step into the world of television. So, we had some similarities in our past, we both worked roughly in the same industry, we shared similar outlooks and principles, and we absolutely shared the same idea that laughing was about the best thing you could do.

Aside from the fact that Wendy is so much fun, she is extremely hardworking and very talented, with this uncanny knack for putting others at total ease. She hugely underestimates so many of her qualities, which, I think most of us would agree, is a quality in itself.

Naturally, she went on to climb the televisual ladder quickly, progressing from researcher to producer on *The Big Breakfast* before going freelance and jumping from one era-defining entertainment format to another. She joined the *Big Brother* production team for their second season, having initially been offered a job on its inception. I'd laughed at the format and told her that it definitely wouldn't catch on with all our British reserve – I really had my finger on the cultural pulse there! She stayed with them right from those very early beginnings of mainstream reality television, seeing it grow to the all-encompassing televisual behemoth it would become in the decades that followed, with *Celebrity Big Brother* and all the copycat productions and spin-offs that then came after it. She set up Hello Halo, her production company here in Glasgow, 14 years ago, and her team have gone on to produce a host of award-winning factual and children's series.

That initial sense of awe would later morph into a sense that I needed to seriously up my game. Wendy was making giant strides in her career, so I felt I really should get on with mine too. She reinvigorated my ambitions. Those few years I'd spent skint and scraping by had knocked me, but Wendy restored my confidence and motivated me.

There probably was a part of me that felt I needed to prove myself worthy of her choice to be with me, but really, I was just as inspired by Wendy's extraordinary drive. She is someone who makes the most of every opportunity that comes her way, whether that's at work, at home, when we are away together, or even when we're out with friends; Wendy knows how to grasp the 'moment' and live life to the fullest. I am so proud to be with someone who is like that, and I naturally wanted to push myself on too. Over the years, she really has brought out the very best in me, and I am very aware that I wouldn't have experienced the same level of success in my career without her.

Wendy taught me how to appreciate the little things so much more. I stopped thinking too far ahead, or too far back, and came to really enjoy the here and now. Just to have someone there who could close the door to any dark thoughts, even for a short spell, was one of her most precious gifts of all.

• • •

It was Hogmanay 2002. Wendy and I were at Norrie and Alison's in Tobermory, and all of our friends had gathered for a long night of drinking and dancing. The bells had come and gone and Wendy and I were lying there, side by side on the floor.

I'd been thinking about it for a couple of years. I'd even tried to orchestrate it earlier with a walk along the coast out towards Aros Park and Calve, but Wendy had strongly objected to a long walk along a narrow muddy path on a grim day. Fair enough, but this wasn't your run of the mill wander in the pissing rain – I was trying to find a meaningful place to propose! This moment, though, was completely perfect. All of our best friends together in one room, with us lying in that peaceful comfort we'd always somehow had.

I didn't go down on one knee and I hadn't even bought a ring (genuinely, I thought I'd better find out what the answer was before I forked out on that!) – but I leant over and quietly asked her if she'd marry me, and, thank god, she said 'yes'.

Eye to Eye

'It definitely knows that I'm here …'

My first leopard encounter in Mumbai and it was staring me down in all its thermal-camera glory. The entire illustrious animal stood clear of cover and captured in a single clean shot. Its eyes displaying as a pair of brilliant white orbs, like two full moons, its thickset body and long tail stretching out behind it.

That moment represented the grand sum of our team's careful planning, execution and belief. It would become one sighting of several, too. We'd found an extraordinary population of leopards slinking past homes and using the very same walkways that, just hours later, would be filled with people. But this was not the moment we were here for. We had come for their hunt, and, in the spot where I was hiding, that meant pigs. Domestic livestock, brought to this part of the city in considerable numbers, equalling easy prey for the city's big predatory cats.

That first sighting was an animal out on the prowl. Always looking for an opportunity, but not actively hunting – not yet anyway. The shift in behaviour of the leopard that gifted us our sequence was palpable. It was crouched down in stealth mode. Creeping on through a tangled web of bush roots, ever so carefully placing each paw so it didn't rattle the shrubs and betray its position. Gradually, it made ground on a family of peacefully sleeping pigs, with their vulnerable piglets nestled close by.

From my vantage point I could frame up the fat black back of an adult pig. It heaved, lifted and fell as it snored; the thermal camera punctured the dark with the white of its hairy body's heat. Then the leopard's powerful neck and shoulders fatefully emerged into the foreground. It was mere metres away.

We were both hunters of sorts. The leopard and me. Calm, poised and steady in the slow build-up to the moment. Both ready to react, to follow the flow and the panic. The cat chasing its piglet prey, the big pig chasing the cat, while I chased after them all with the camera's lens.

The leopard snatched a piglet from the front of its parent's snout, gripping the tiny pig right across the back of its neck and sprinting away. The mother pig gave chase, and both animals carved a crashing path through the bushes in my direction. The young pig squealed out in desperation, the leopard quickly getting ahead to clear ground, an expert at navigating tight environments in the total dark.

The piglet and its parent stood no chance. The leopard bounded up and over a high wall as if it were no more than a short hurdle, before it consumed its prize in the crook of a tree.

It was over for all of us. Months of planning, days of waiting, years of training – for two minutes of truly extraordinary action.

. . .

It was right at the end of the trip when the largest leopard broke its cover with confidence. It strode towards me in a manner that landed somewhere between a casual prowl and an active hunt. An ambiguity in its approach that was as unnerving as it was compelling.

We were both a ghostly white. The leopard in my thermal camera, my face framed by an infrared diary cam.

'Look at the size of him …' I whispered, almost breathless as I suppressed the sound of my voice, maintaining my murmur and keeping my calm. 'He's coming up, he's coming up, he's coming up.'

This animal, in all its predatorial majesty, was most definitely aware of my presence. But what else could I do other than lean in to my instinct to film?

It was close. Close enough to see the brilliant heat of its nostrils. Close enough to see the livid scars on its legs. Close enough to hear it breathe. Close enough to hear my own breath, as I gulped it back down and swallowed.

It paused. Now just a metre and a half from me. One paw held in the air. Ears erect. I pursed my lips, steadied my camera and focused on the animal, hyper-aware that I'd never been this close to a leopard in all my years of filming them, and very much alive to the possible danger this situation could present. But very much still filming.

It readied to move off, then thought again. Paused. Weighing me up. Crouching as if to pounce. We were eye to eye now. I dared not breathe. Gently, I placed my fingers over my mouth and held every ounce of my body and camera in a focused fear.

The moment I had worked for, the capture of the hunt, had been and gone. This was a very different moment, one in which my elevated status as earth's supposed top species was being directly confronted. This was literal living in the moment. The leopard cradled my entire life in whatever it decided to do next. But I just kept filming.

And so, it departed. With a sideways leap into the depths of an Indian night.

Afterword

I've tried to tell you as much as I can about the story of how my life in wildlife all began, but there are other stories of important people, whose lives and friendships I haven't quite had the room to close. I hope you don't mind me doing so here.

Firstly, Norrie. We might've developed separate lives and interests after he got that horse of his own, but we always remained best friends, and that continued deep into our adult lives.

Devastatingly, my dearest, oldest friend had a massive cardiac arrest a few years ago. He survived, but he was left as a shadow of the exuberant, extroverted looney he once was.

I'm not sure if any words can adequately express the role he played in the shape of my early life's journey. He took centre stage in our group of friends, and when he wasn't directly providing me with an escape, he was giving me the confidence to go and try things that I, quite frankly, would never have dared to attempt were it not for him.

I even met Wendy through his wife, Alison – they had all studied at the University of Glasgow together. If I was to line up all of the many lucky events of my life, meeting Norrie, then Alison, and then finding Wendy are the three where I know I've been the most deeply blessed. I owe them all so much, but I hope that what I've written of the times Norrie and I shared on Mull goes some way towards immortalising the memories of the many incredible times we had.

Thank you, Tash.

Next, my mentor Nick Gordon. Our work in Sierra Leone may have come to an abrupt end in the late spring of 1991, but our very next long-term project in Venezuela started up that autumn. We went on to have so many incredible adventures together, in West Africa and South America, and the impact Nick has had on both my life and career was profound.

He wrote me the most beautiful letter when we finally finished working together. It included many lovely words about how much luck he wished me going forward in my own career, how proud he was of me, and, most poignantly of all, how he would always be there.

In April 2004 we lost Nick, aged just 51, to a massive heart attack. He had been hospitalised and warned about his irregular heartbeat in the weeks before, he had even given up caffeine, but he couldn't give up filmmaking or that hunger for adventure. He died on the jungle border of Venezuela and Brazil while shooting a seven-part series called *Secrets of the Amazon*. There's no good way to go, especially not for someone who had so much more life to live and give, but perhaps there was something consoling about the idea of him slipping away in the heart of a forest that he had loved so much. The jungle was his place, and he was once moved to say: 'I went into the tropical rainforest for the first time and that was it. I simply fell in love with the heat, the humidity, the snakes, the insects, the animals, the natives. I knew I couldn't leave it. I was a rainforest man.'

I'm sure the stress and pressure he always put himself under couldn't have helped his health, and I doubt his recurrent bouts of malaria did him any favours either, but Nick Gordon was a wildlife filmmaker with an unmatchable commitment and passion for his work. He was very brave, kind and infectiously enthusiastic. A person with whom even the briefest of encounters could not pass without a fond memory of a man who possessed such a bubbling eagerness. He had an uncanny knack for helping others obliterate their own fears and self-doubt. Only a few minutes in his company gave you a spring in your step and a belief that you could achieve absolutely anything.

When Nick died, it left a deep void that could never really be filled. I felt desperately sorry for his whole family, especially Emma, who was only 16 at the time. At least I'd had the benefit of proper time with Nick. We worked shoulder to shoulder for five and a half exceptional years, filming extraordinary wildlife and forming a lifelong friendship that was utterly irreplaceable. At first, I recalled those words in his letter to me and felt so deeply sorry that he was no longer here. I spoke to Wendy about it, and she wisely countered that Nick will always be there in the incredible opportunity he gave me, in all of the things he taught me back then, and everything I went on to do in my career as a result of the extraordinary faith he put in that 17-year-old daydreamer from Tobermory.

Nick really believed in me, at a time when few others did, and, as a result, I was finally able to believe in myself. My gratitude to him for that is inexpressible.

The 'Timber Wolves', my siblings, are hovering around the half-century now. We all remain very close, while still maintaining that independent streak that runs through our generation of Buchanans. We are comfortable together but well able to cut our own pathways through life's grand bush too. Of course, the playful piss-taking and banter has carried on from childhood, except now it doesn't cross the line into a roll-around on the carpet with our mum cooing about how 'it'll all end in tears!'

My biggest brother, Sandy, having left home at 16, did return after Alastair was gone. Though he studied at catering college in Clydebank, he returned to Tobermory and, but for a stint in hotels and on the trawlers, he was at the fish farming for his whole working life. Cruelly, when still a very young man, he was diagnosed with muscular dystrophy (MD). There are several types of MD, but in essence it is a genetic condition that causes your muscles to progressively weaken. Sandy's type is facioscapulohumeral MD, which progresses slowly and isn't usually life-threatening, but is nonetheless really horrible, and those fishing jobs represented just about the most physically demanding work in the UK. Once his muscles began to decline, he inevitably had to give it all up. There is no cure for MD, and everything we take for granted is a struggle for Sandy. He lives in pain, a life that is unimaginably hard. Not that he lets you know any of that though, save for at the very worst of times. My brother bravely shoulders it all, meeting those challenges head-on, in much the same way that he's always lived his life. I still look up to him and whenever I'm feeling a bit strung out, demotivated at work, or like I just can't be arsed to do something, I think of him, pull myself right out of my hole and get on with it. He's one of the most inspiring people I know. His determination, grit and good humour in the face of so many challenges always lift me out of whatever wallow I find myself in.

Stewart also left school at 16. He did a youth training scheme as a linesman on the mainland, and like Sandy was drawn back to Mull. Back on the island, he split his time between working in an ironmonger's shop, serving little old grannies everything from drawing pins to bike chains or a bottle of whisky, and heading off to bar work in the evenings. Stewart was absolutely loved by all the customers and his bosses. Another Buchanan trait is to burn the candle at both ends and Stew, on occasions, would burn it in the middle as well! Frequently, his boss at the ironmonger's would ring our mum up to find out why he wasn't in work. She'd then hammer on his door and find him asleep and fully clothed from his pub shift the night before. He'd peel himself from bed, run out the door to the local clothes shop, buy himself an entirely new outfit and make it into work, with smiles all round. Soon, he was working in the Tobermory whisky distillery and from there he flew up the rungs to become the global ambassador for a group of major Scottish whisky brands. The boy has done well for himself. We're proud of Stewart; he found his own path and grabbed the opportunities that came his way with both hands. (And I still wouldn't dare challenge him in karate!)

Like Sandy and Stewart, Maggie did stints on the mainland over the years, both studying and working. She lived with us in Bristol for a year, to help us after our second child was born, and spent another year with us after we moved to Glasgow. But ultimately, the lure of Mull saw her settling down and raising her own kids back on the island. There is a contentment and ease of life on the islands that many people miss when they move to the mainland. She is the type of person who is valued by everyone who knows her. She's funny, caring, empathetic and intelligent: a real laugh to be around. She's the only one of us that showed any real academic promise, and is a real worker too. When she was only 11, she was already out earning decent money, cleaning people's houses, and she worked with our mum in a restaurant too. Now, she's a working mum to two kids, Oran and Evie. Having previously run whale- and dolphin-watching tours on Mull, she now works for a holiday cottage company and even makes her own Scottish tablet to sell in shops.

Wendy and I have been married for 20 years this year and have two wonderful children, Lola and Harris. My marriage to Wendy, and our kids, are the things that I am most proud of in my life. The force of our connection has remained as constant as it ever was, and the security we've built is the springboard for us all to try and grab the opportunities that life can offer – but it is our safety net too. In that respect, nothing is more important to me than Wendy and our children.

Although I am often taken away with my work, I always make sure that when I am home, I do the best I can to give as much of my time and attention as possible to our home life. School holidays became sacred, and, when the children were really young, I'd love indulging them on all their camping trips, walks in the woods and the great discovery of all the tiny wonders our natural world has to offer. Being with Lola and Harris as they learnt how to explore the world for themselves was a huge vicarious thrill that helped me to feel all those simple childhood joys a second time around.

I hope Lola and Harris think we are pretty cool parents. That they can always have a proper laugh with us both, but that they also know we are always here whenever they need us. I know I'm probably a bit of a pushover as a dad. I probably shouldn't admit this, but I think they both know that I would do anything for either of them (even stuff they could probably do for themselves), just to make sure they've always got the most support, and the best start, that we could possibly give.

Lola and Harris have grown to become amazing young adults. In a major shift from all the scrapping I did with my siblings, I'm very happy to say that they always played really well together as children, and care for each other greatly today. From being a shy, concerned wee girl, Lola has grown into a positive, independent young lady. Outgoing, funny and up for anything. A chip off Wendy's block in so many ways. She's definitely got that very same magnetism and good energy that lights up a room. She's a remarkably skilled artist too. She got into the Glasgow School of Art and has an extraordinary eye for detail in all the work she produces. There's a lot of wild themes and natural influences in her art, but it's eclectic and can often be quite dark. She once wanted to paint a portrait of a human hanging up like a carcass in a butcher's, and, ever obliging dad I am, I trotted off with her on a cold and grim afternoon to get it done. It was only once I was stripped down to my underpants, hanging upside down in a tree with large hooks around my ankles, that I really did hope that no one spotted us and called the police!

Harris is chilled out and laid back, but he's also a very deep thinker and has an ability to really interrogate any argument, theory or thought, breaking it right down in forensic detail until he feels he properly understands it from every angle. In that way, Harris is someone who will find something he likes and study it deeply. I've seen him really go in on ants, sharks, Pokémon and Naruto, but music has remained his biggest passion. He's a naturally talented pianist. He's come a long way from the wee fella who could never sit still in nursery or school, who was apparently always 'lazy' or 'underachieving'. Within just one week of being in class with the excellent Mrs Patterson, Harris was identified as being dyslexic. He was lucky enough to be in a school with a fantastic Support For Learning team, which really turned his school days around, and now he's at the University of St Andrews studying economics. He has a kind and gentle soul that is plain to see, but also an air of intrigue about him, which is most apparent with his frequent private smiles; as if the invisible man has just whispered something amusing in his ear. It's pretty mind-blowing to consider our baby boy is now a towering six-foot-three student, who is also getting far too comfortable at whipping his dad's arse at badminton!

Despite a few twists and turns, I hope that Lola and Harris would say that I've been a good dad. I have tried to be serious when I've felt a bit of seriousness was required, but mostly I've found myself trying to show our children all the great joys to be had in life too. I think life is serious enough as it is. You've got to indulge the daftness, arsing around, and all the nonsense, *especially* as a parent. My own mum was a great one for that. After all, when everyone is smiling, life really doesn't get any better, does it? And a tear-streaming giggling fit is actually heaven on earth!

Finally, my mum. The love and respect I have for her transcends words. Always fun to be around, we had a great relationship, and we still do. She is an amazing, resilient woman, who had to put up with an awful lot, on her own, from a very young age. Not only did she do her best, I think she did better than many of the parents that had none of the challenges she faced.

And she did eventually find the happiness she very much deserved. After years of juggling several jobs, she began working in the Tobermory Distillery (where Stewart would later work). That's where she met John in the early 1990s.

The first time we properly spent time together, John was keen to impress just how much he loved my mum and what she meant to him. My mum clearly loved John too, and it was obvious she was in a relationship where she finally felt valued and safe.

John is one of life's thoroughly decent men. He's charming, great company and he gives our mum every bit of love he has to give. Back then, it felt to us all like this could be our mum's 'happy ending', and now, some thirty years later, I am really happy to say that it worked out that way.

Acknowledgements

At the start of writing, I naively believed that in a book of 85,000 words, there would be room to touch on every moment of consequence and every person of significance.

But if I've learned anything from this process it's that I've been lucky enough to reflect back on a rich life full of incredible friends, family and experiences that have shaped who I am today. This is not an account of all I've seen and done, nor of every individual who has enriched my life and taught me more than I could have hoped to learn. Instead, this book treads one particular path through the years, as I attempt to make sense of how I got here. As a result, there are far more omissions than I would like, but I challenge anyone to capture a full account of their life in just 85,000 words. Perhaps another book will remedy that!

Still, I want those who matter to be present within these pages, as they have been present in my life. This is my way of honouring a few individuals who, though not in the body of this tale, have profoundly impacted my life – not as an afterthought, but as a tribute to the support, guidance and inspiration they've provided.

To a few who are no longer with us, I offer my gratitude for their shelter, cups of tea, and some of life's quiet teachings: Dick Balharry, Netta and Willie MacDougall.

Jo Sarsby, my agent, for being the champion you are, for getting me on track (and keeping me there).

Mike Birkhead, producer of some of the best wildlife documentaries of the past 20 years, a huge debt of gratitude for the opportunity and coaxing me out from behind my camera. As you predicted, wonderful changes have come my way.

Johnny Keeling, head of the Natural History Unit but before that just a pal, for finding my funny bone in every possible situation and making me feel less inappropriate.

Nick Allinson, sound man and old chum, for bringing giggles and good vibes to adventures past, present and future.

Firm friends from the beginning.

Marcus McEwan, for being effortlessly funny and for your ability to translate the way you see the world from a uniquely wonky angle.

Alan Malloy for your solid dependability, zero bullshit approach to life and your tolerance and participation of a whole lot of nonsense over the years.

Colin MacIntyre, for the musical memories, your creative gusto, and for always having your laugh in first gear and your foot halfway off the clutch.

Juliet Knight, for your cool, your calm and your company and for my funniest and fondest memories of dark Edinburgh nights.

Jamie Spencer, for being the architect of unforgettable weekends for over three decades.

Marj and Tom Nelson, always inspiring, always a warm welcome and always up for a laugh.

And finally deep appreciation and respect to Will Millard for helping shape and give texture to this story – we (you) did it!